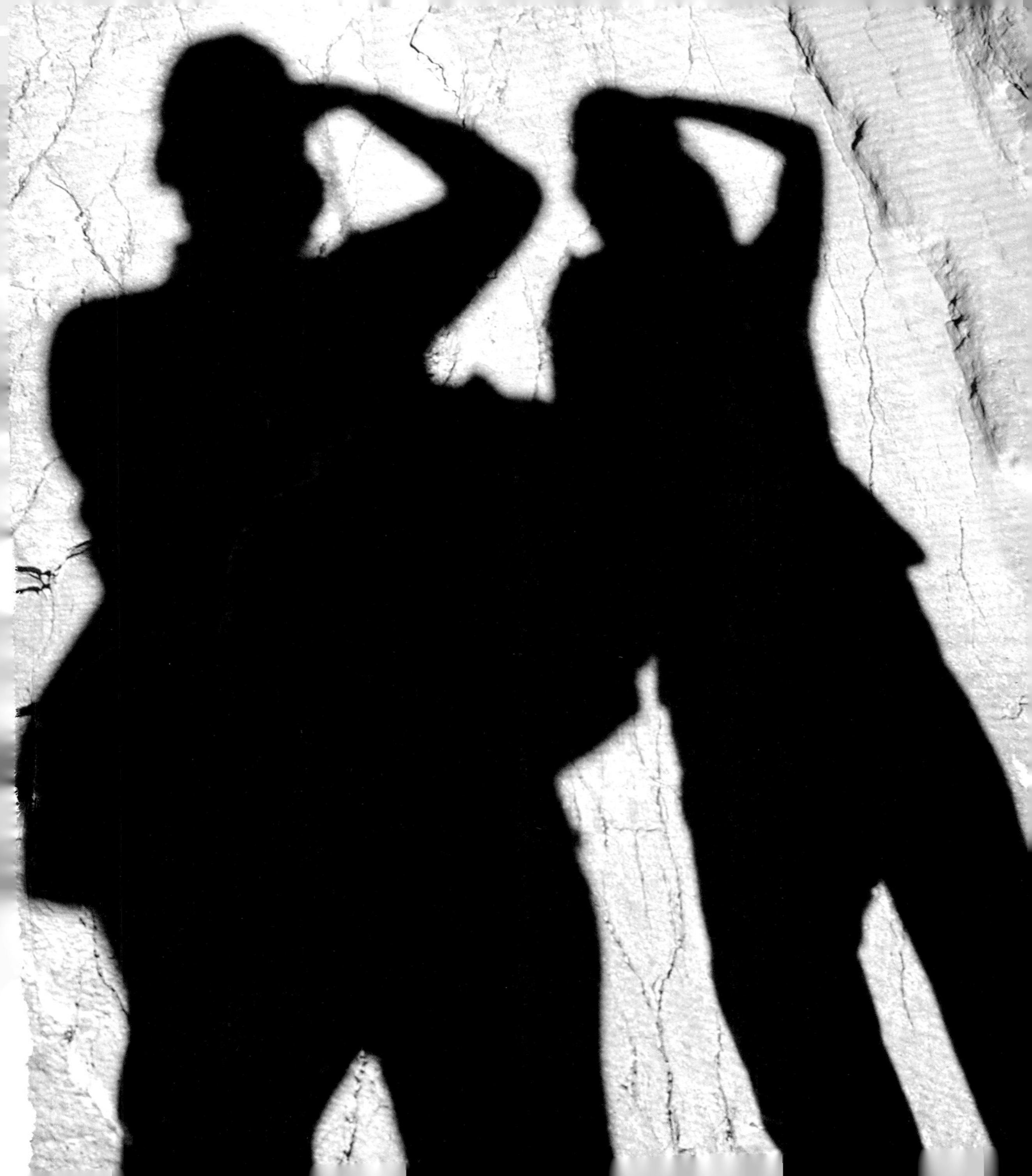

Diane Jonte-Pace and David Pace

Where the Time Goes

I realized these were all the snapshots which our children would look at someday with wonder, thinking their parents had lived smooth, well ordered lives...never dreaming of the raggedy madness and riot of our actual lives.

– Jack Kerouac, On the Road

David and I met in the summer of 1970. I had gone on a month-long backpack trip with two professors and a dozen students from the University of California Santa Cruz – it was a course on the sociology and ecology of the Sierra Nevada. At the end of the trip I borrowed my parents' car to drive my new backpacking friend Lauri to her boyfriend's house. She had told me about her boyfriend, David, a UC Santa Cruz student and musician who had recently released a record with his band. When we arrived at David's house, I was surprised to find that all of the furniture in the living room had been turned upside down. David was playing the saxophone. Together with his housemates, who were playing trombone, French horn, and accordion, he was marching around the overturned sofa. Lauri was quite a sensible person – "Why would she have such an idiosyncratic boyfriend?" I wondered. Although they have remained lifelong friends, Lauri and David broke up a few months later. The following year David and I took a few classes together. In 1972 we moved in together.

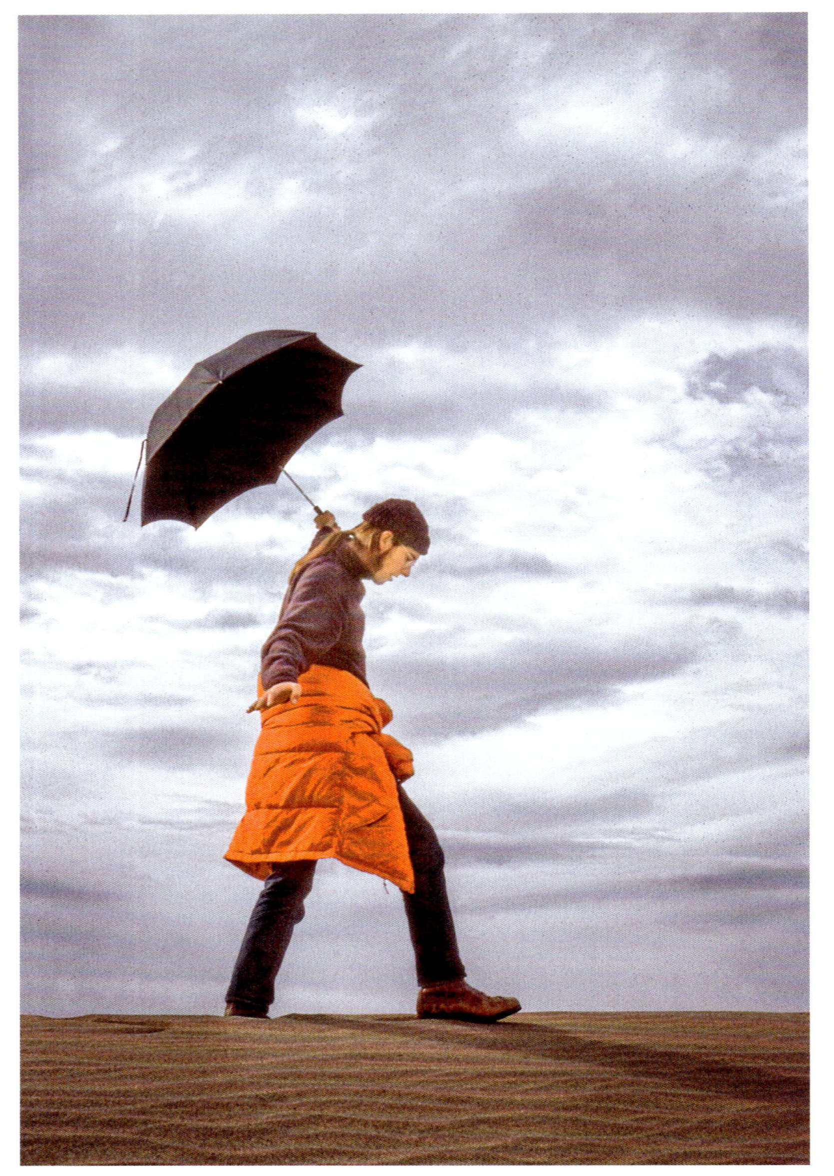

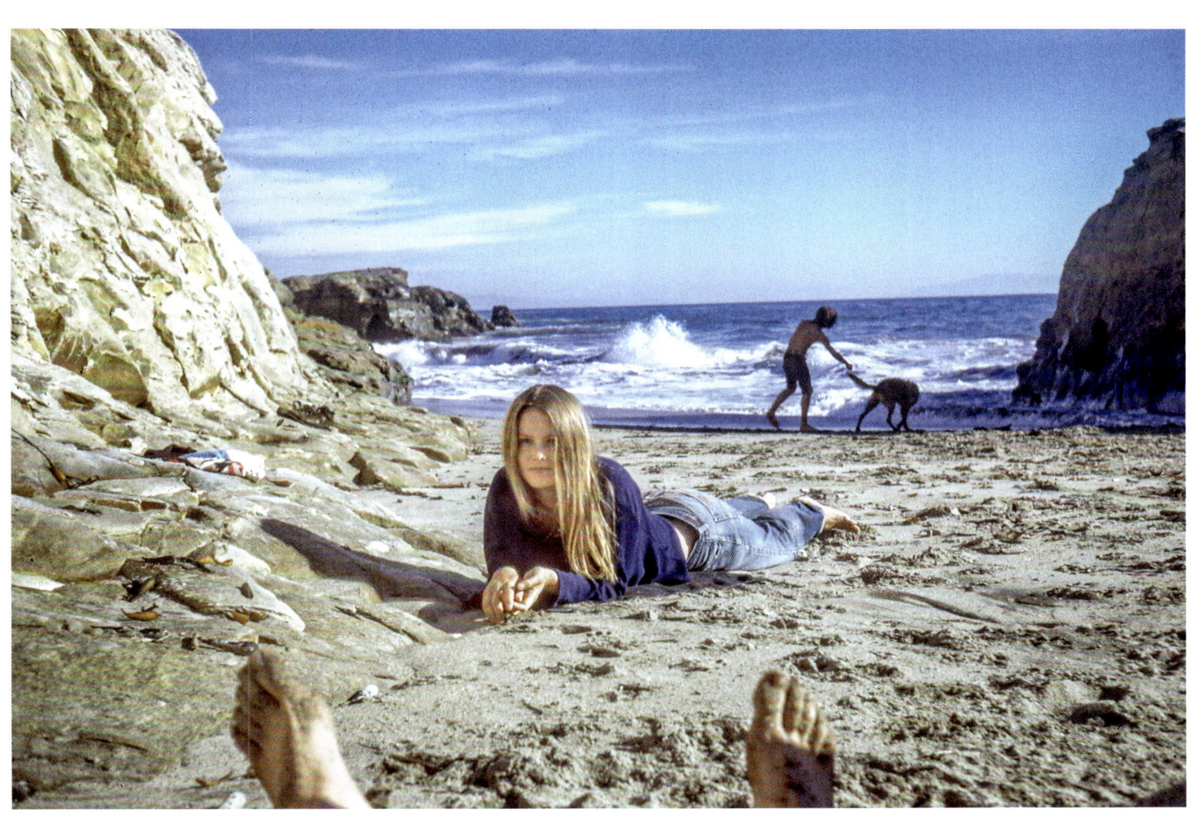

SANTA CRUZ, CALIFORNIA 1972 | 7

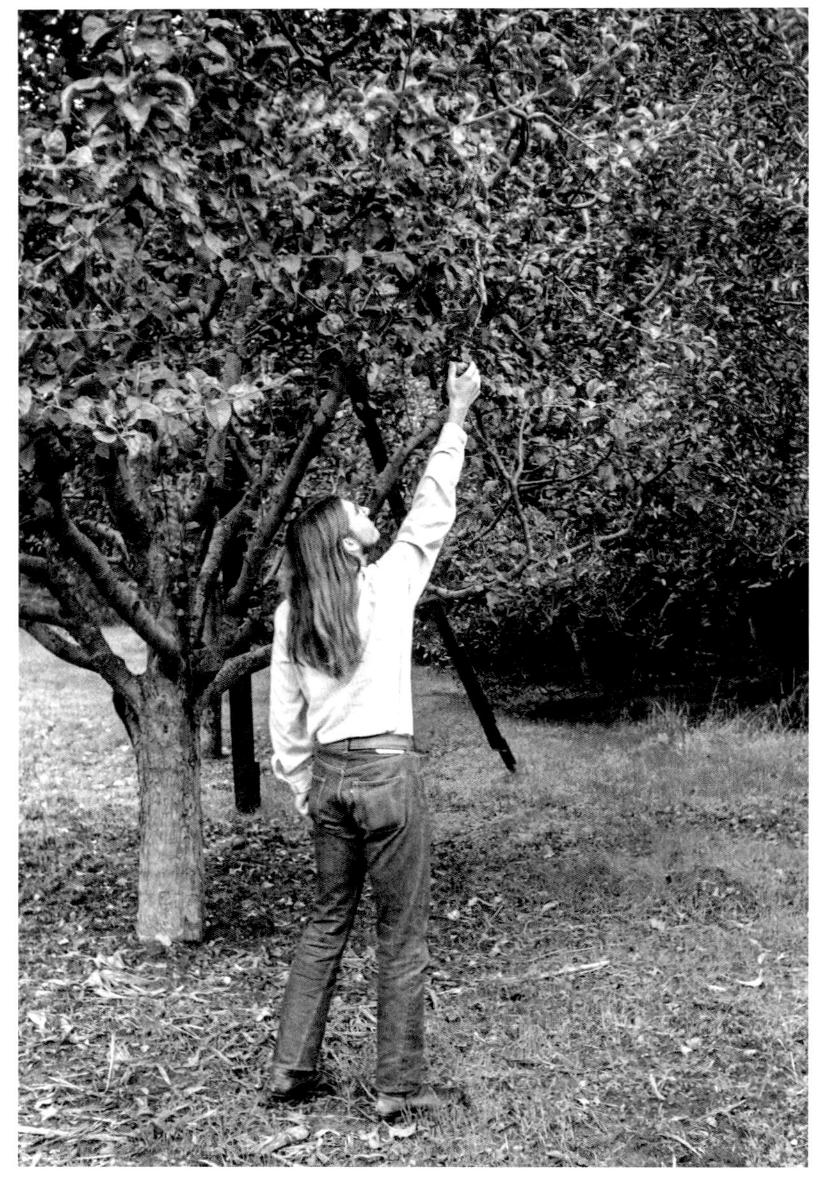

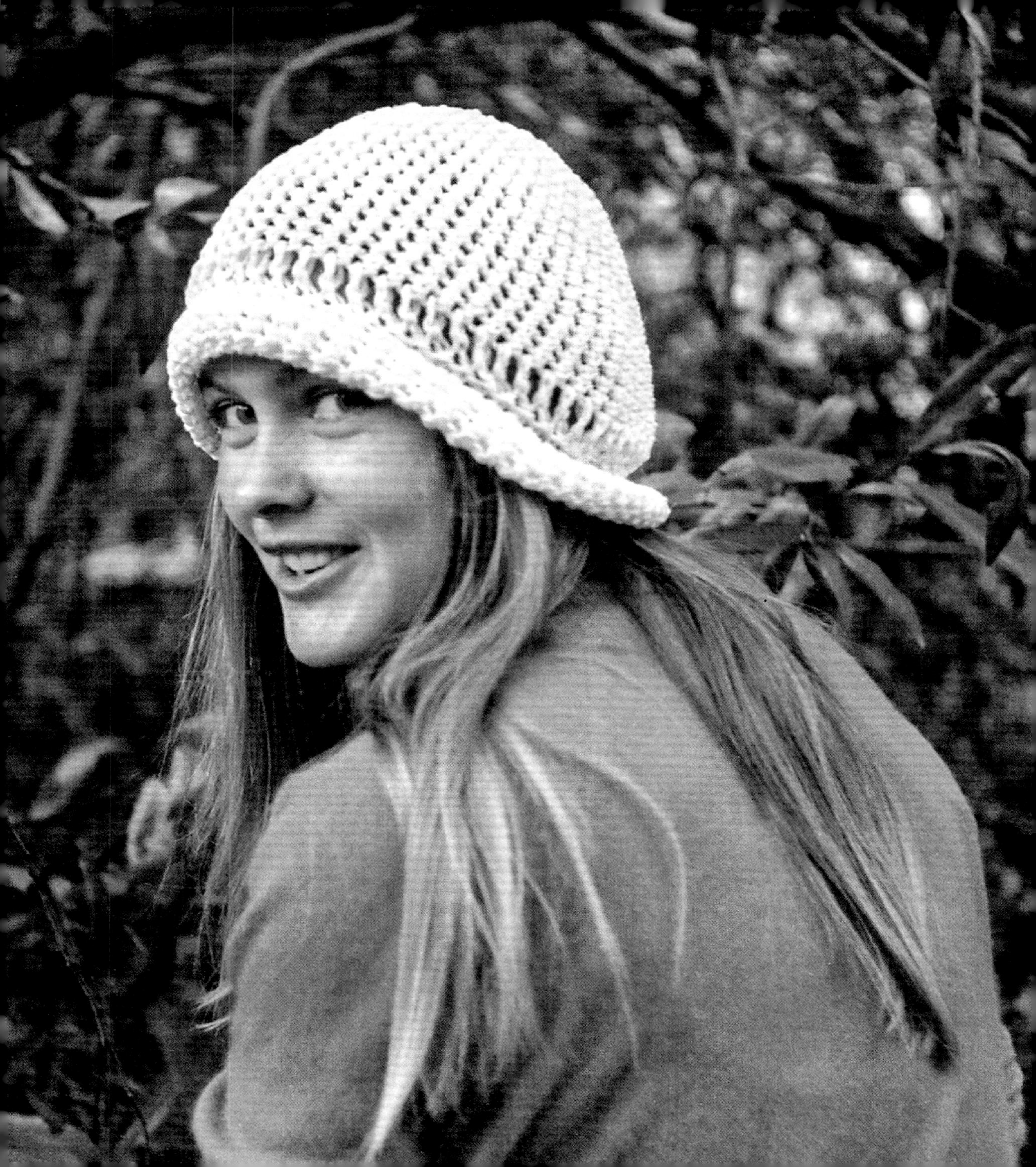

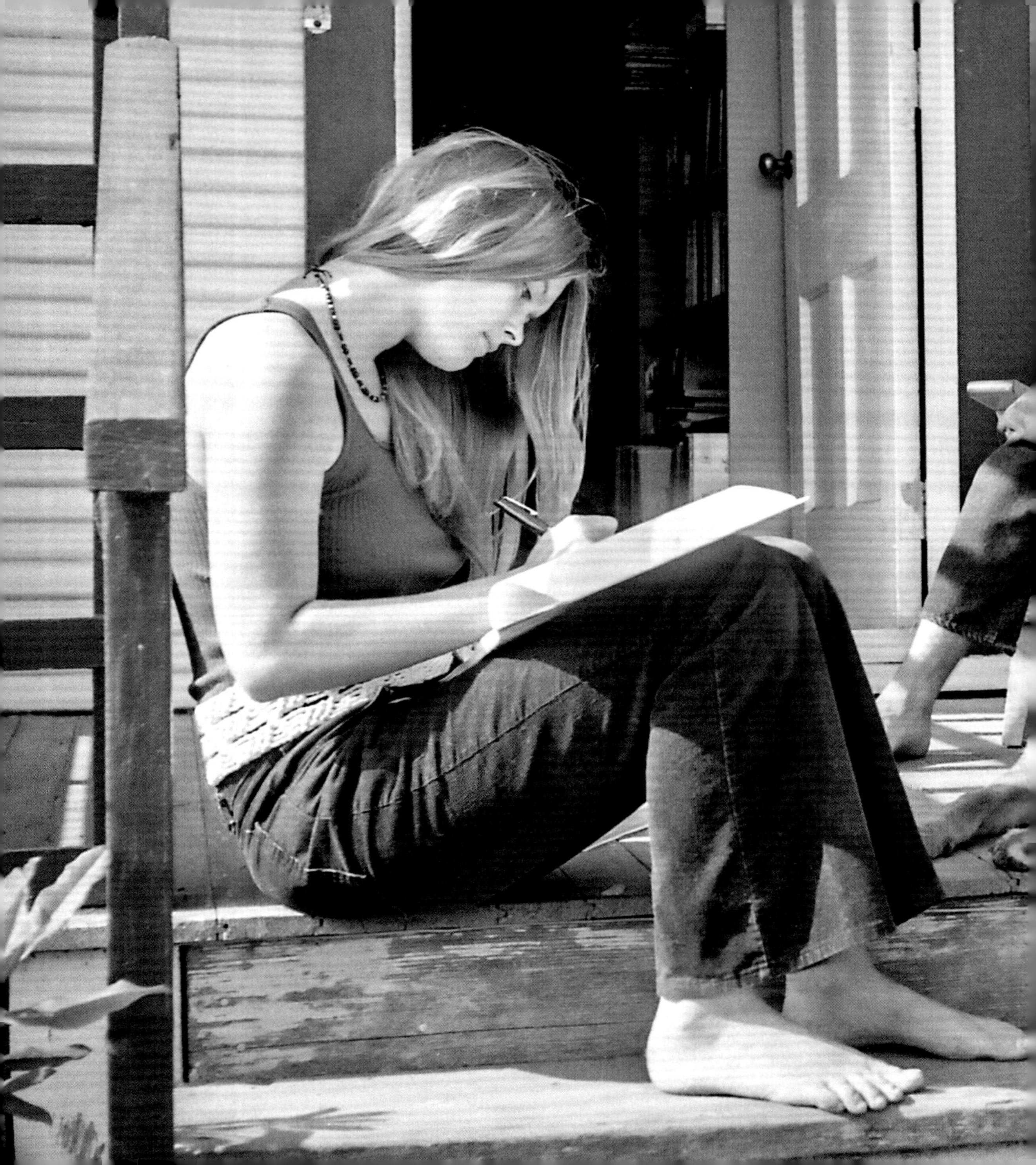

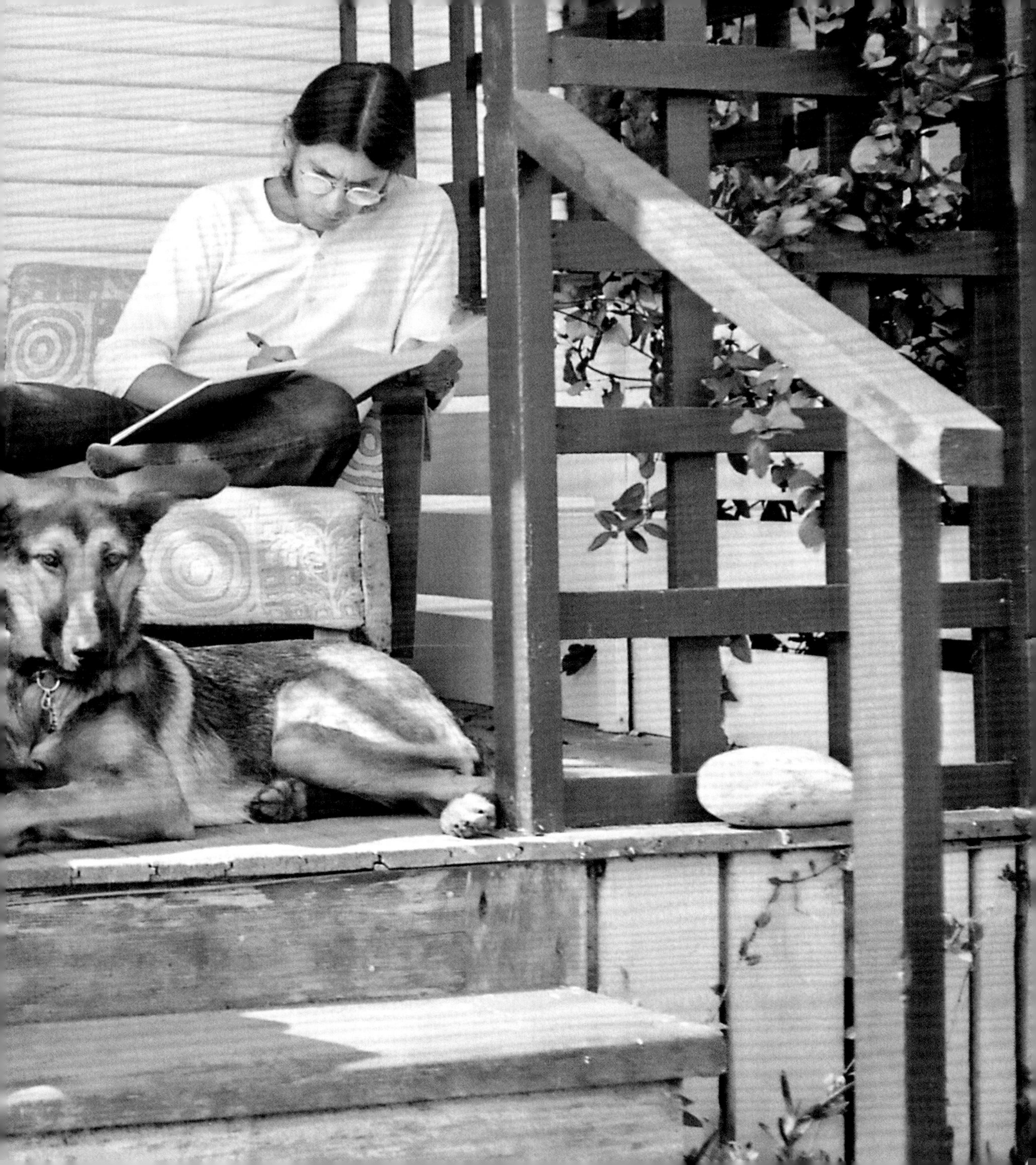

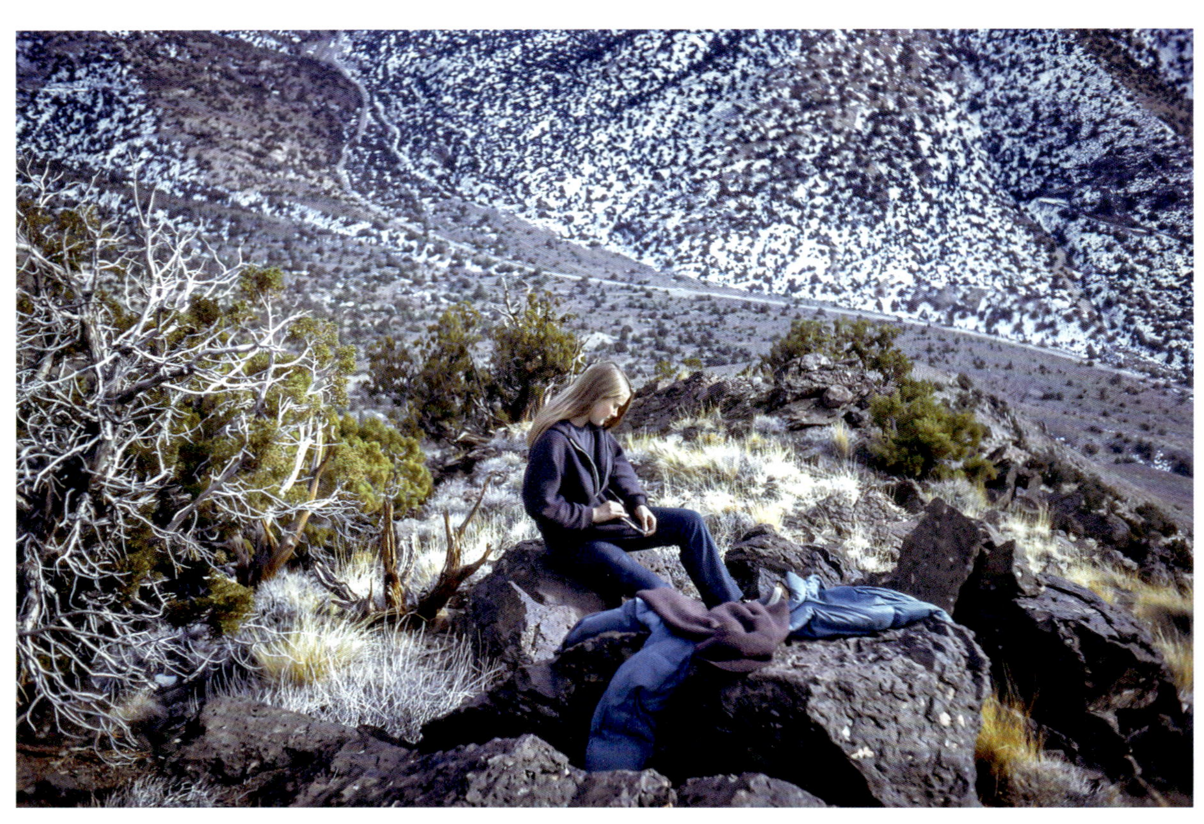

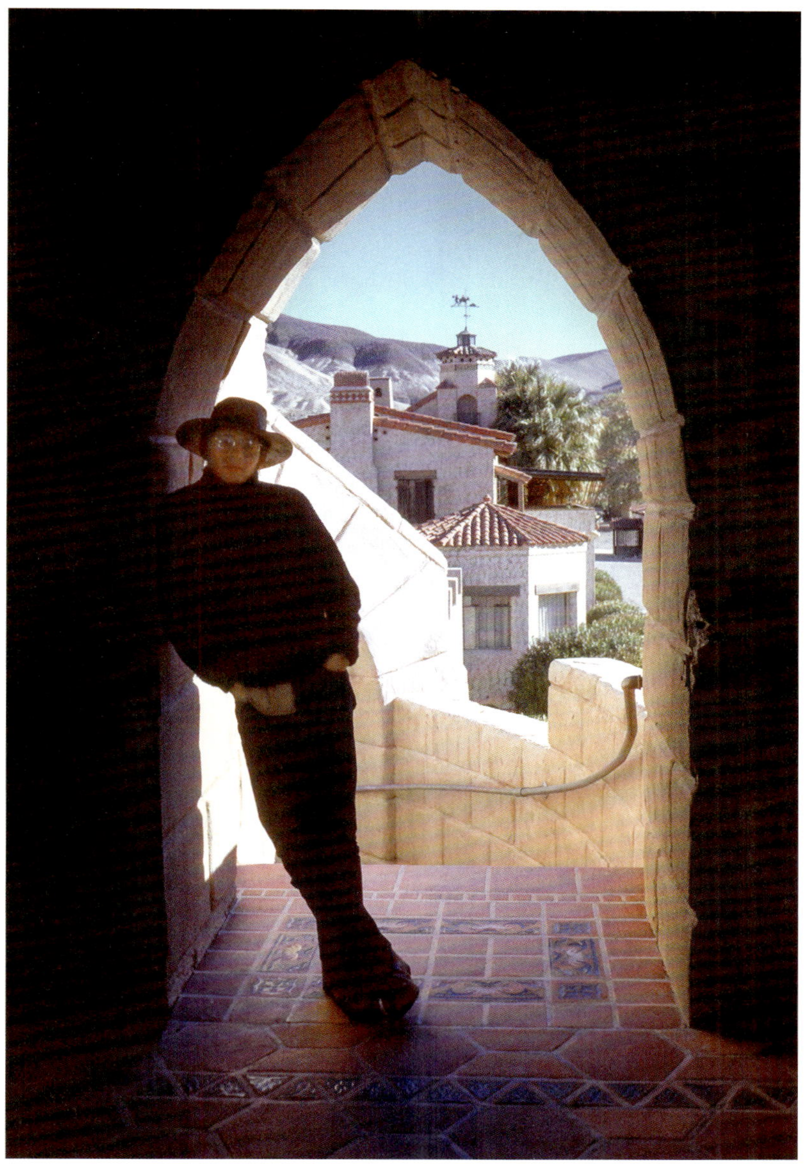

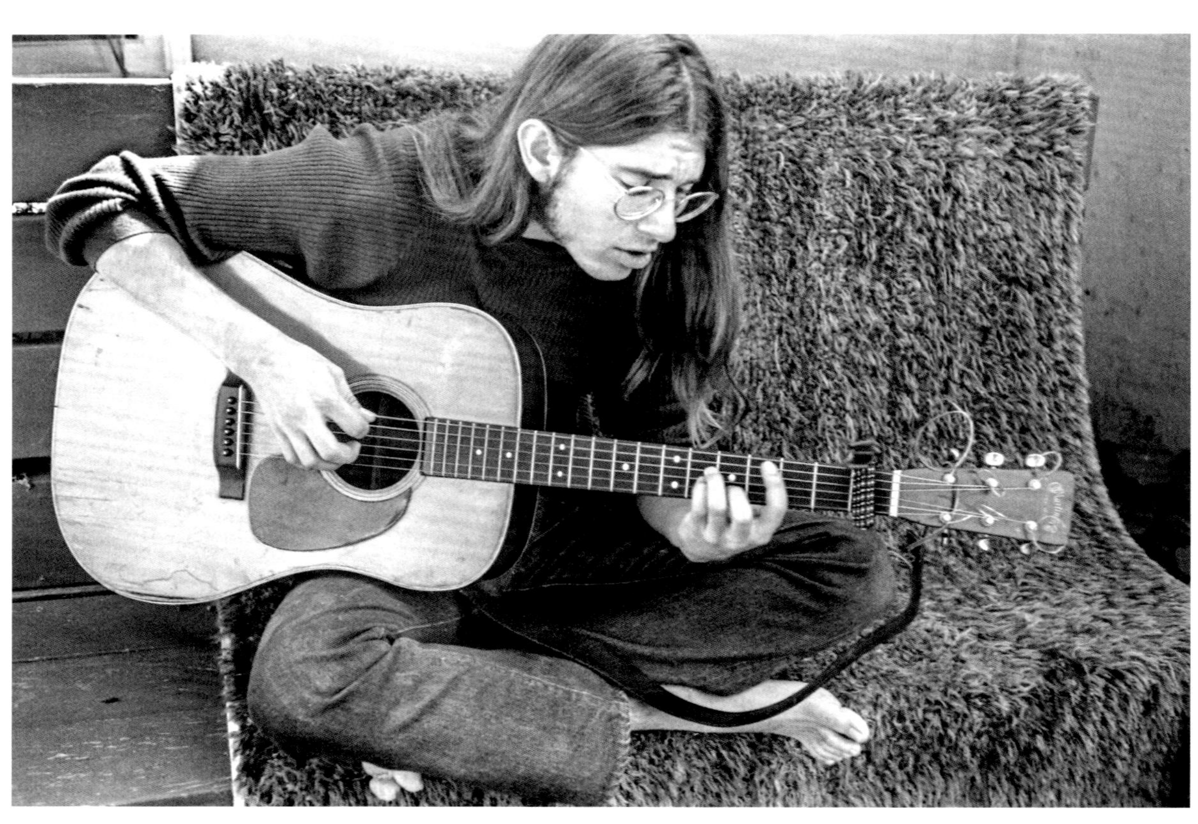

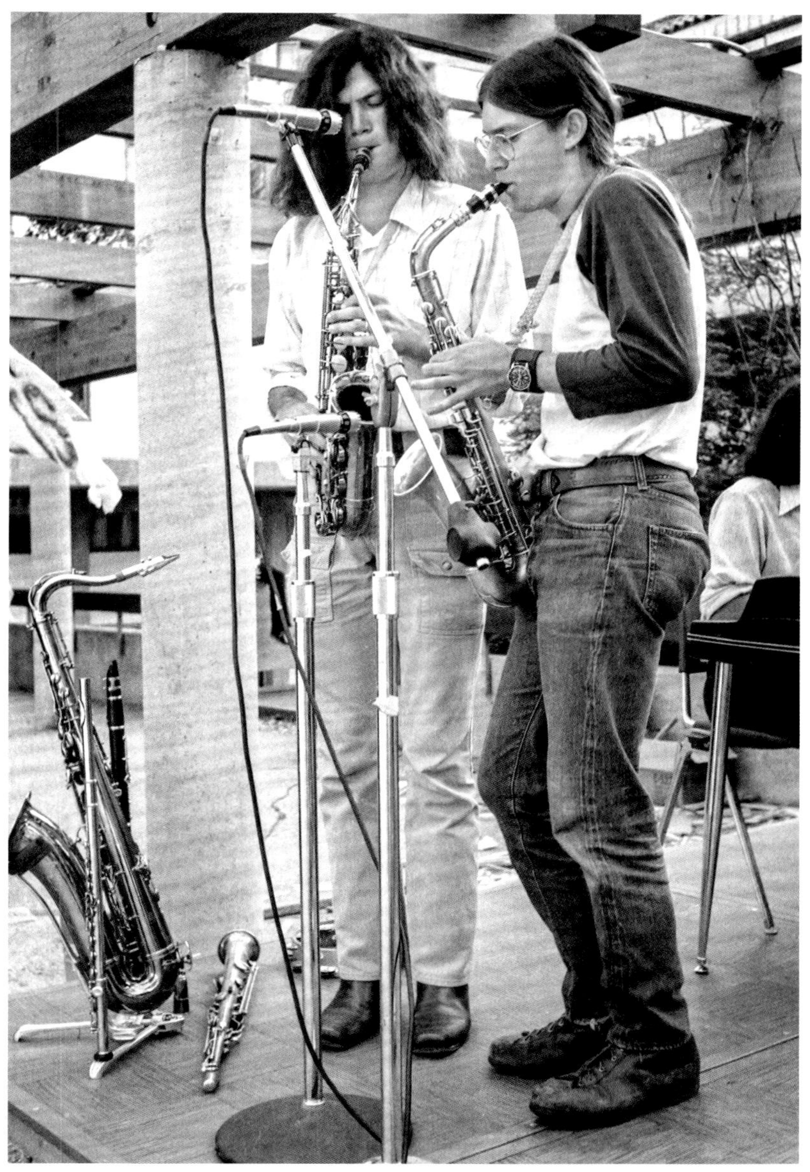

All paths are the same:
they lead nowhere…
Does the path have a heart?
If it does, the path is good; if
it doesn't, it is of no use.

In the summer of 1973, when we graduated from college, David was singing, writing songs, and playing guitar and saxophone with his band. It was a full life for him. But I had other plans. I said goodbye to David and flew to Europe to travel for a few weeks before starting a year-long depth psychology program at the Jung Institute in Zurich. I traveled through Austria and the former Yugoslavia with friends, returning near the end of the summer to Vienna, where I found a letter from David. To my surprise, he wrote that he would be arriving in a few days and wanted to spend the year with me in Switzerland. I met him at the airport – he arrived with a backpack, a guitar, and a pile of books. We spent a night or two in Vienna, and then used our Eurail passes to take a train to Athens. I hadn't expected him to join me – I hadn't wanted to break up the band – but I was overjoyed. David's decision marked an important turning point in our relationship. It was a sign of commitment. And, although his departure did cause the band to break up in 1973, David continued to write music and play in other bands while I was pursuing a doctoral degree at the University of Chicago, and a career as teacher, scholar, and academic administrator at Santa Clara University in California.

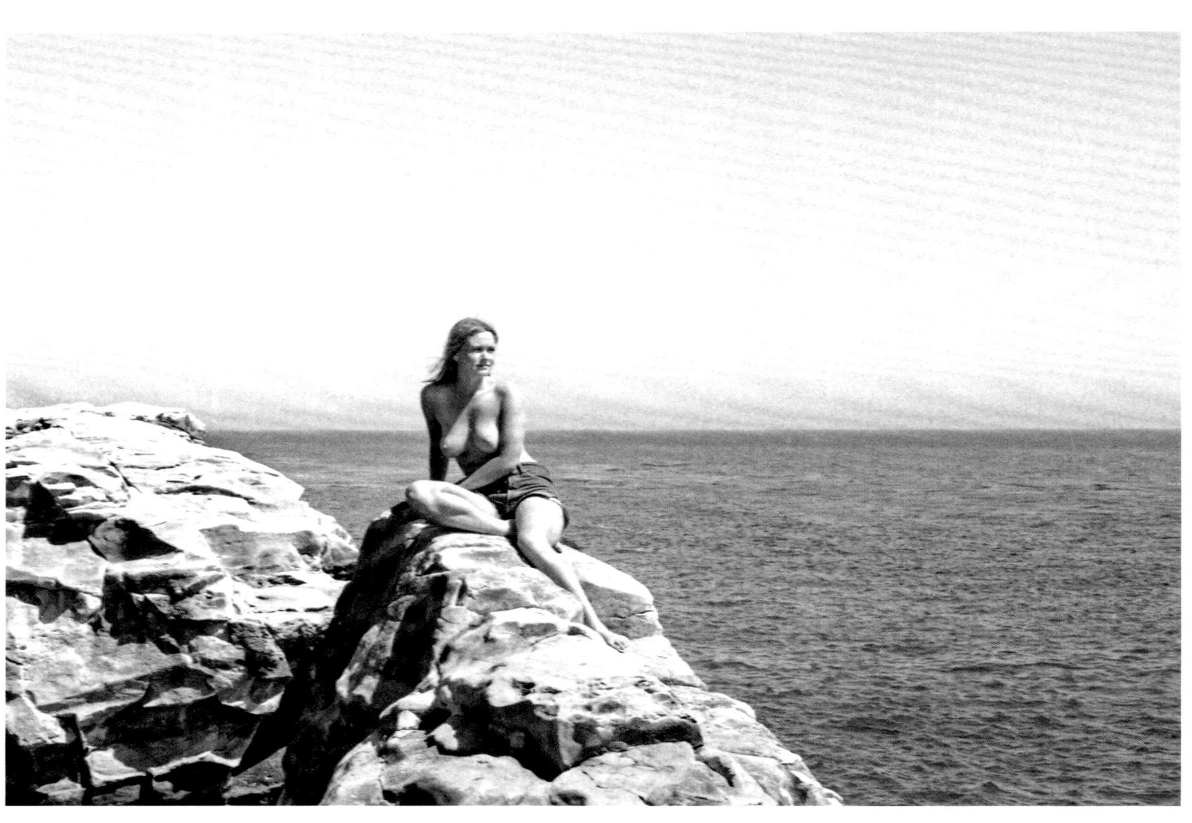

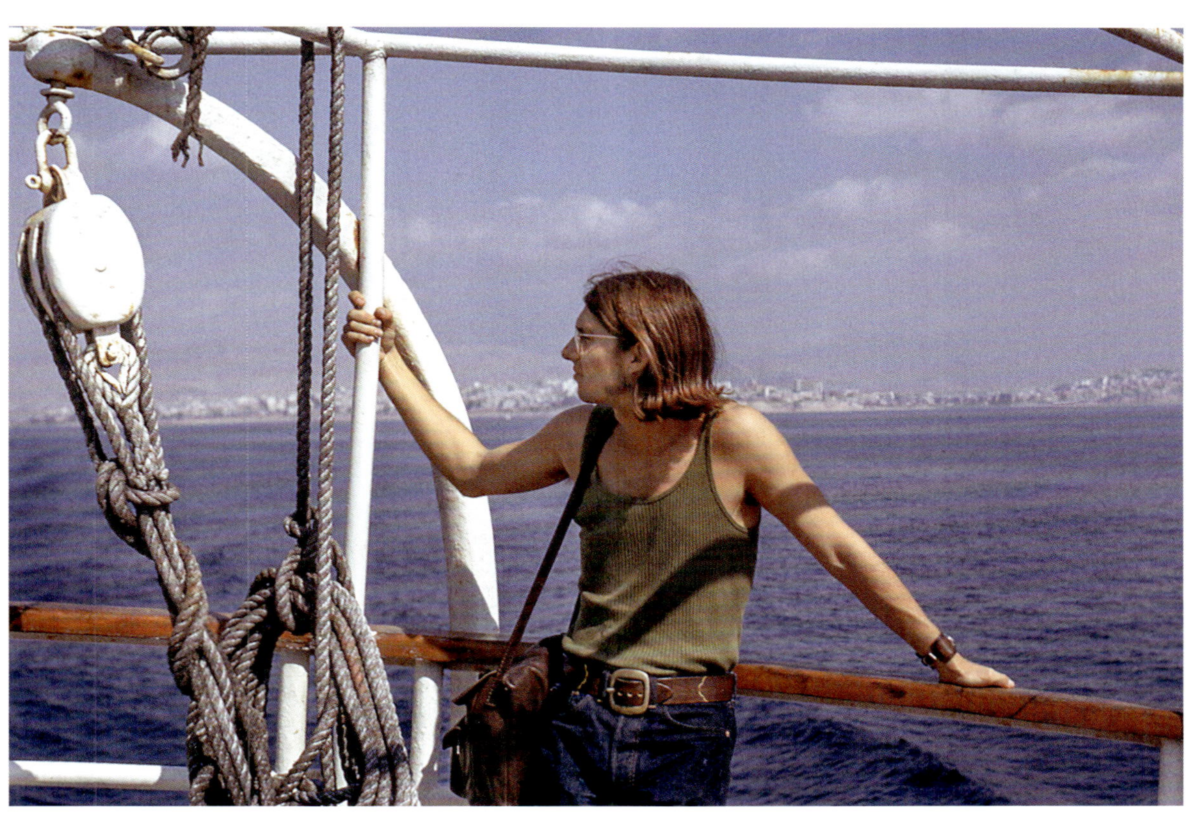

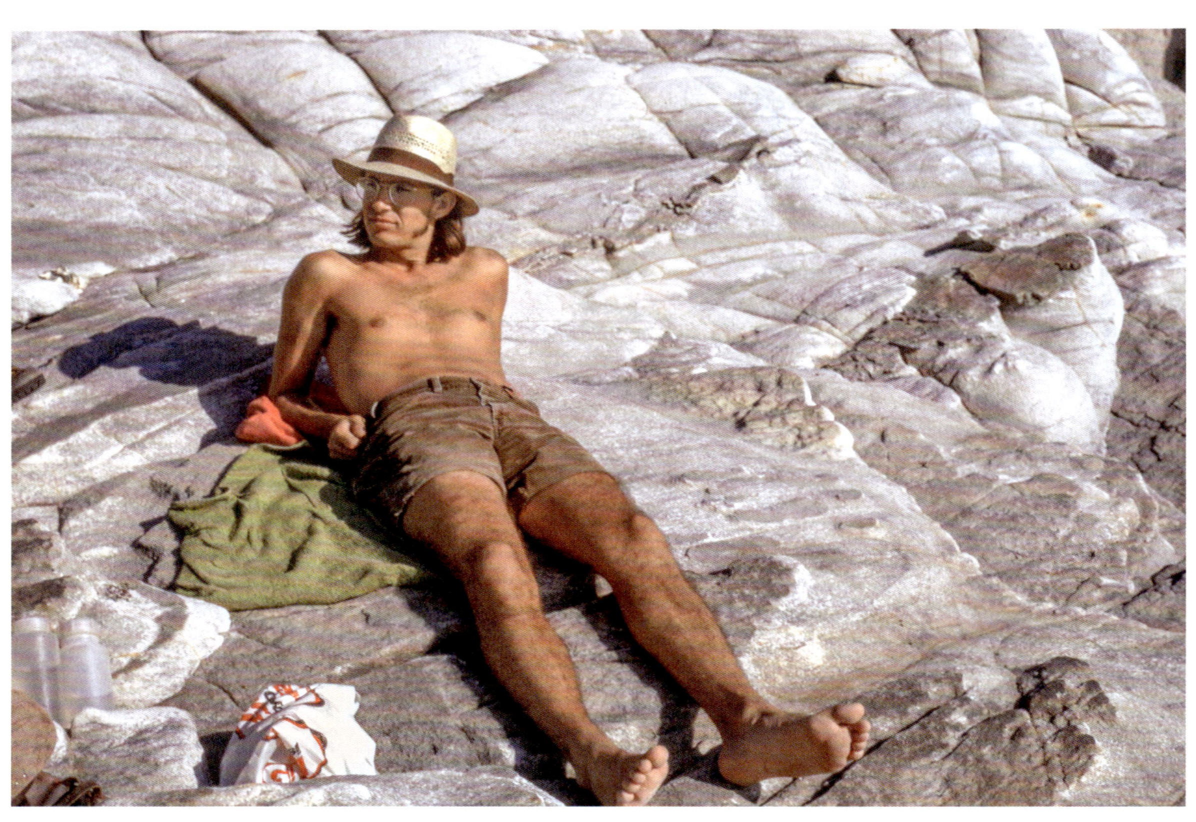

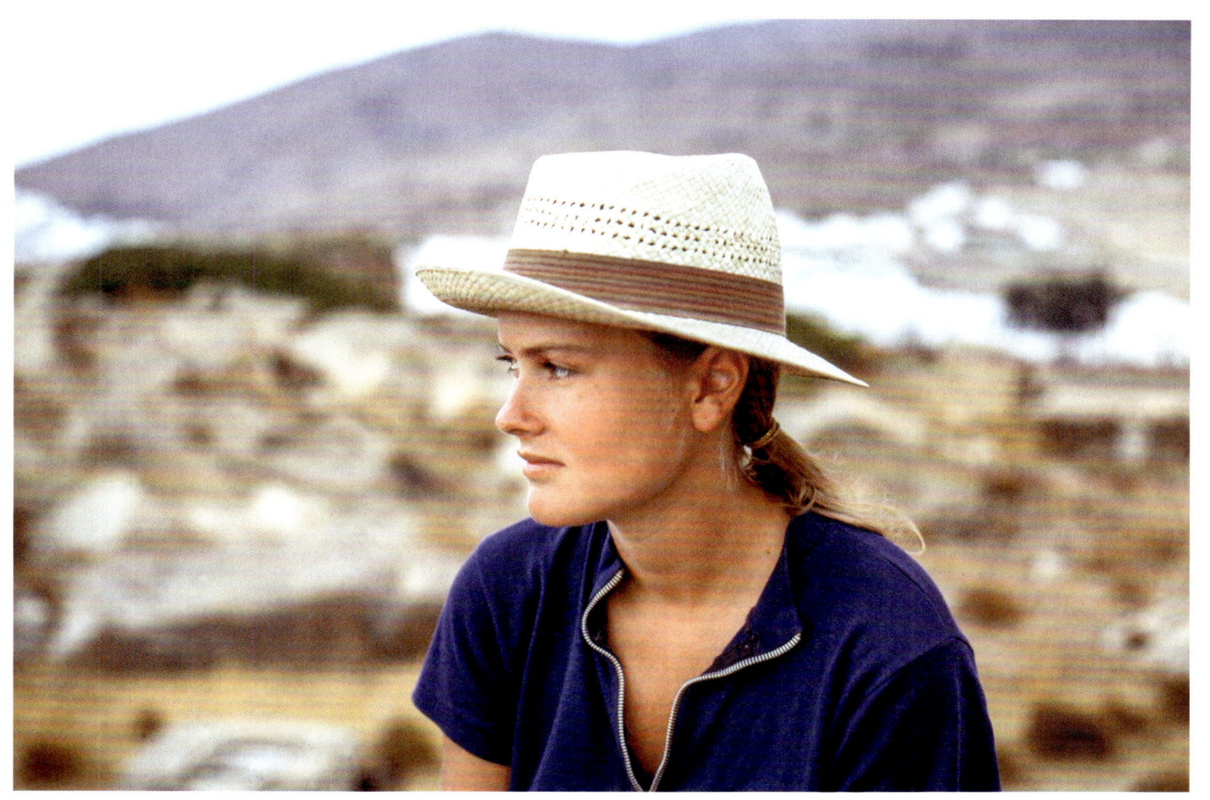

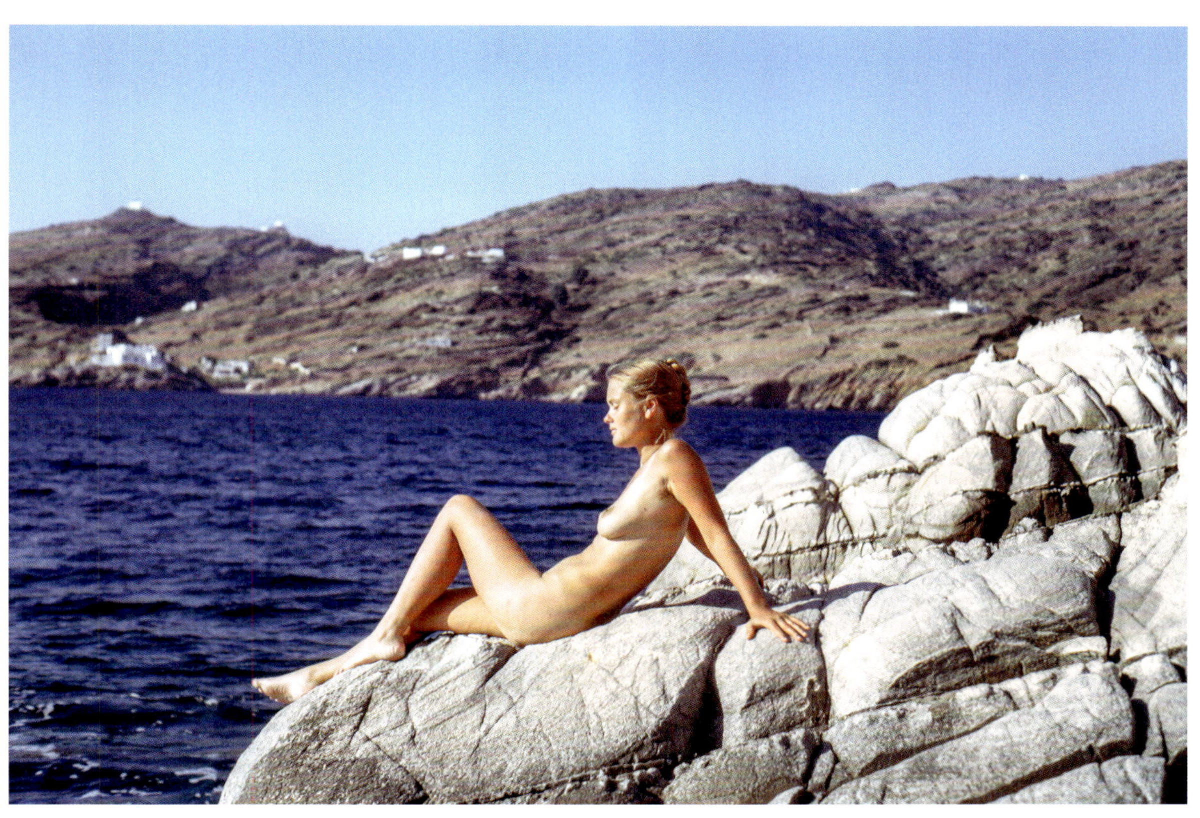

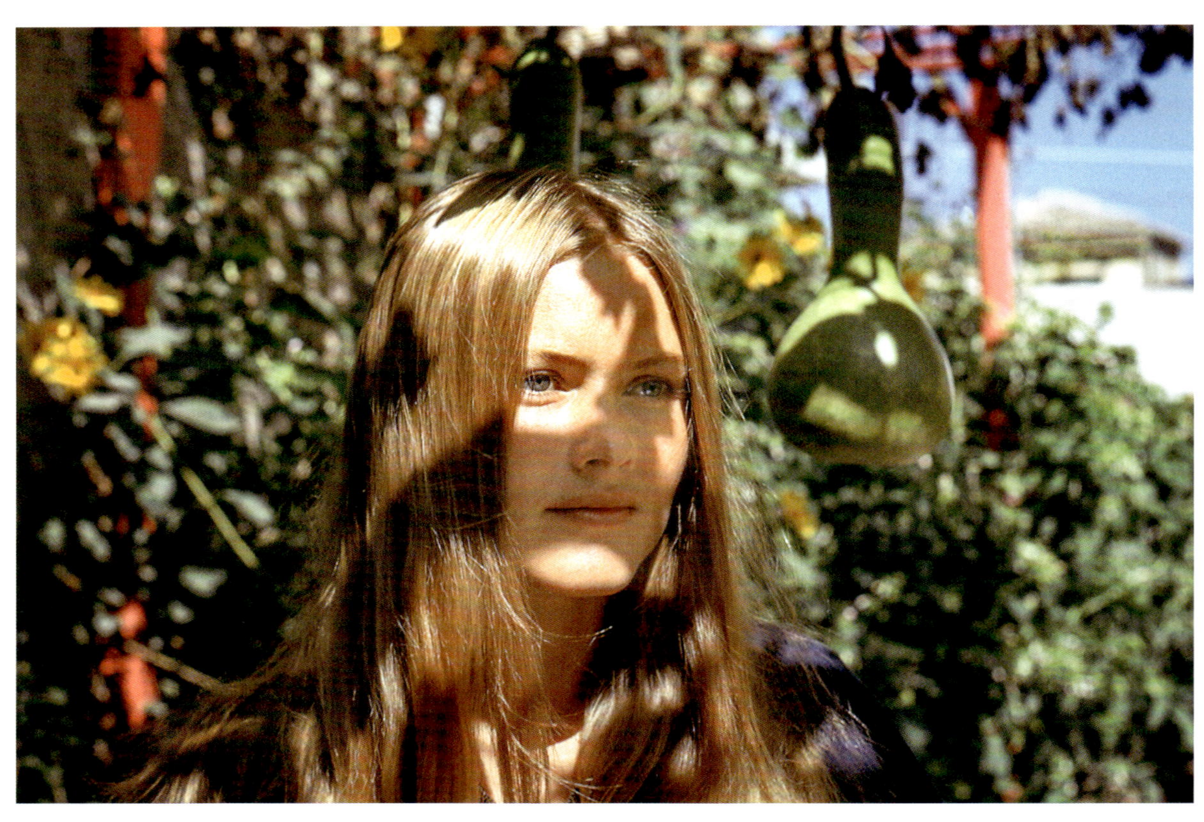

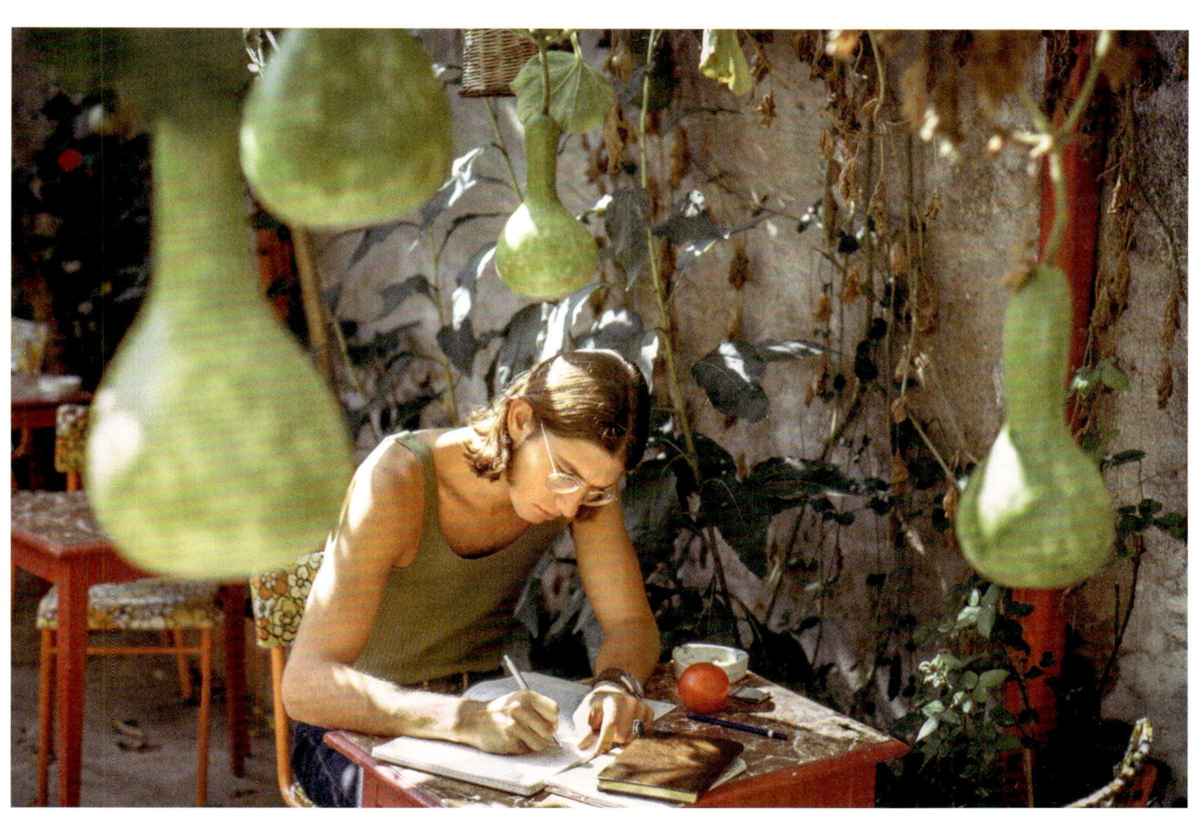

HERAKLION, CRETE 1973 | 25

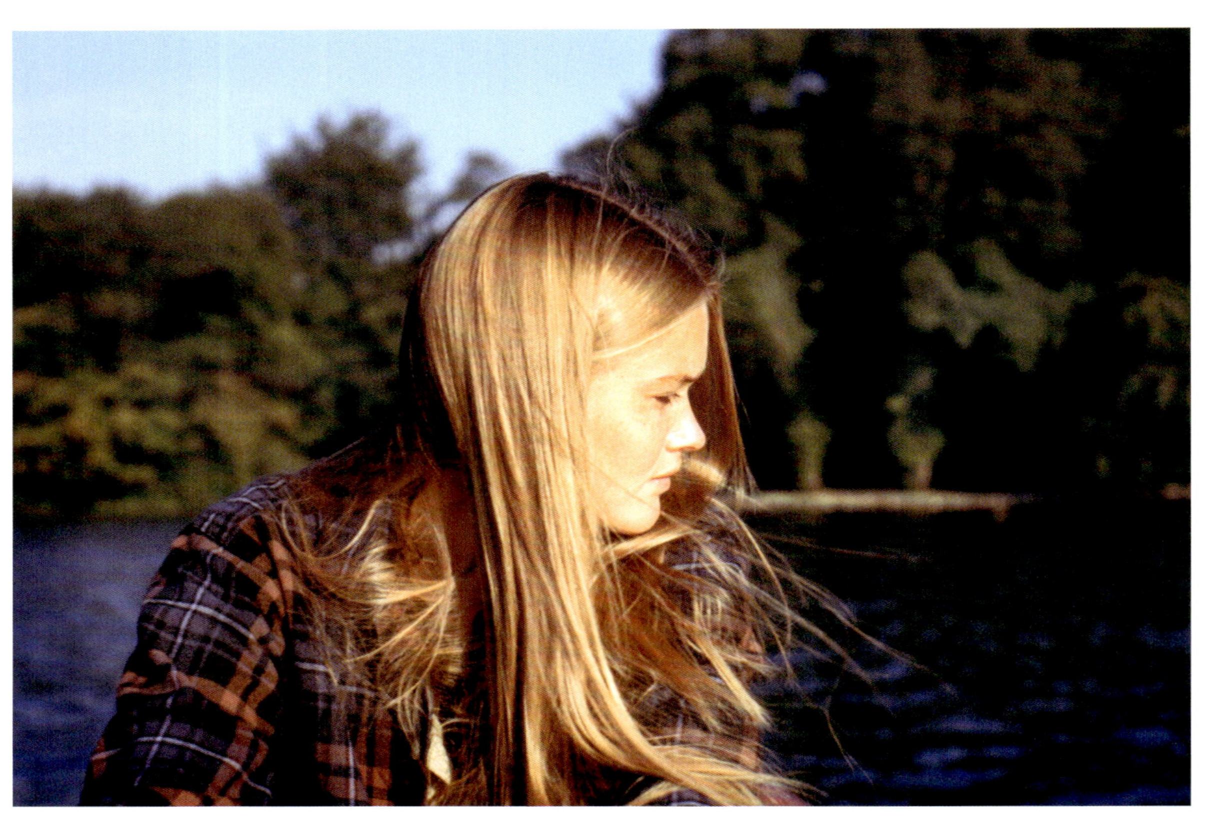

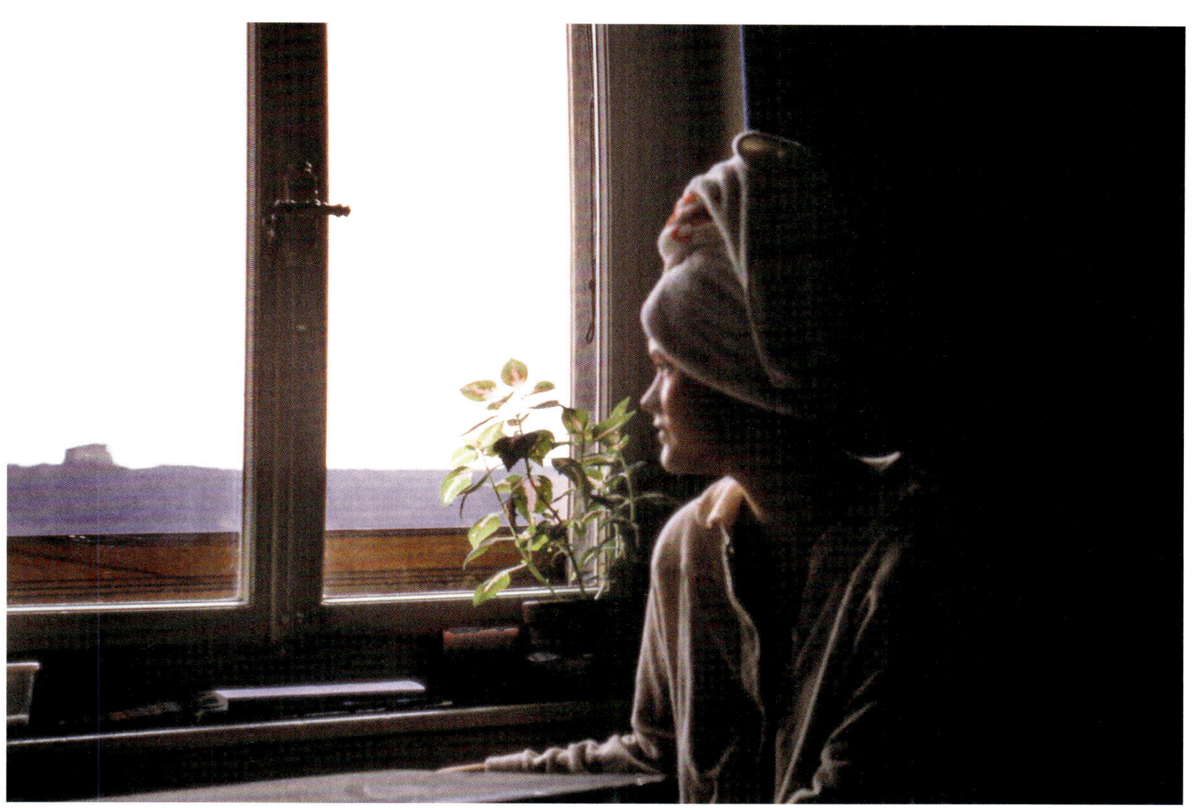

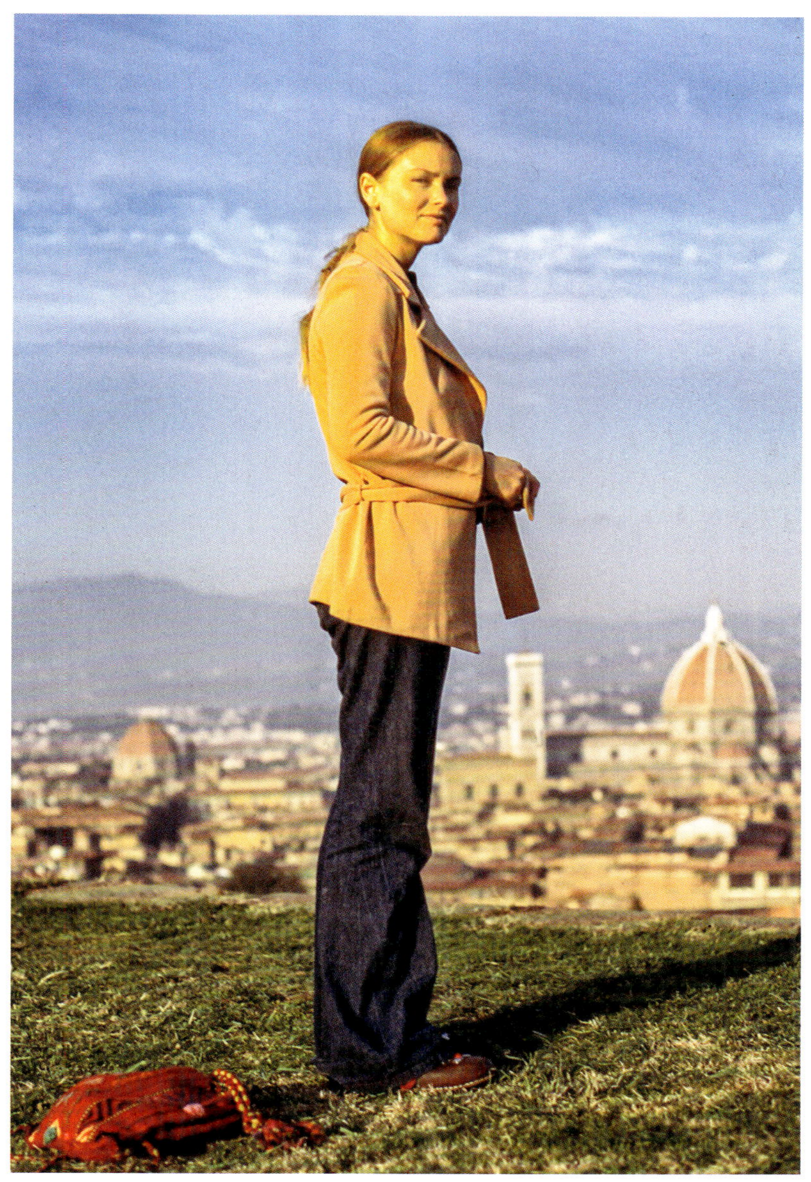

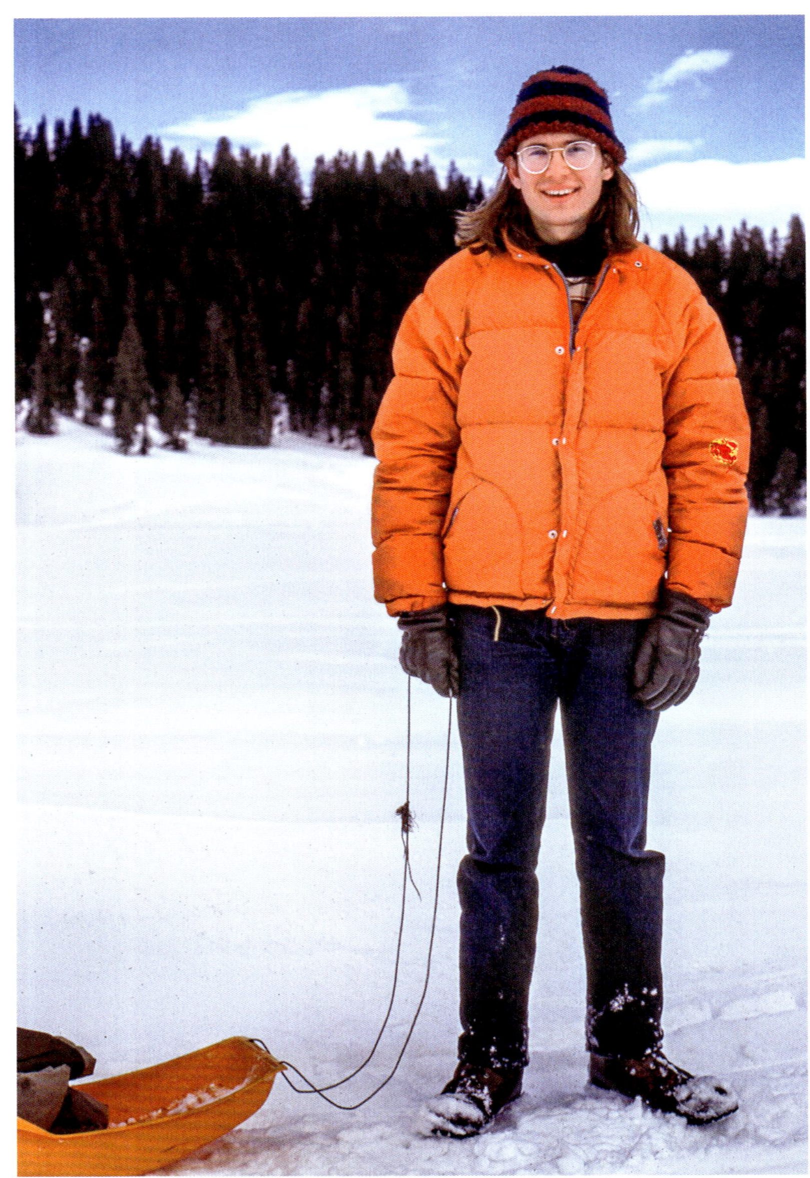

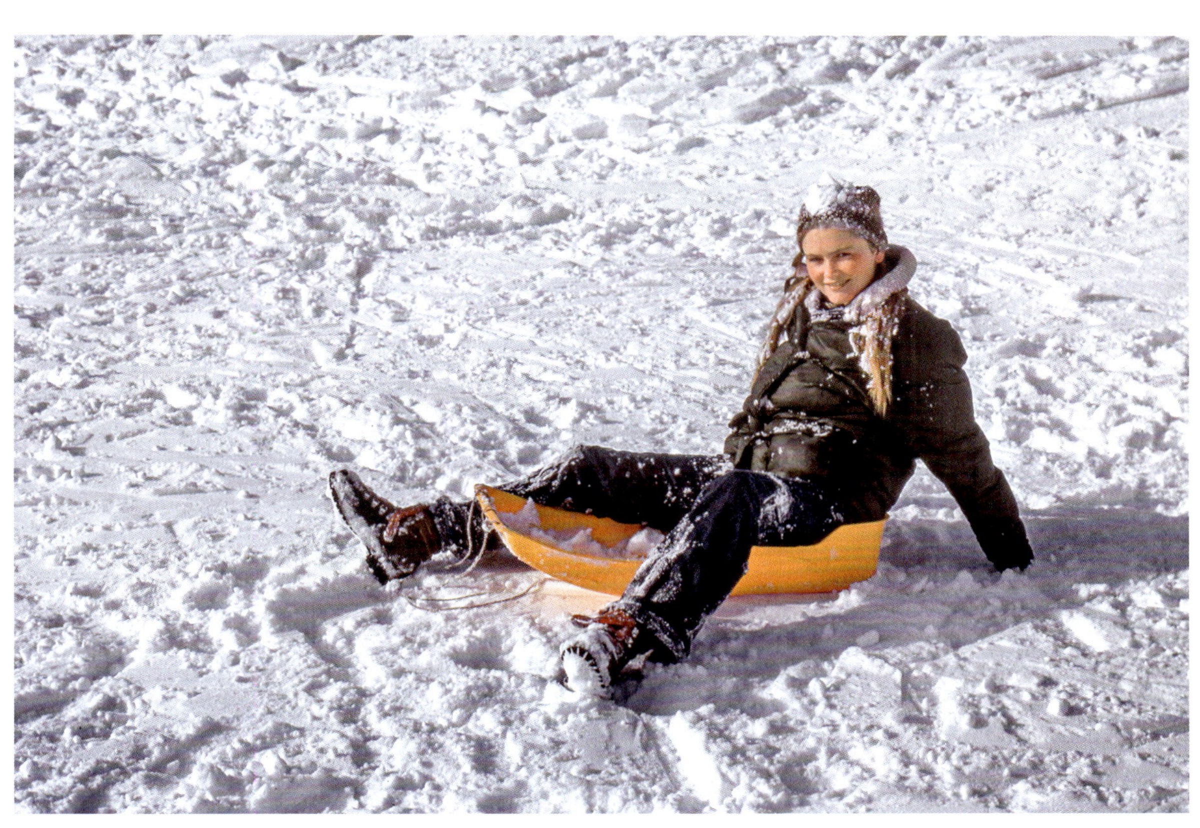

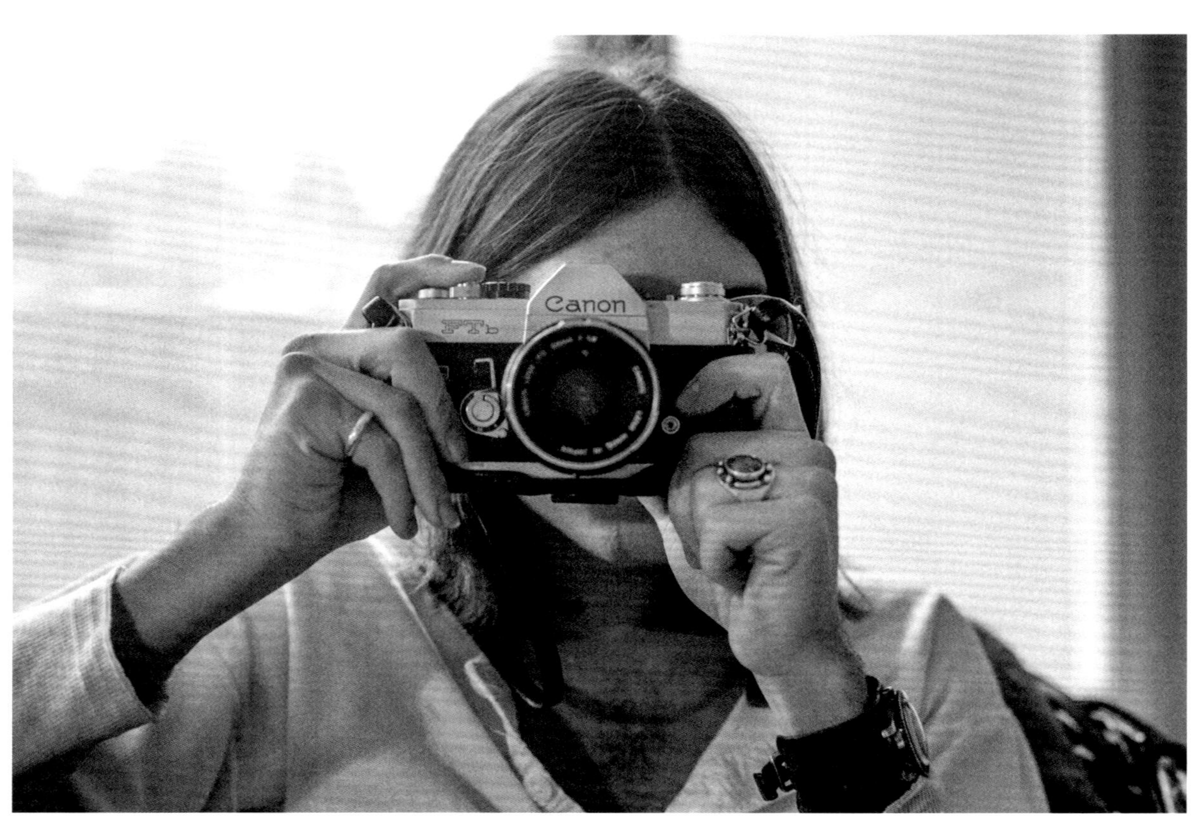

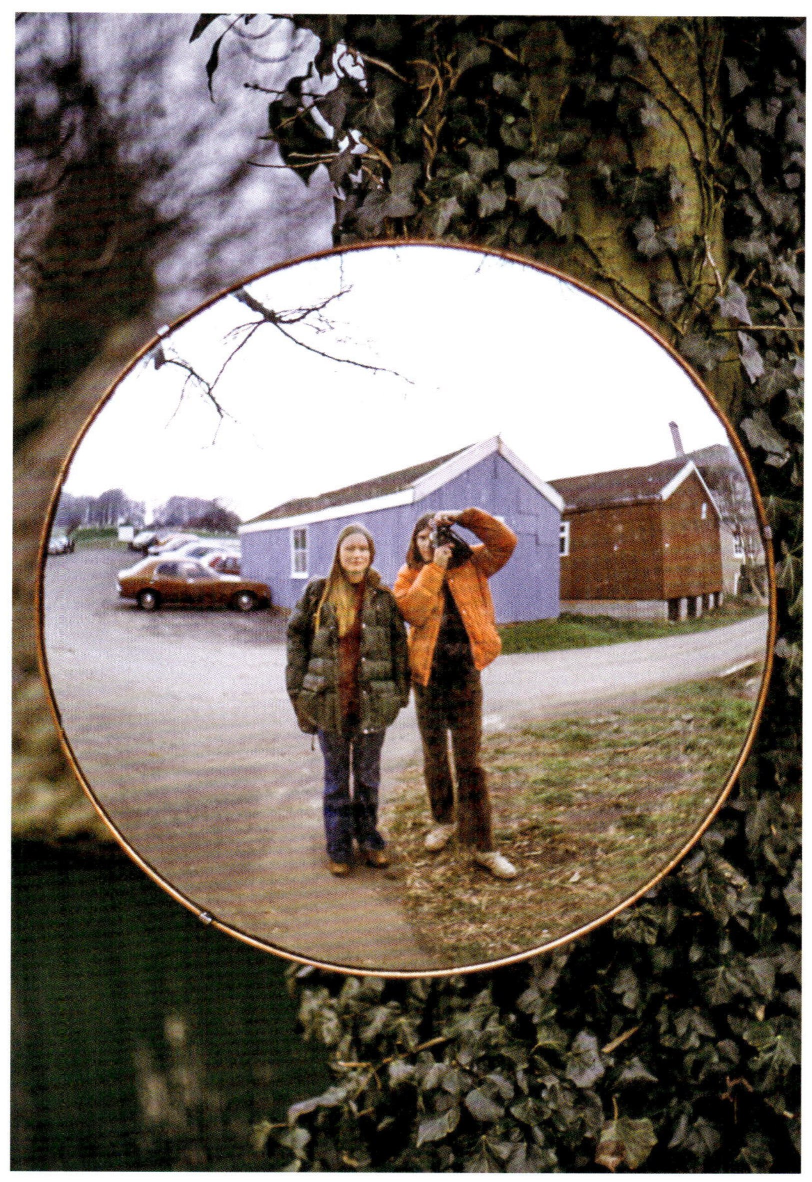

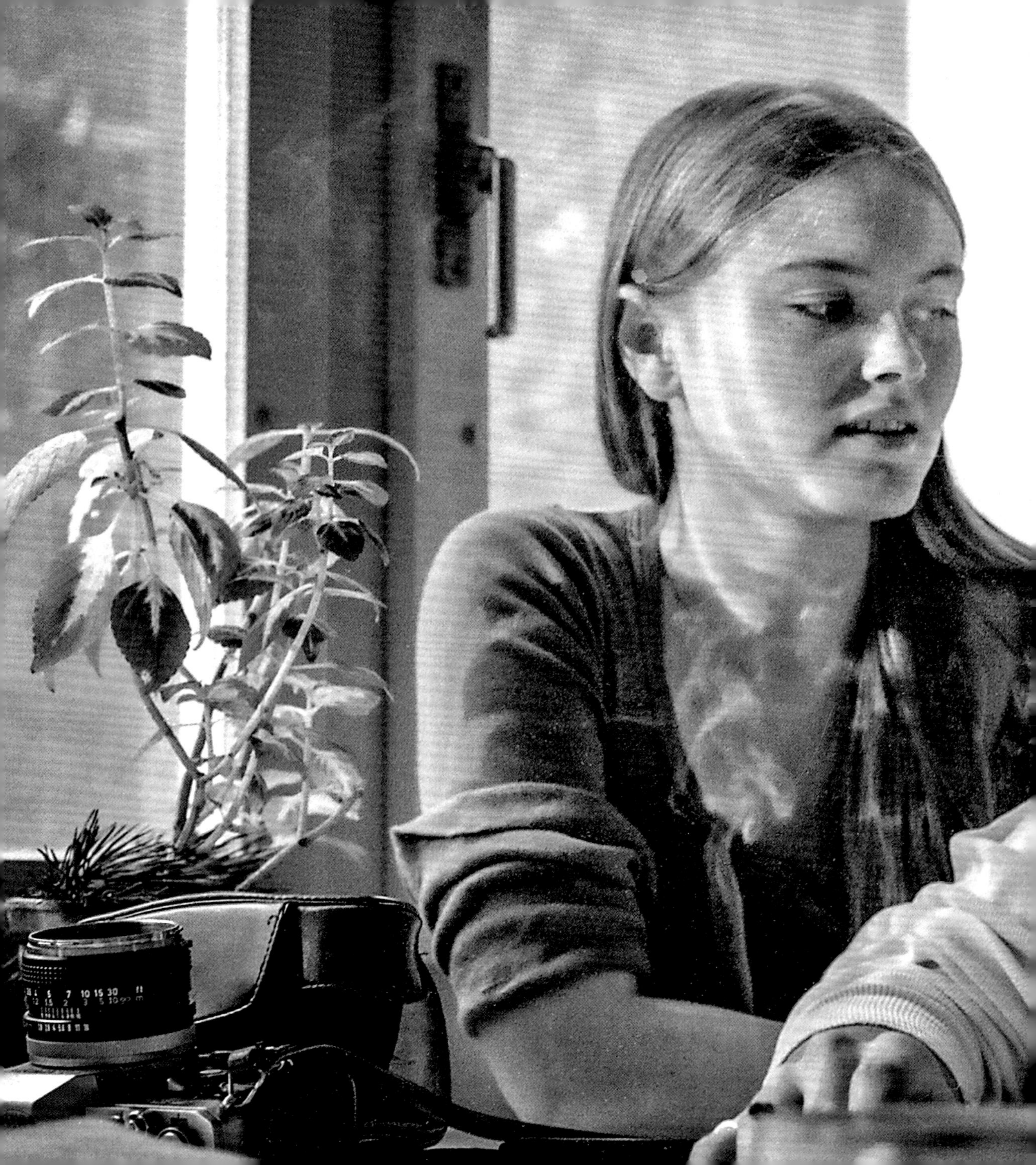

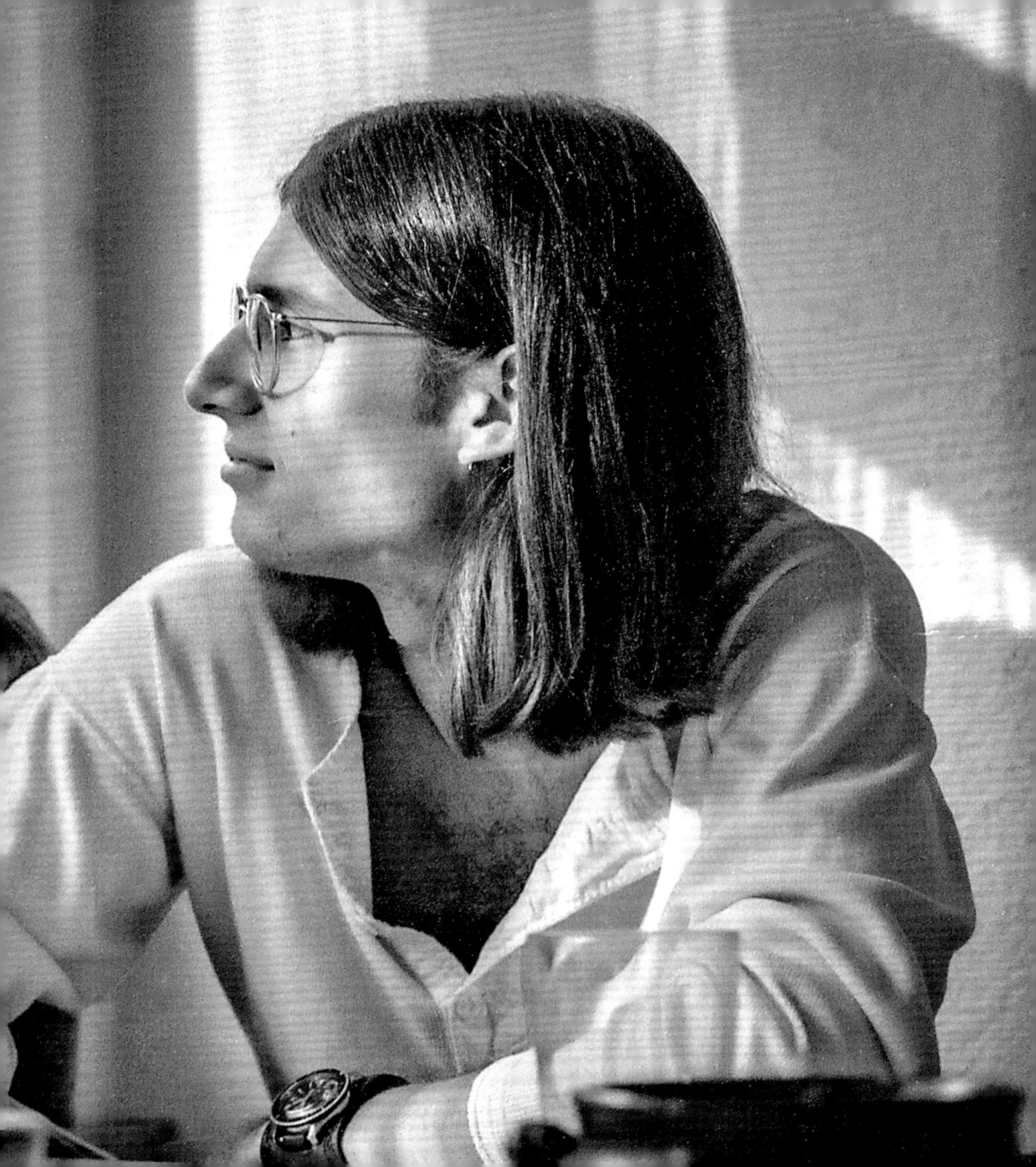

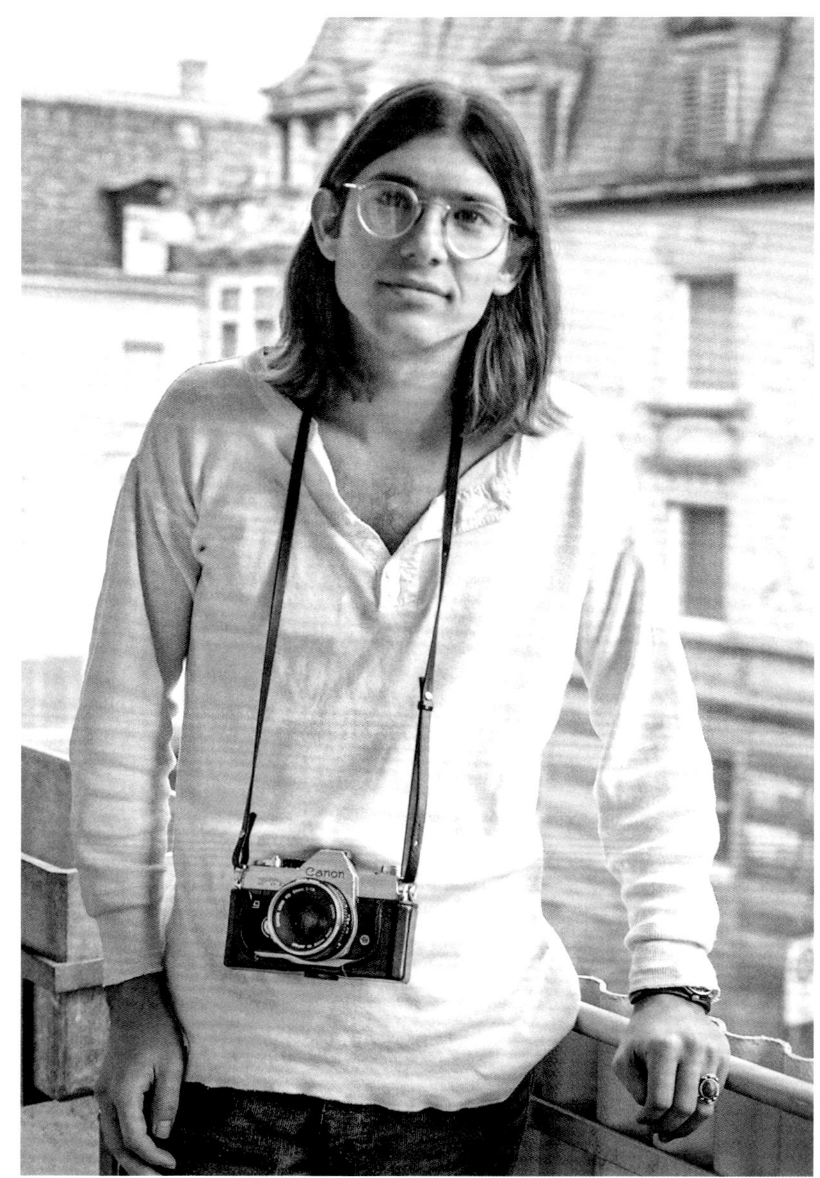

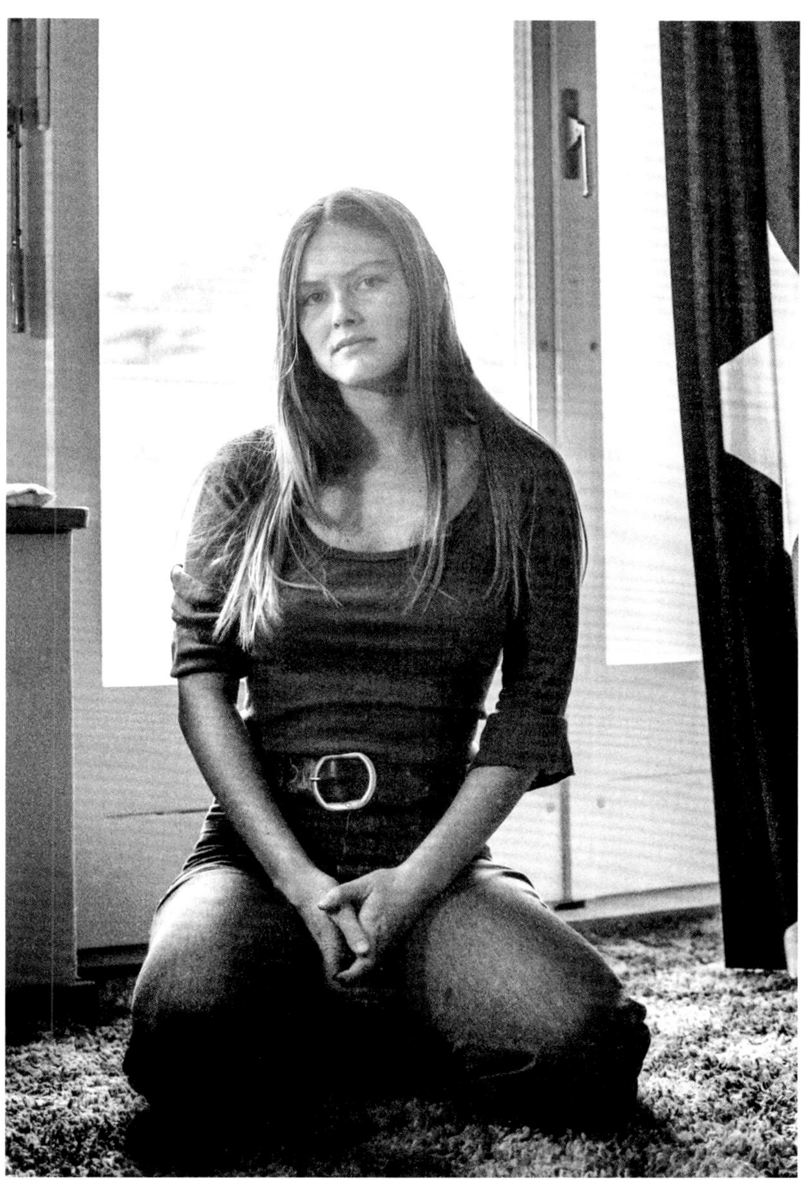

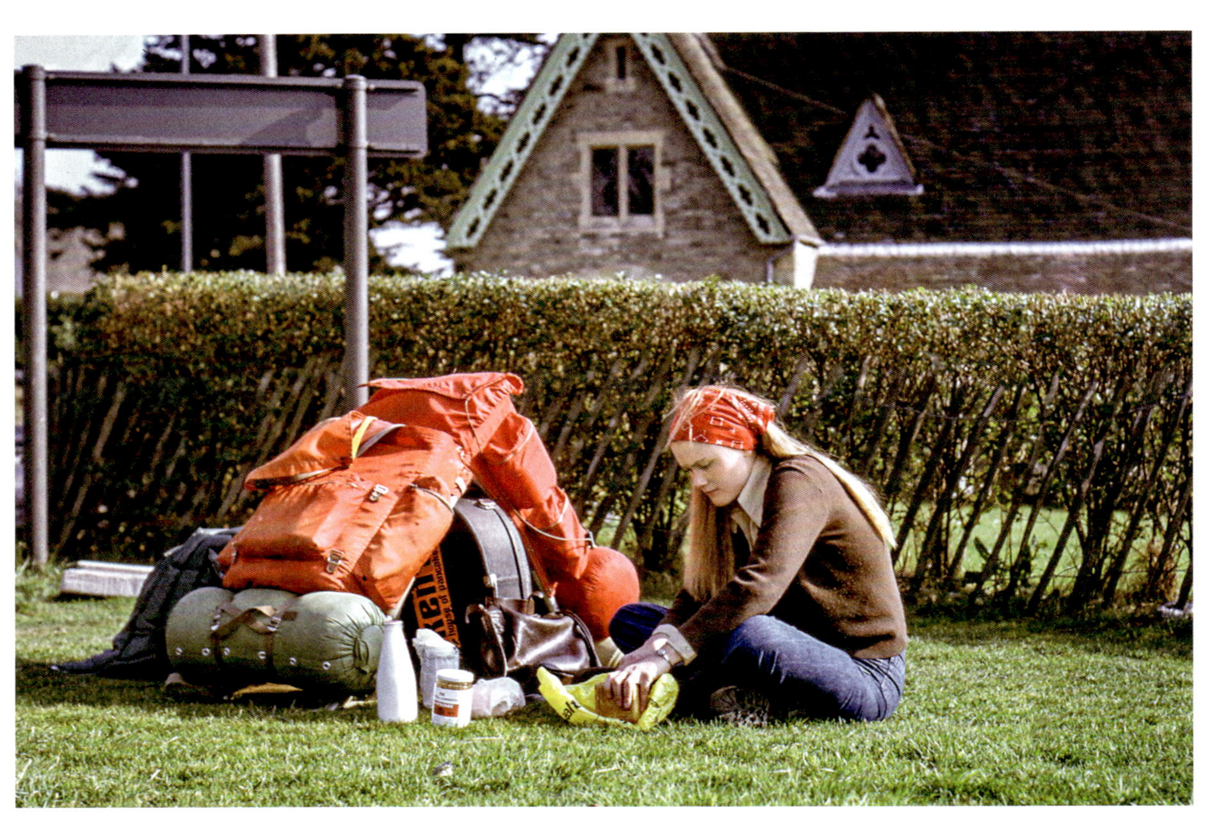

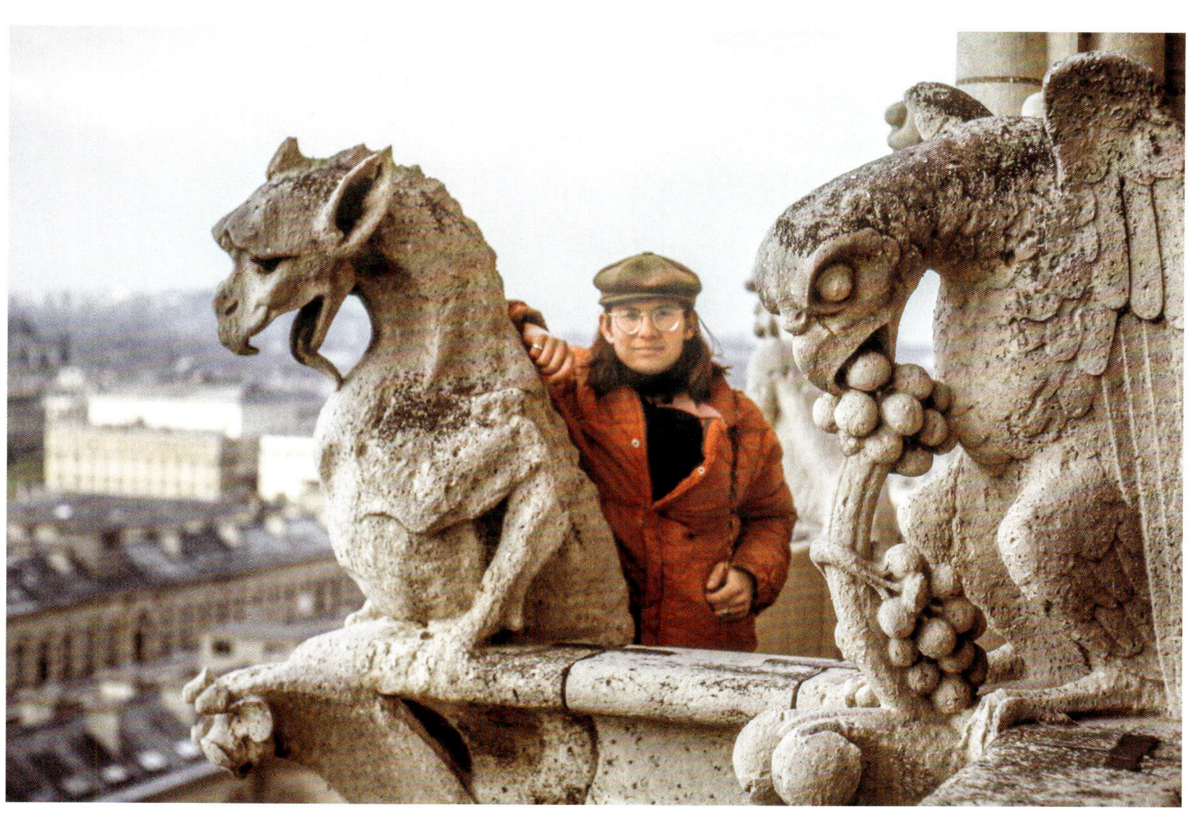

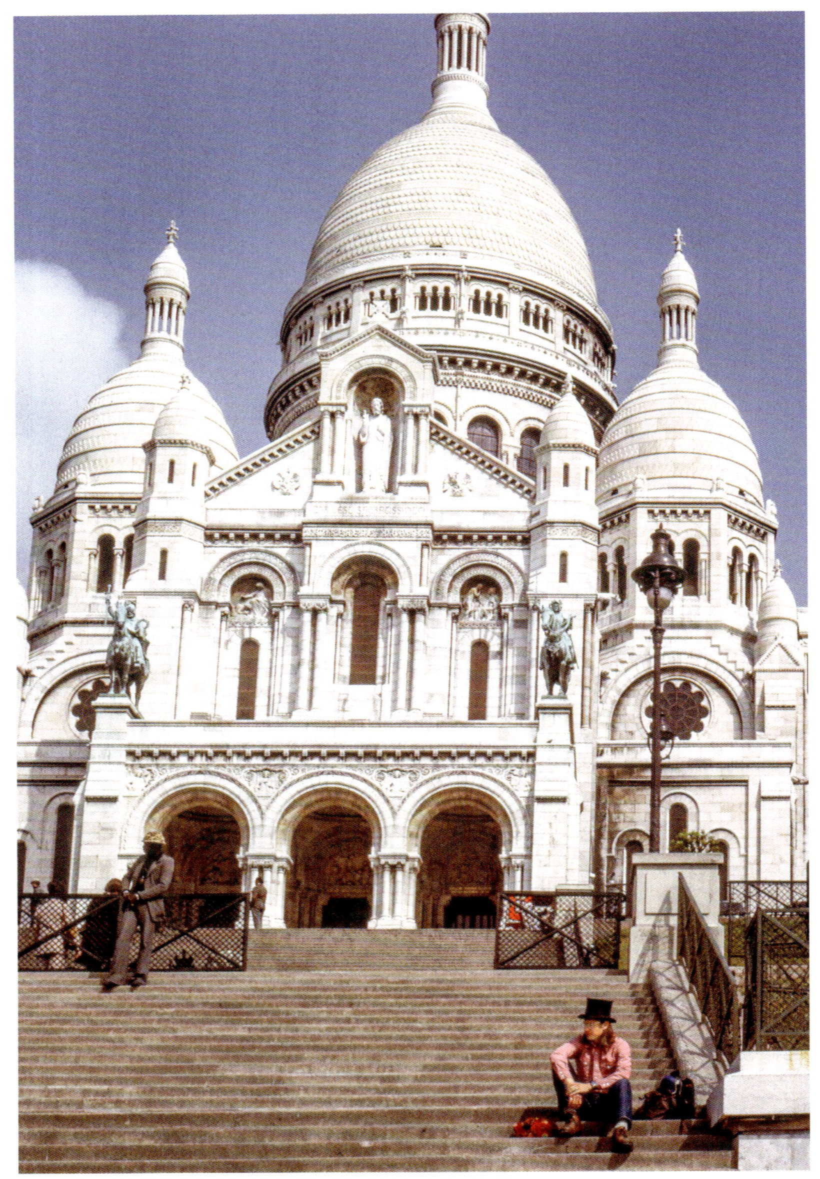

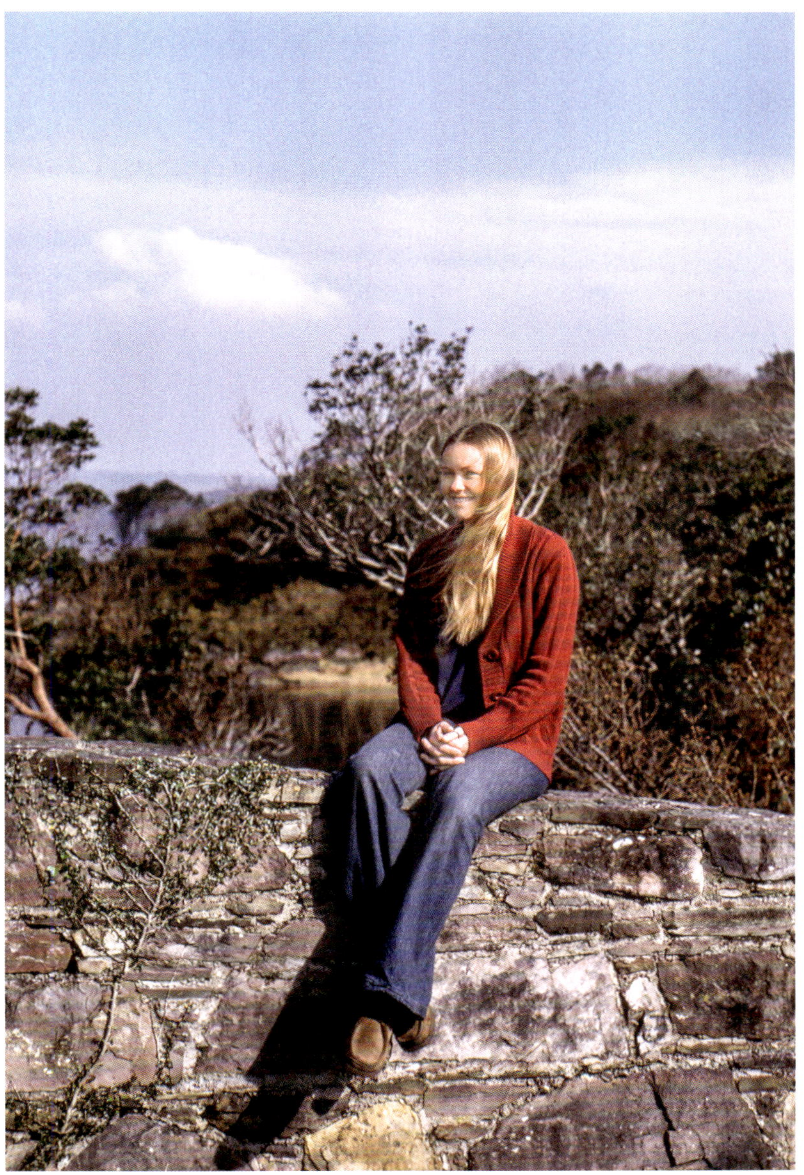

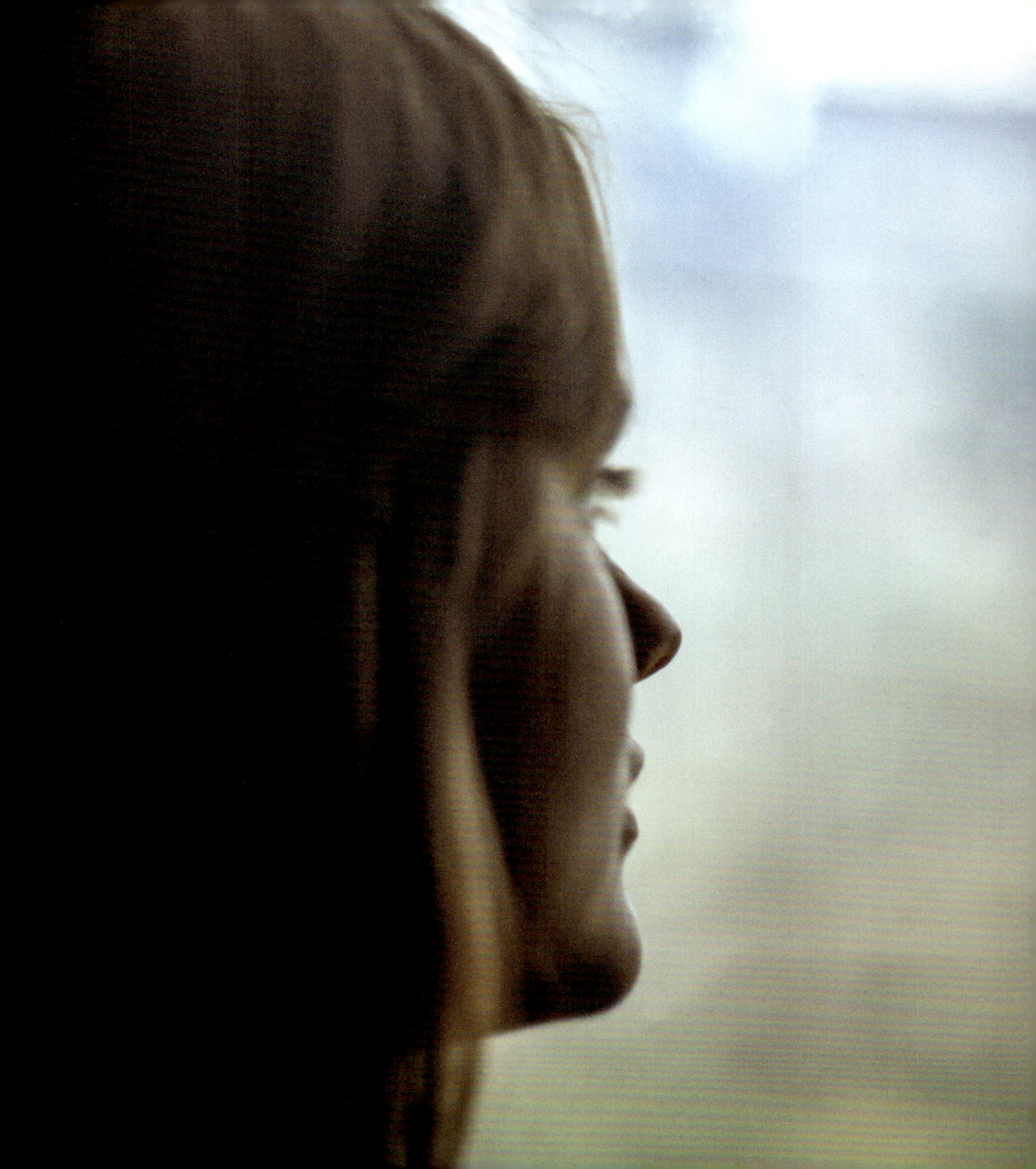

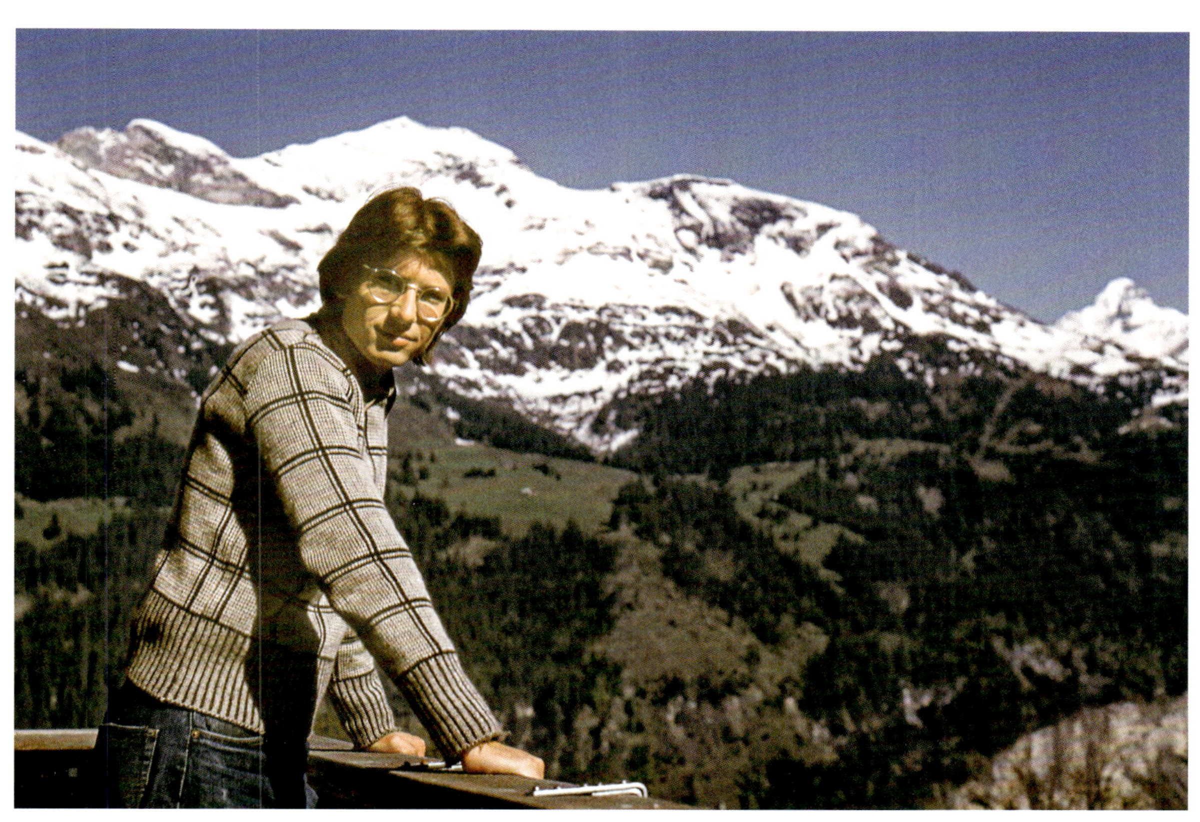

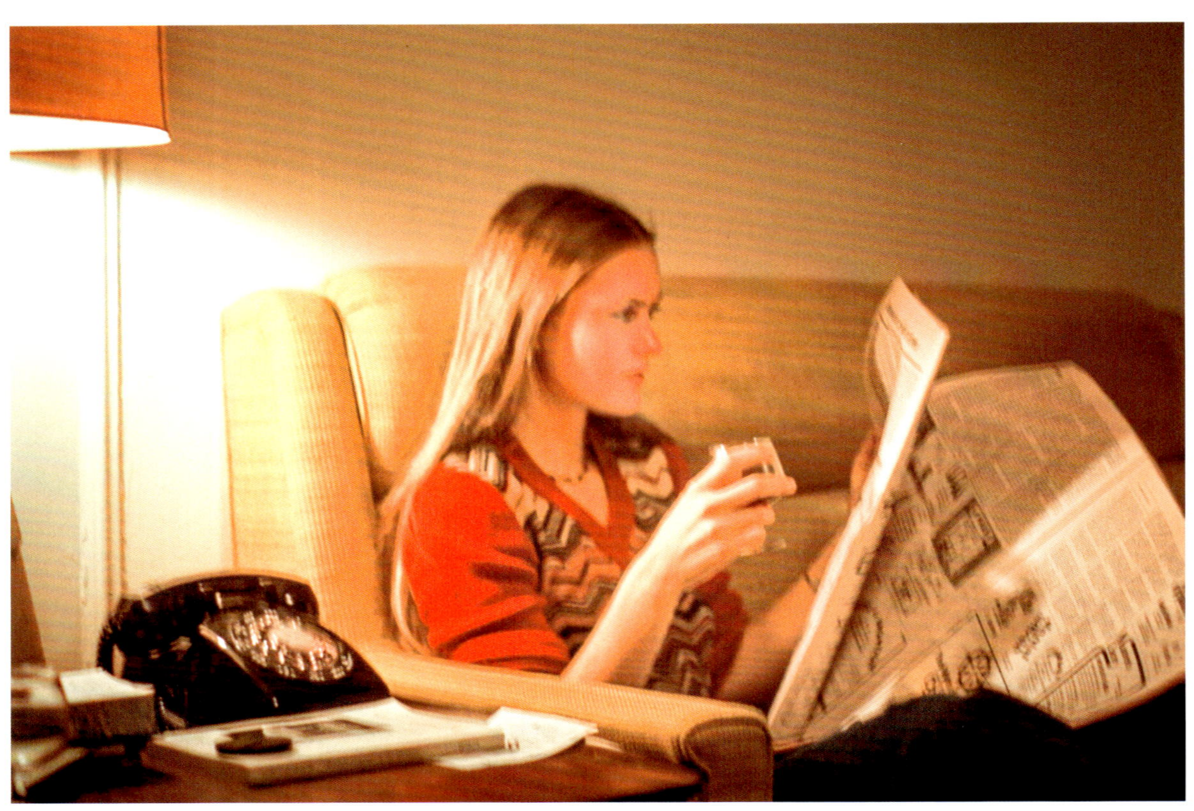

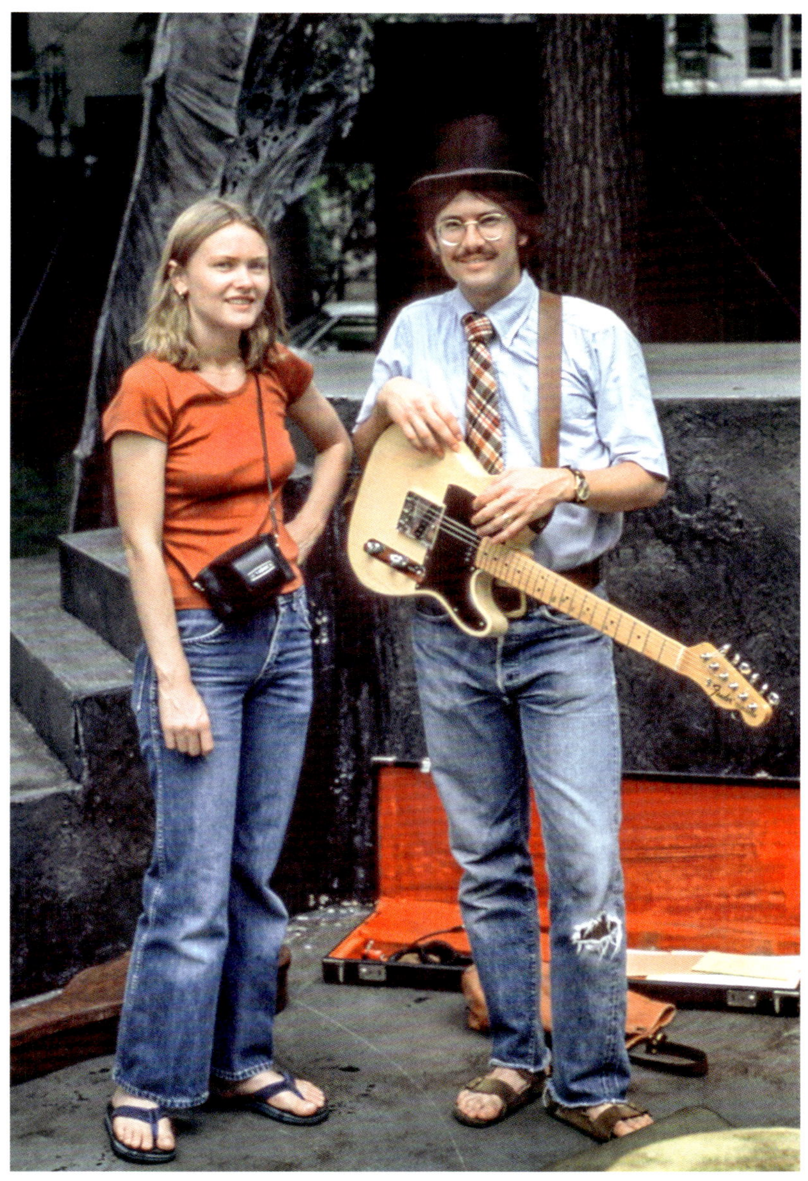

Make sure you marry someone who laughs at the same things you do.

– J.D. Salinger, *Catcher in the Rye*

David and I were married in 1976. We have been meditators since almost the beginning of our relationship. We deepened our practice shortly after our wedding by participating in a two-week silent Vipassana retreat. We still meditate for half an hour every morning.

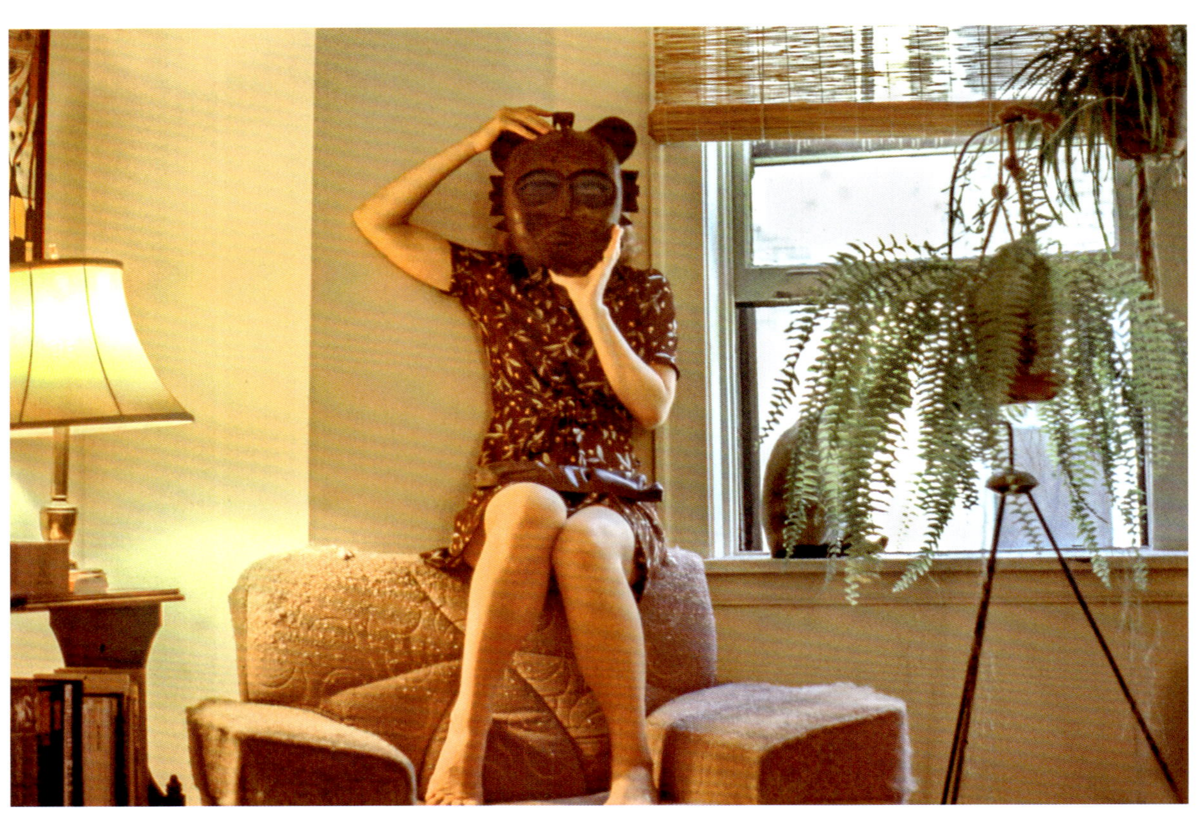

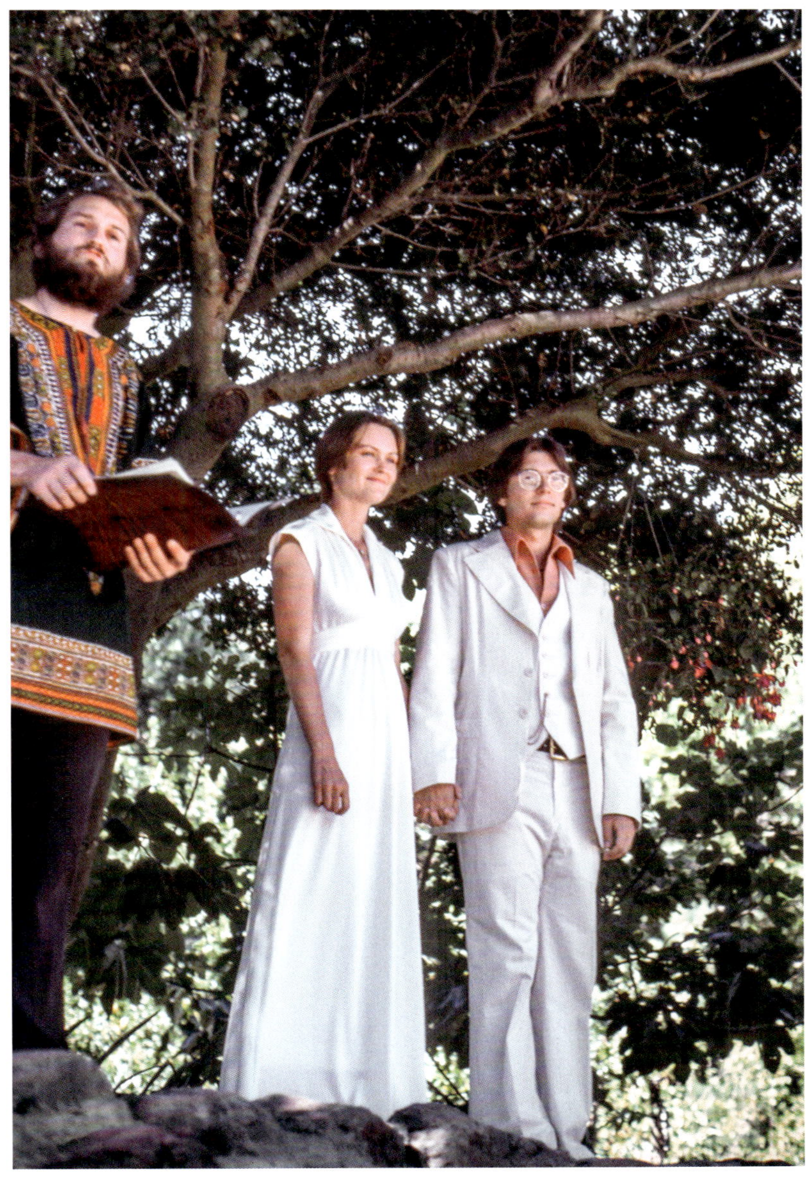

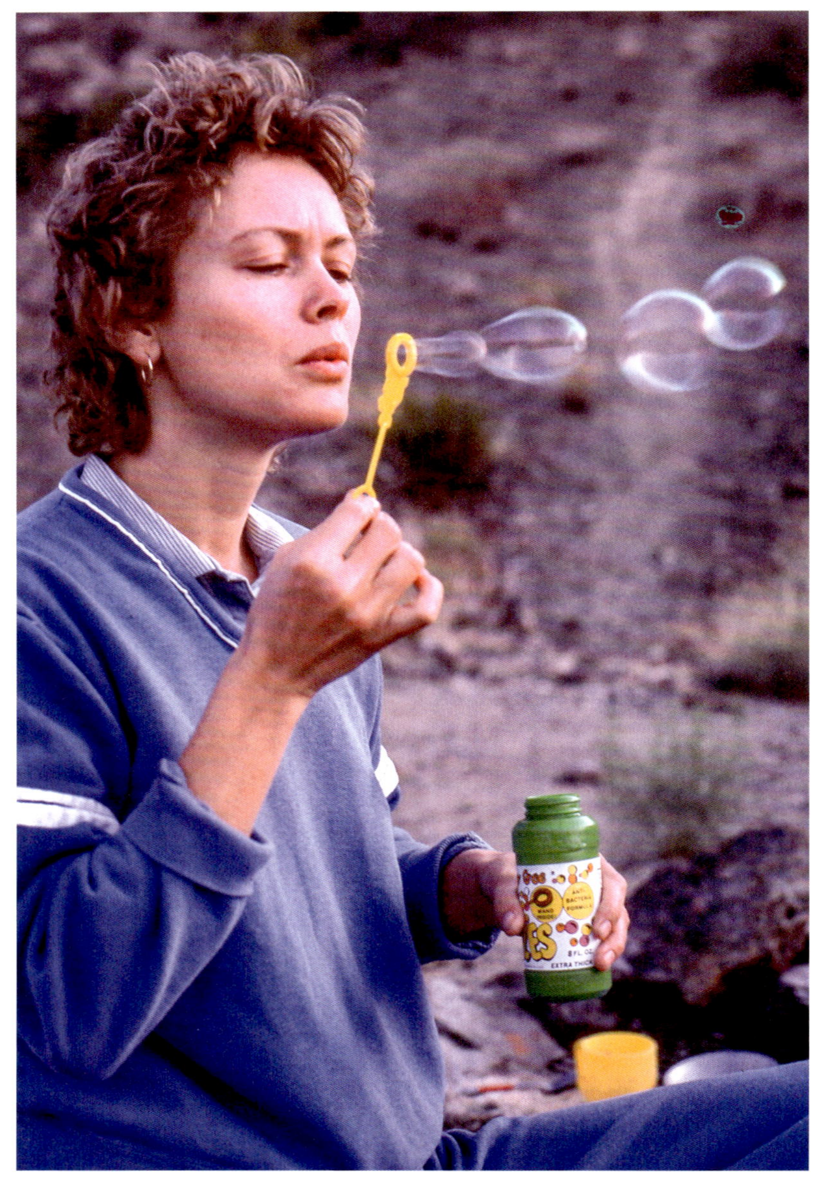

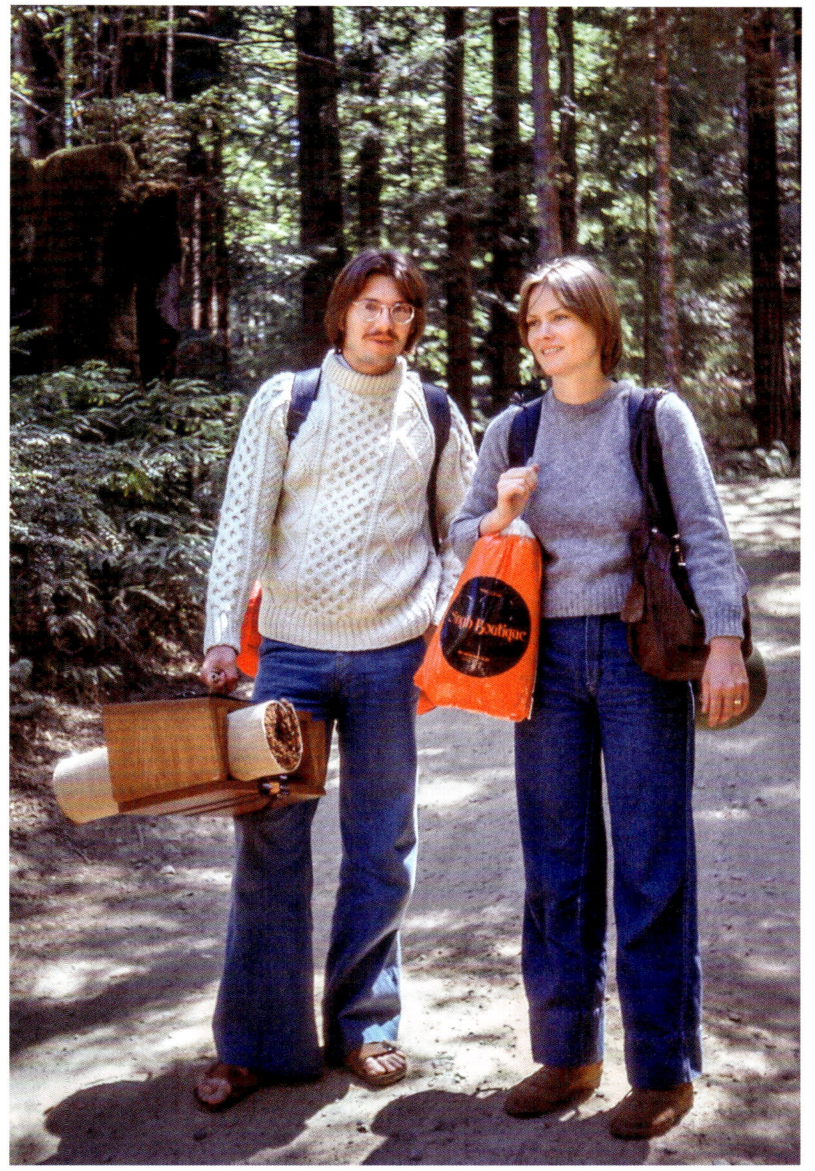
Sign Boutique

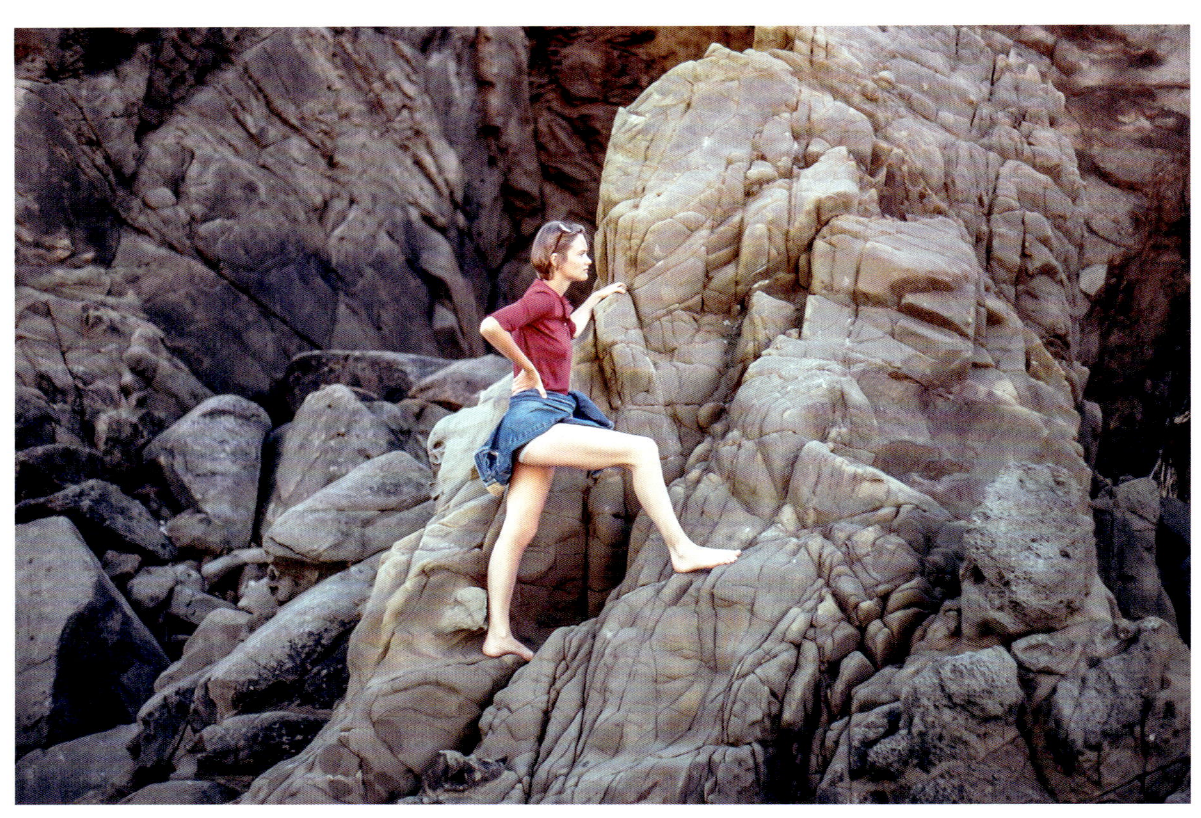

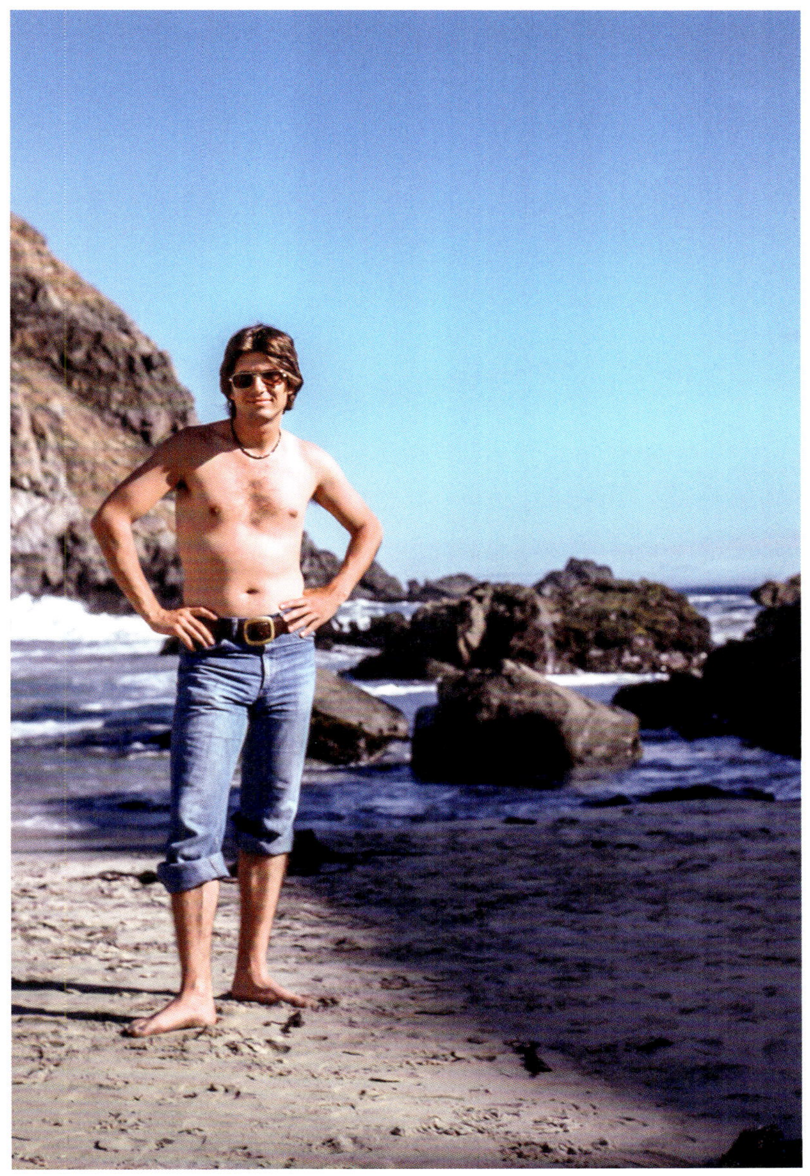

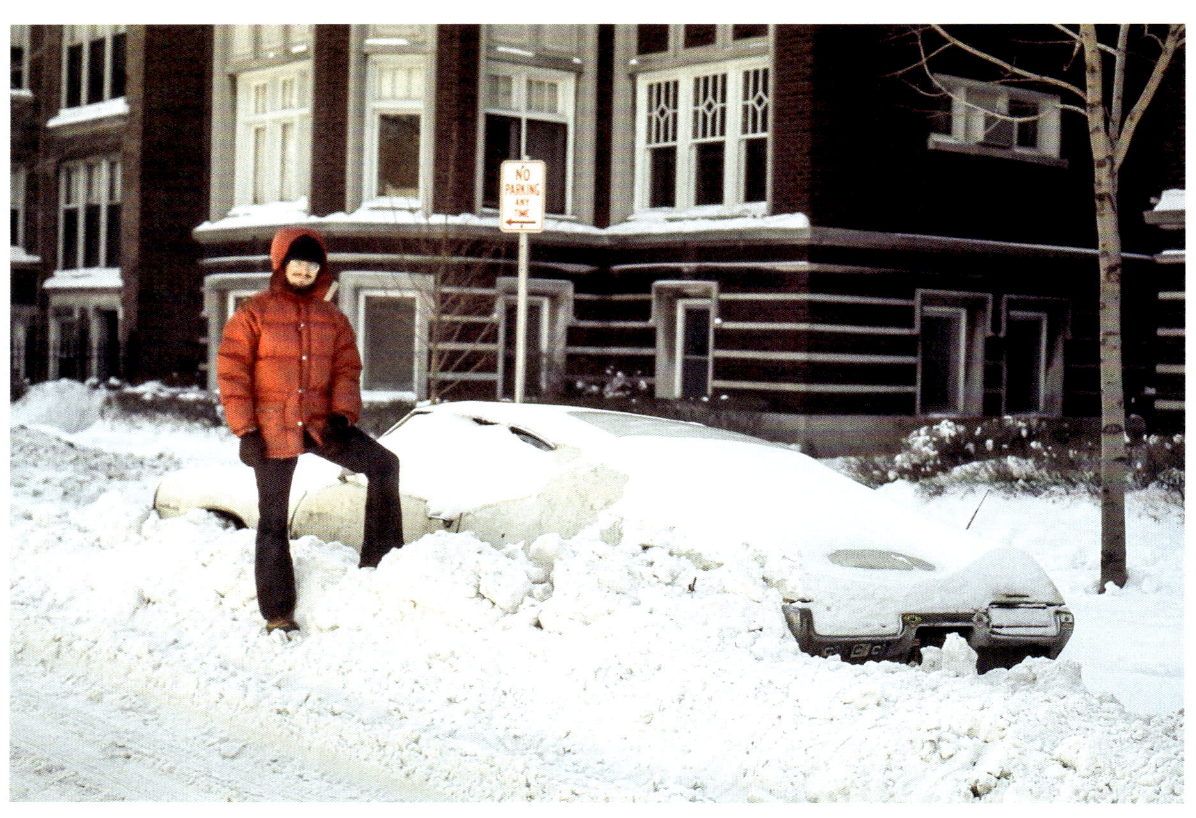
NO
PARKING
ANY
TIME

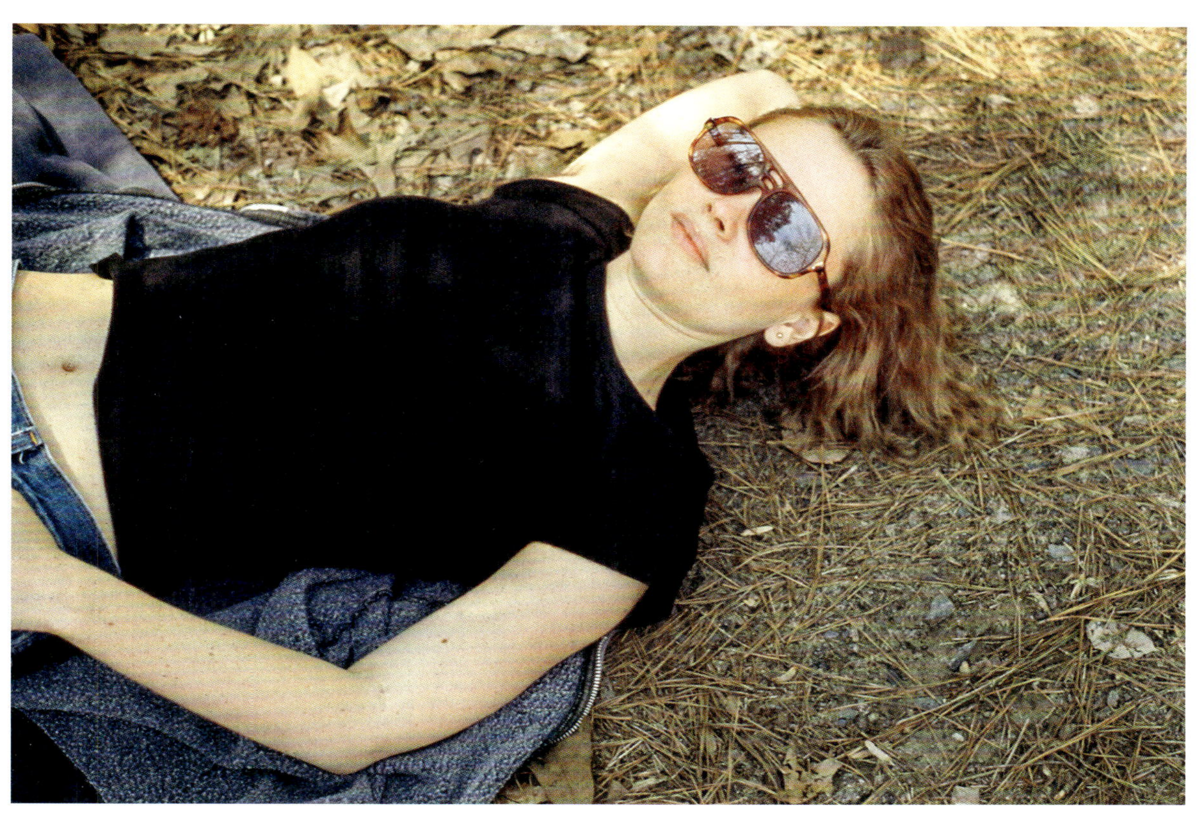

DURHAM, NORTH CAROLINA 1978 |

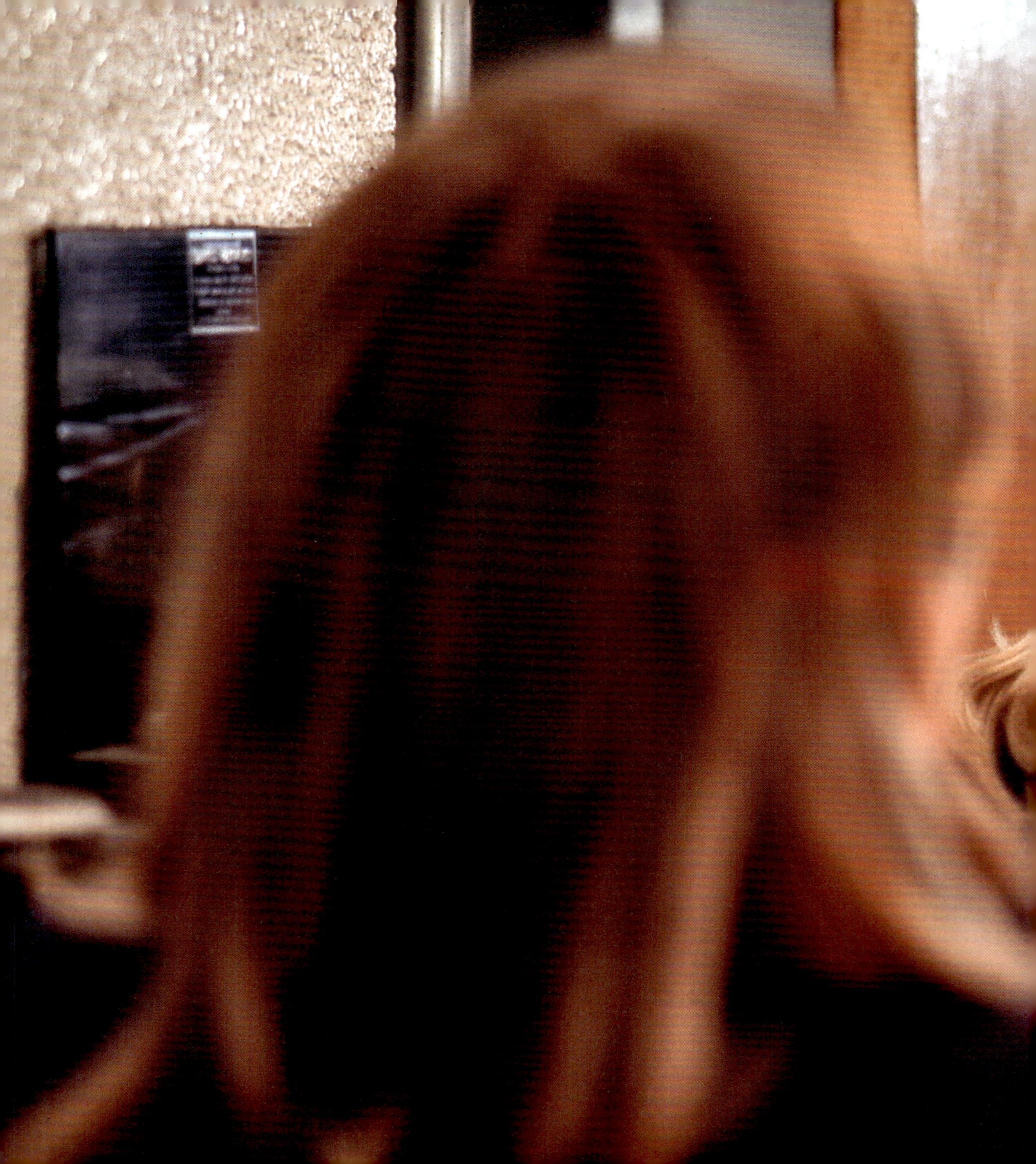

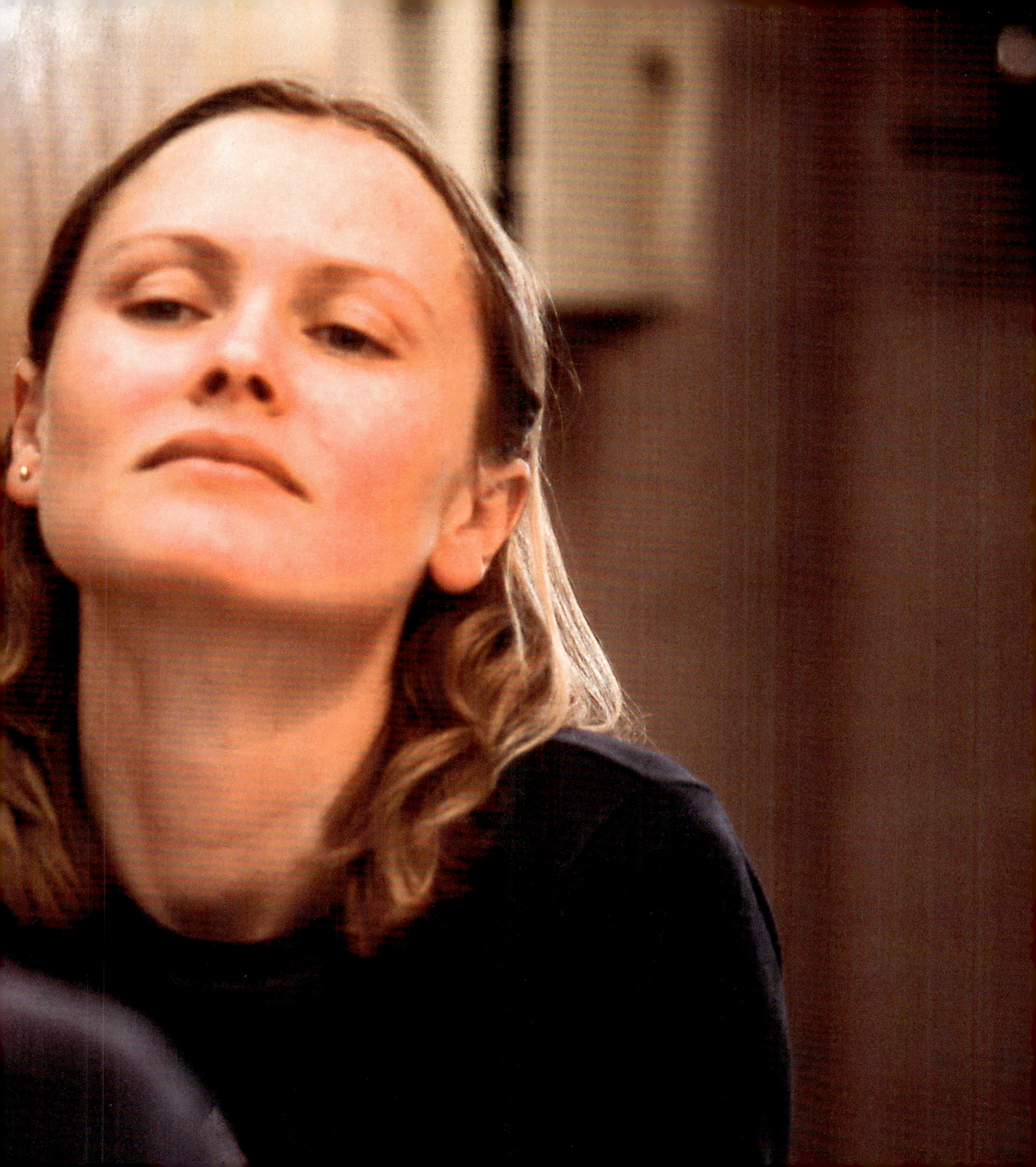

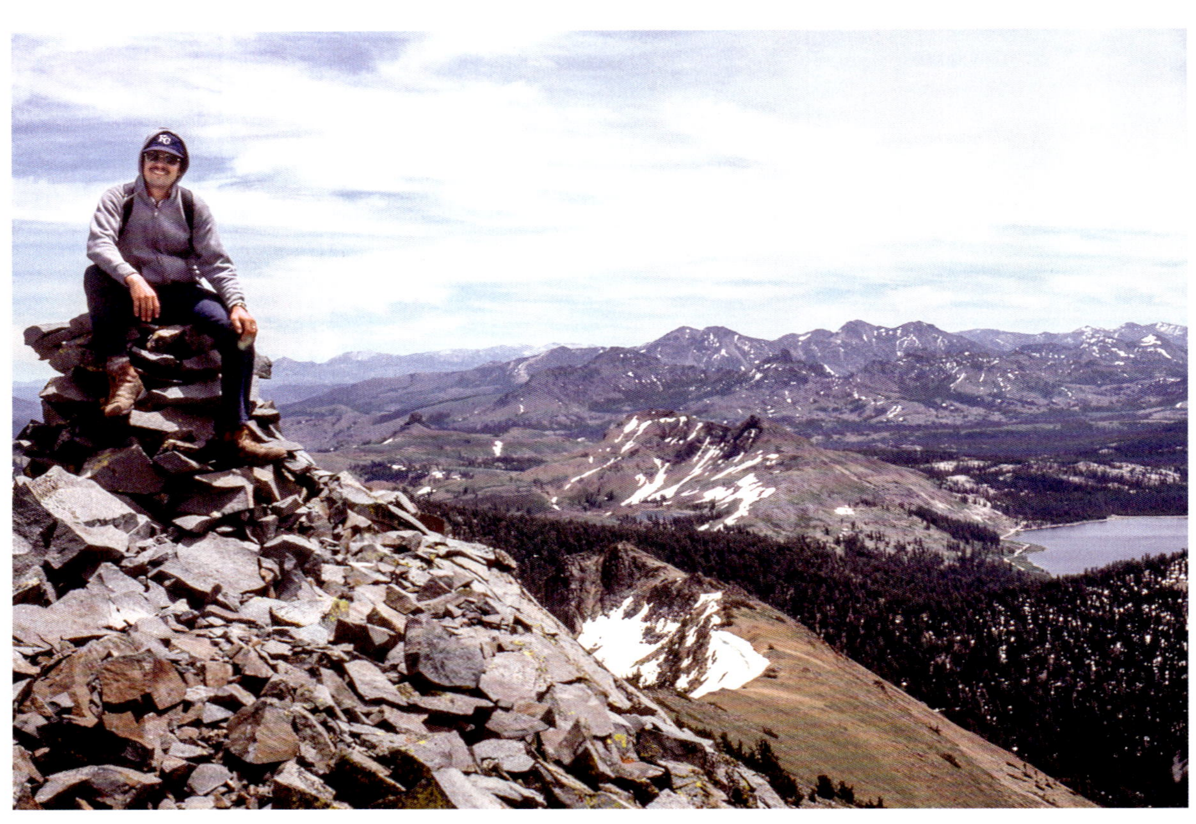

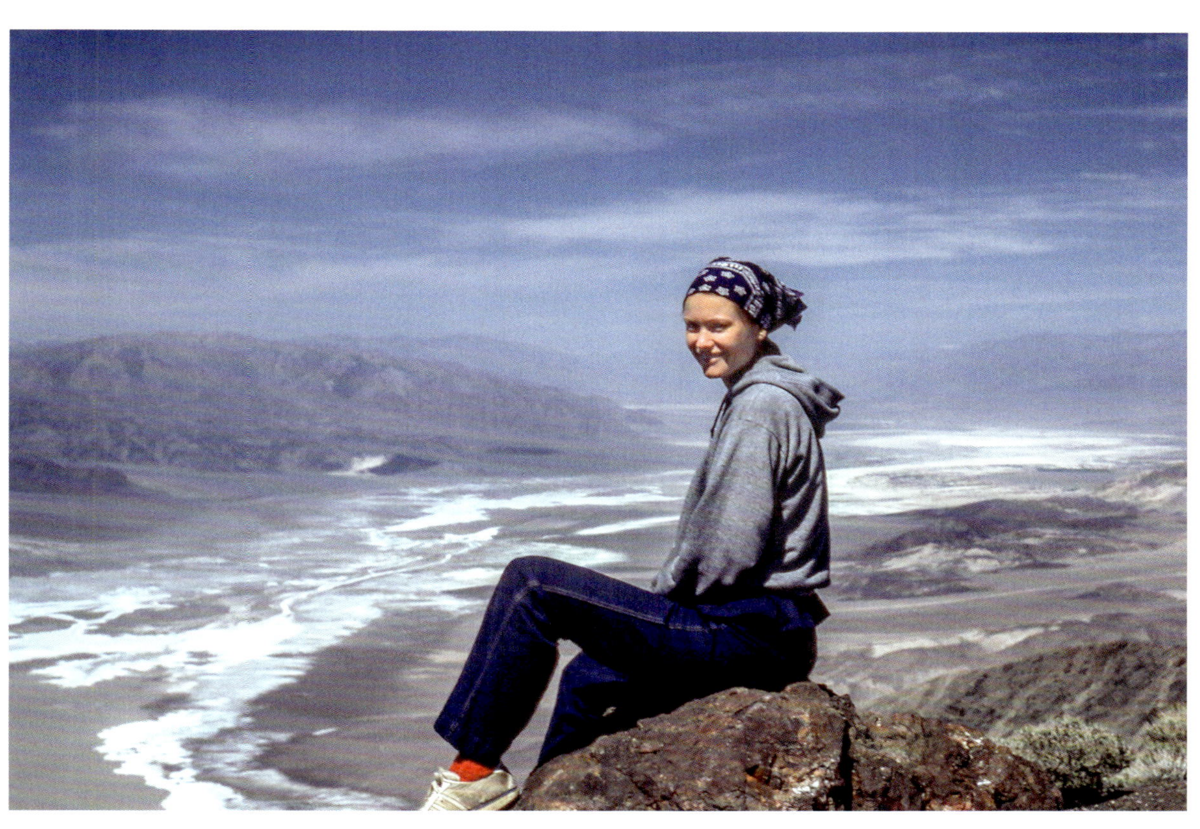

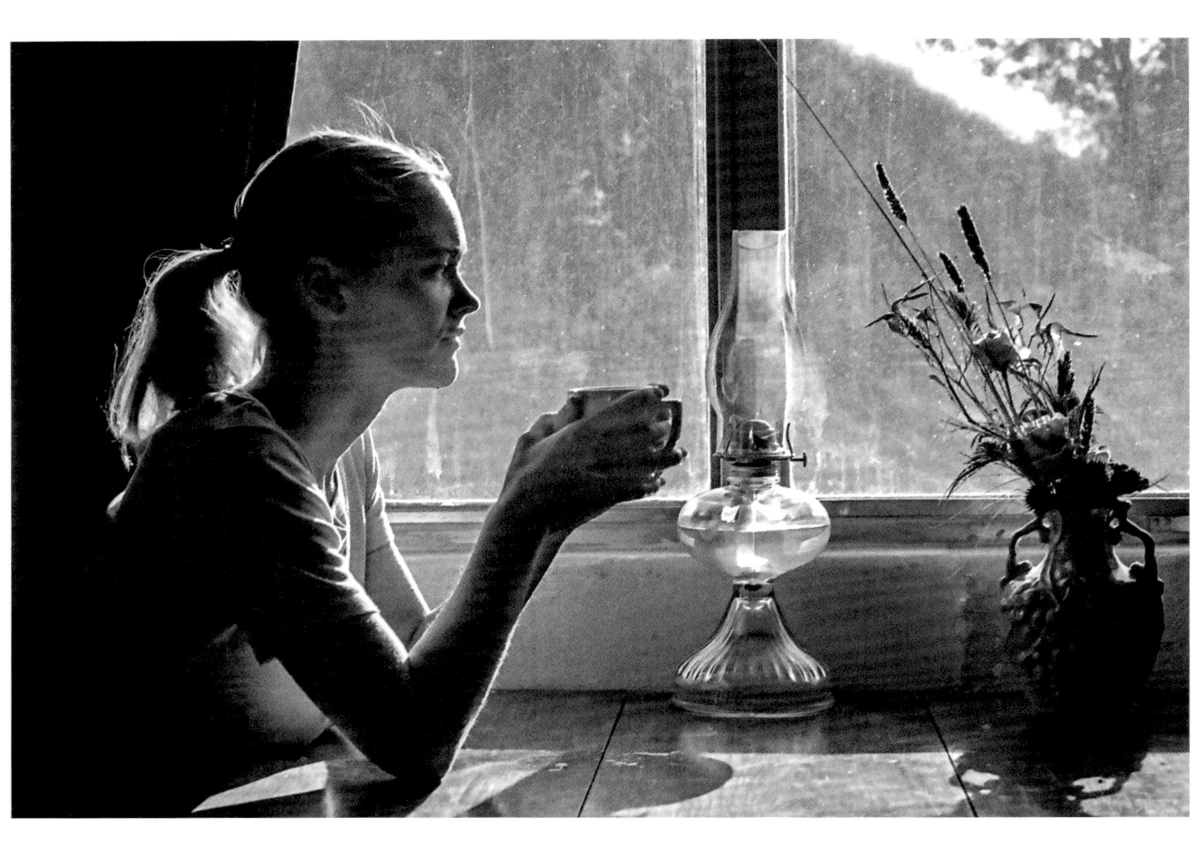

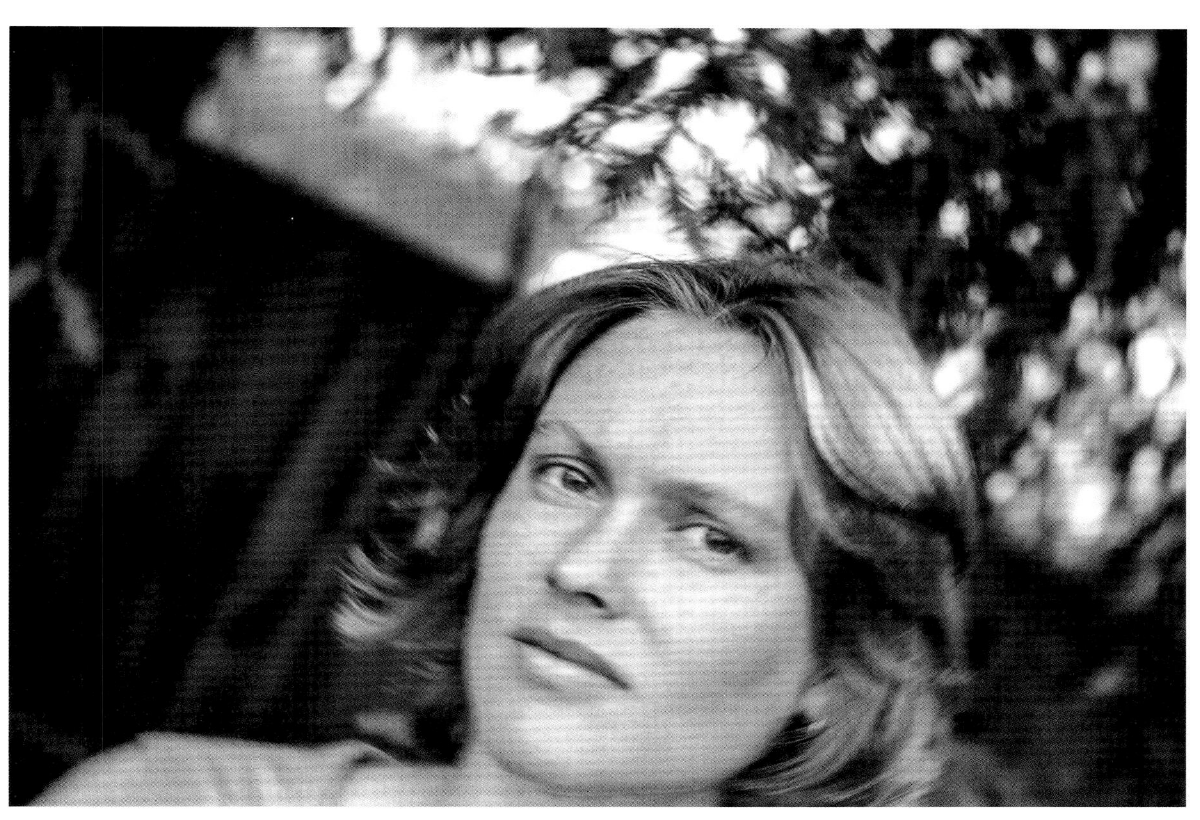

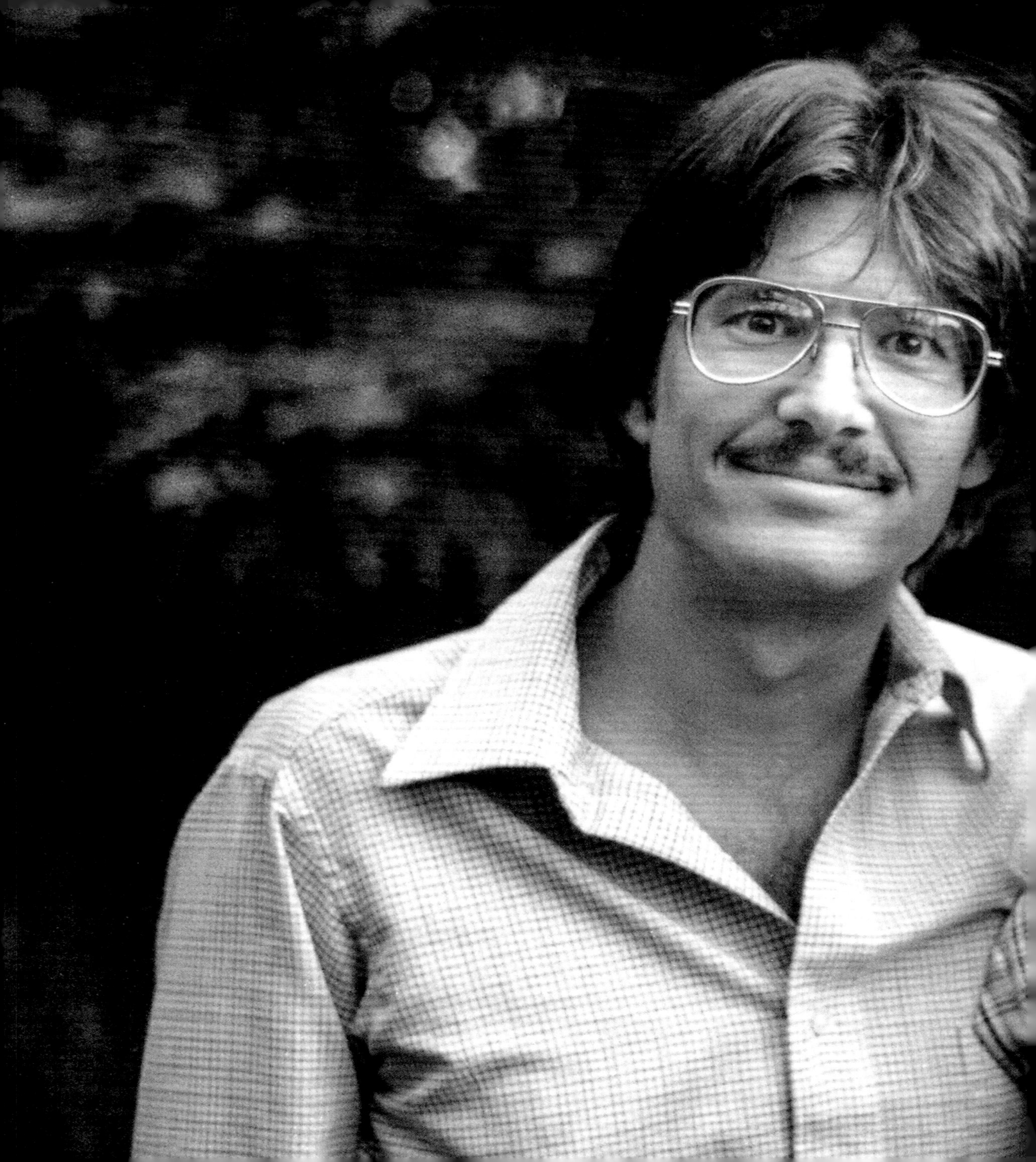

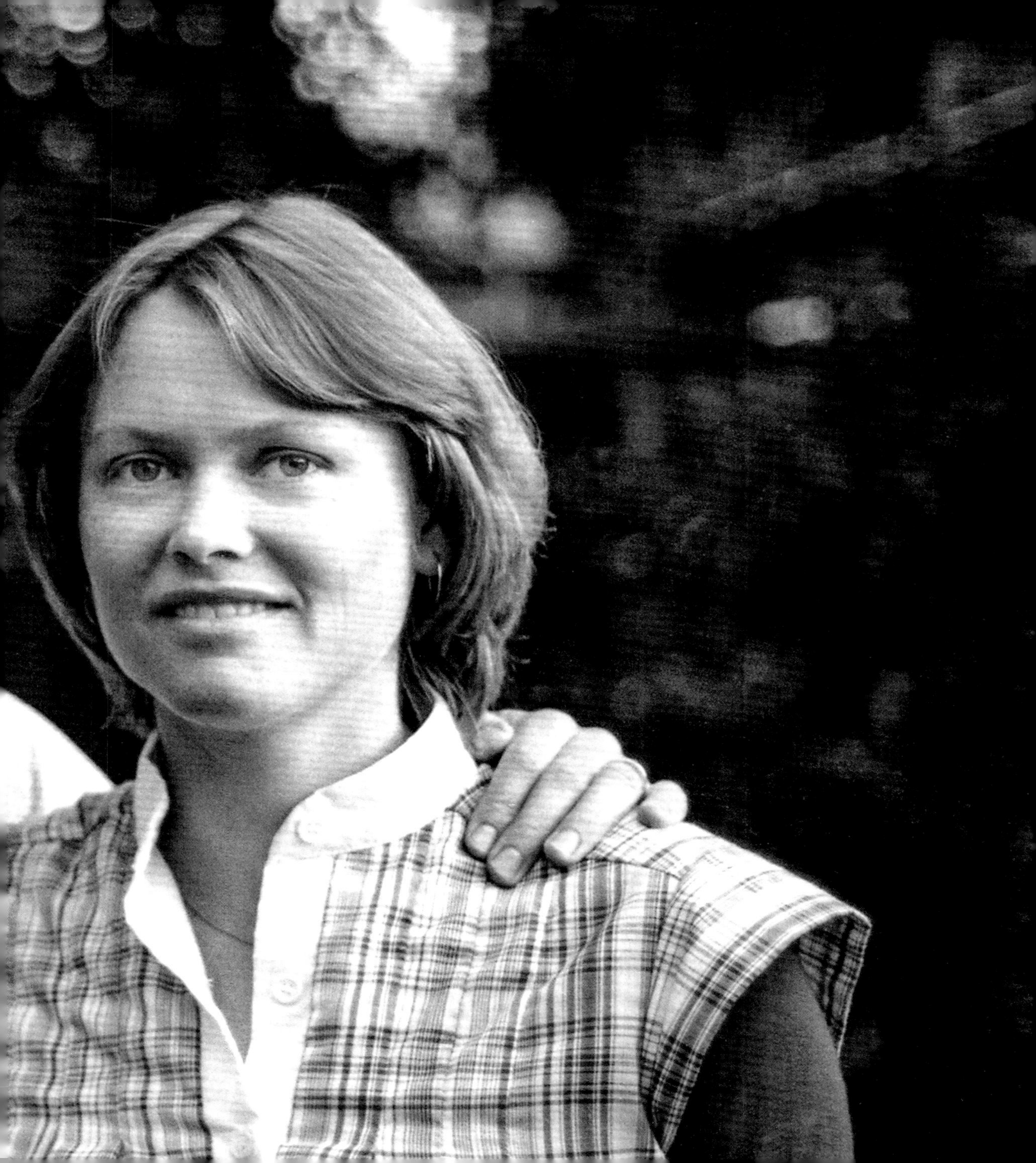

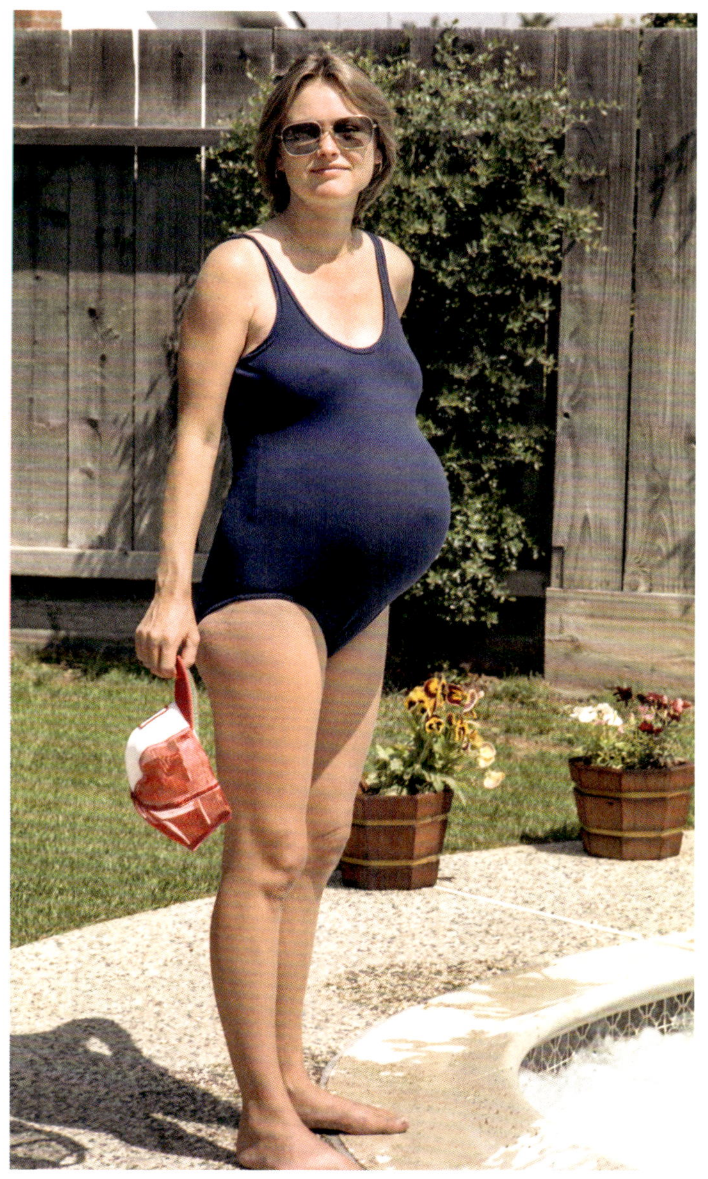

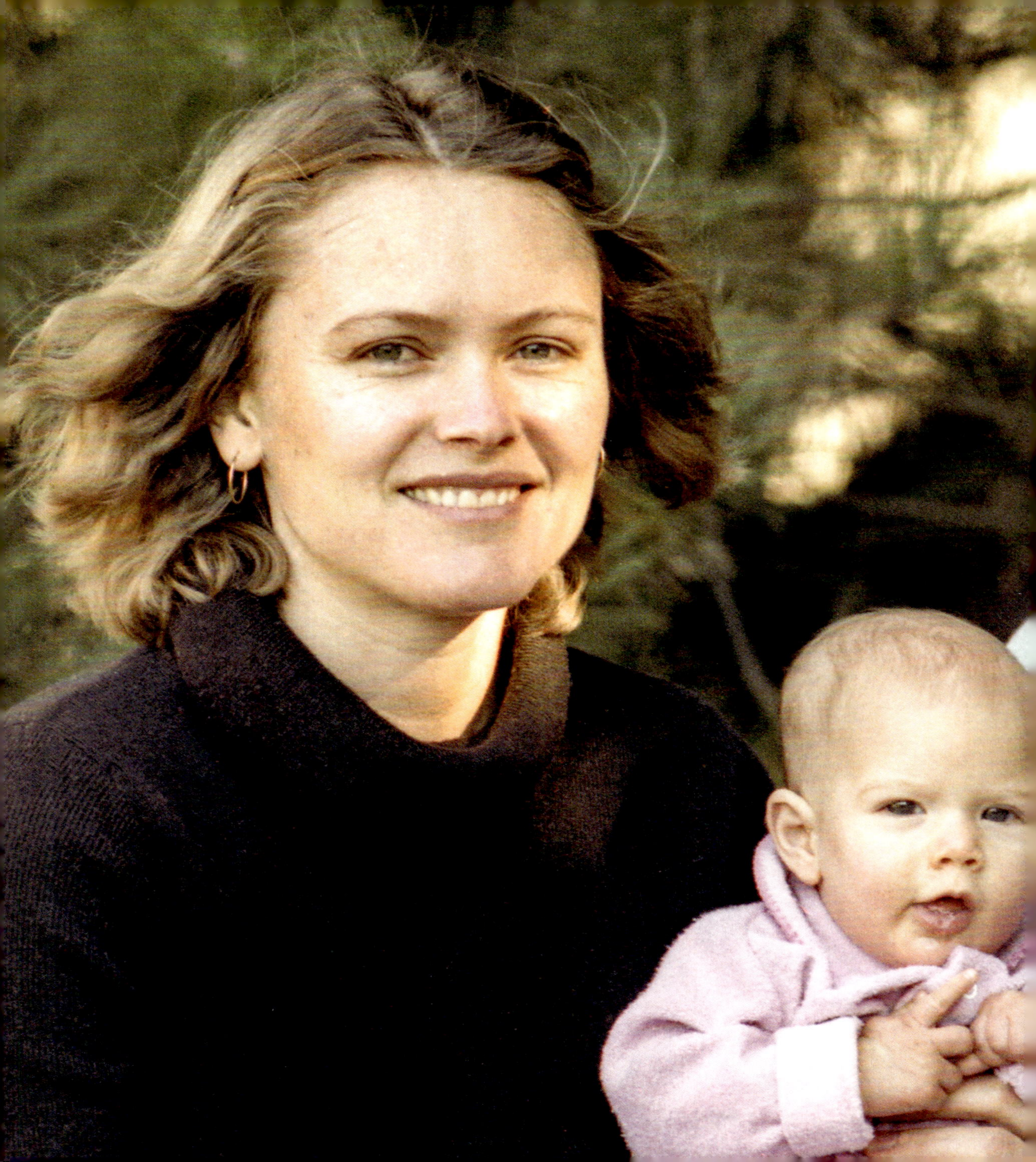

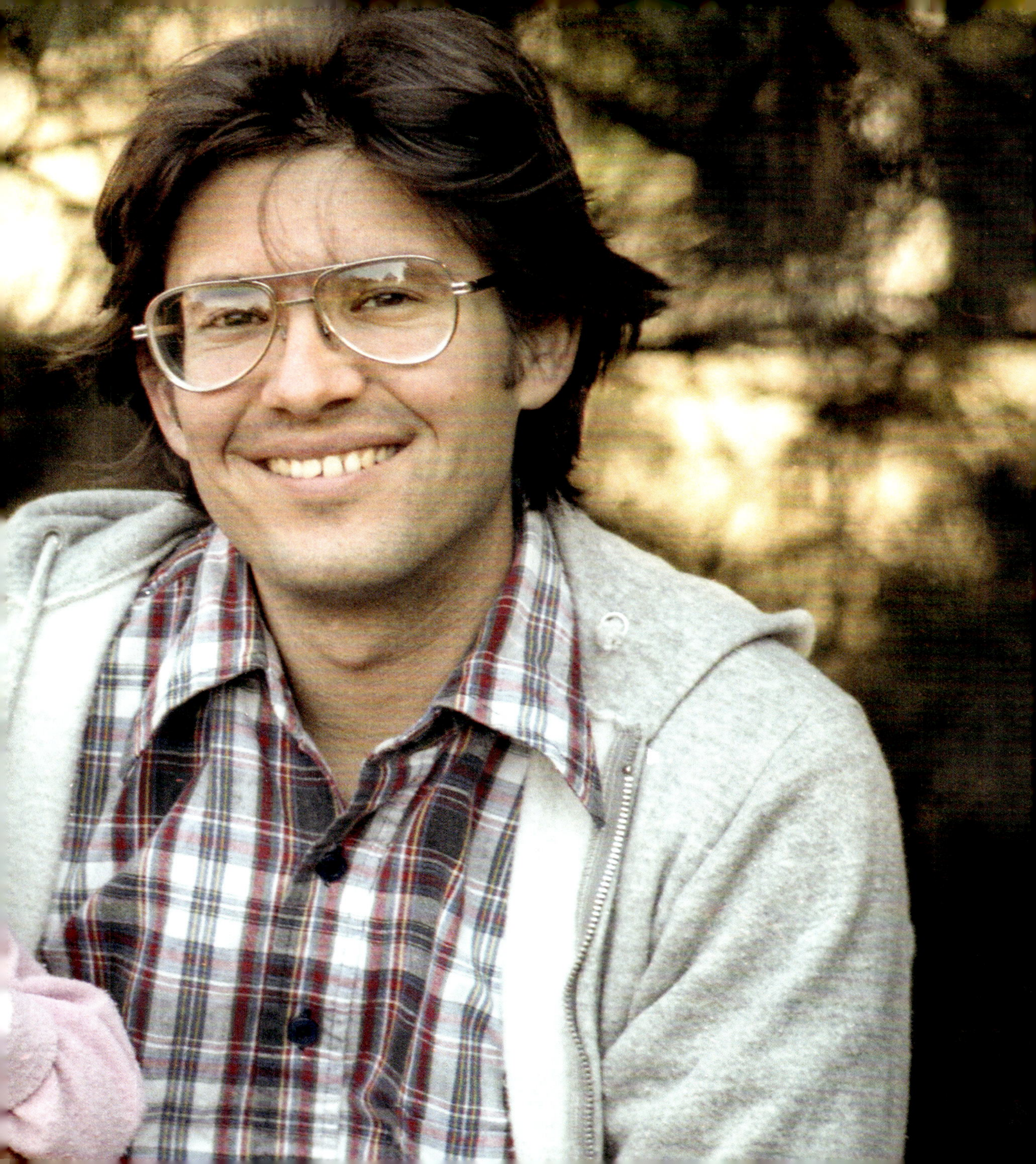

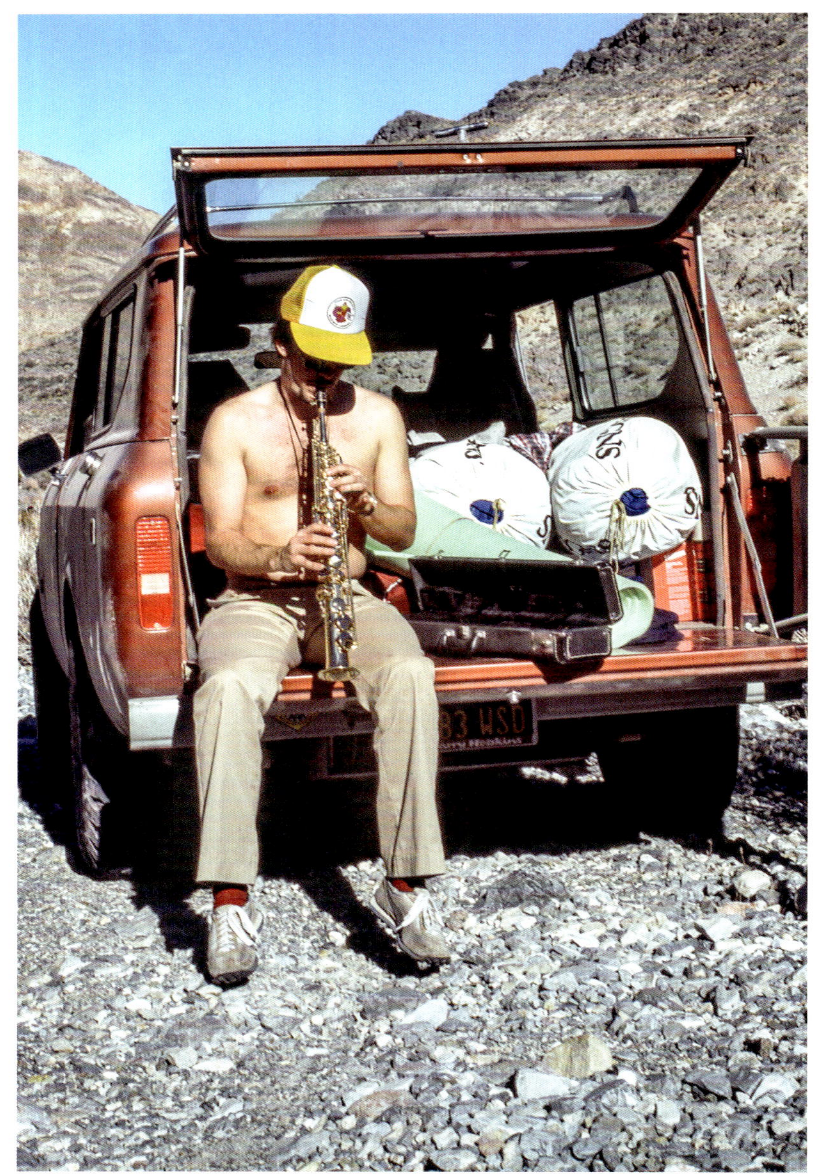

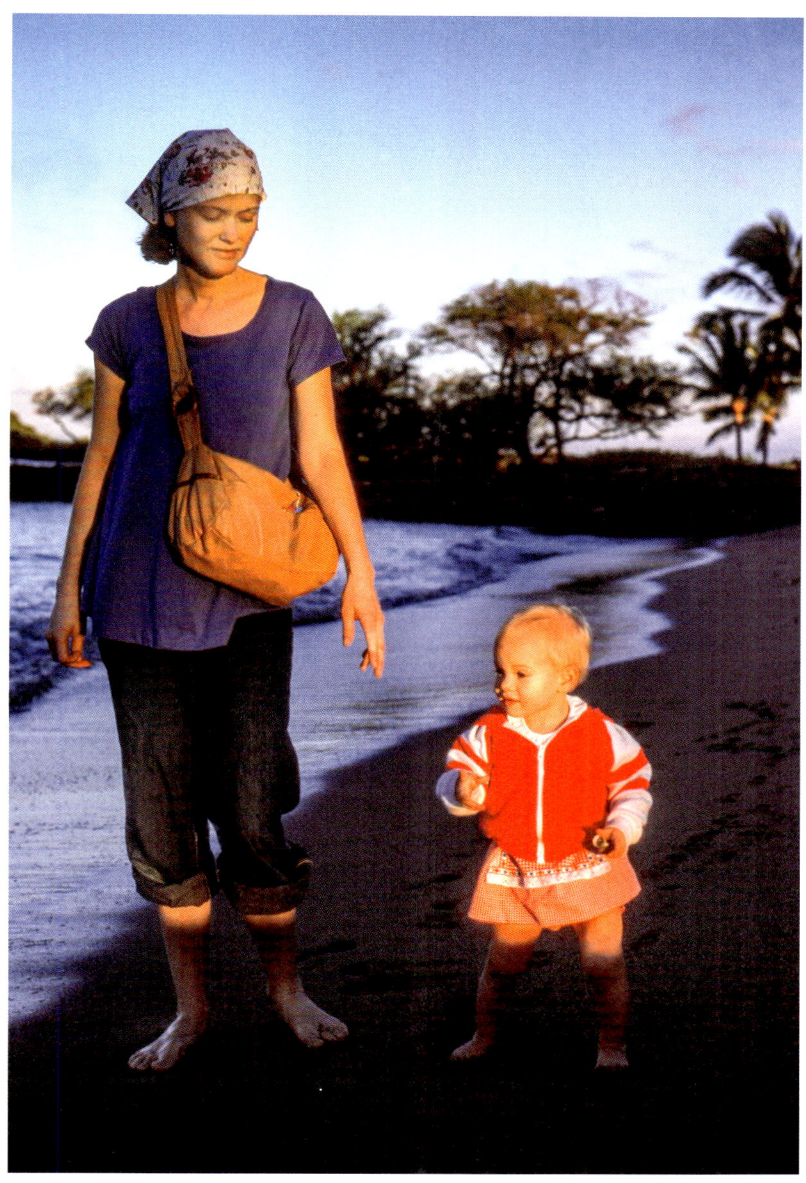

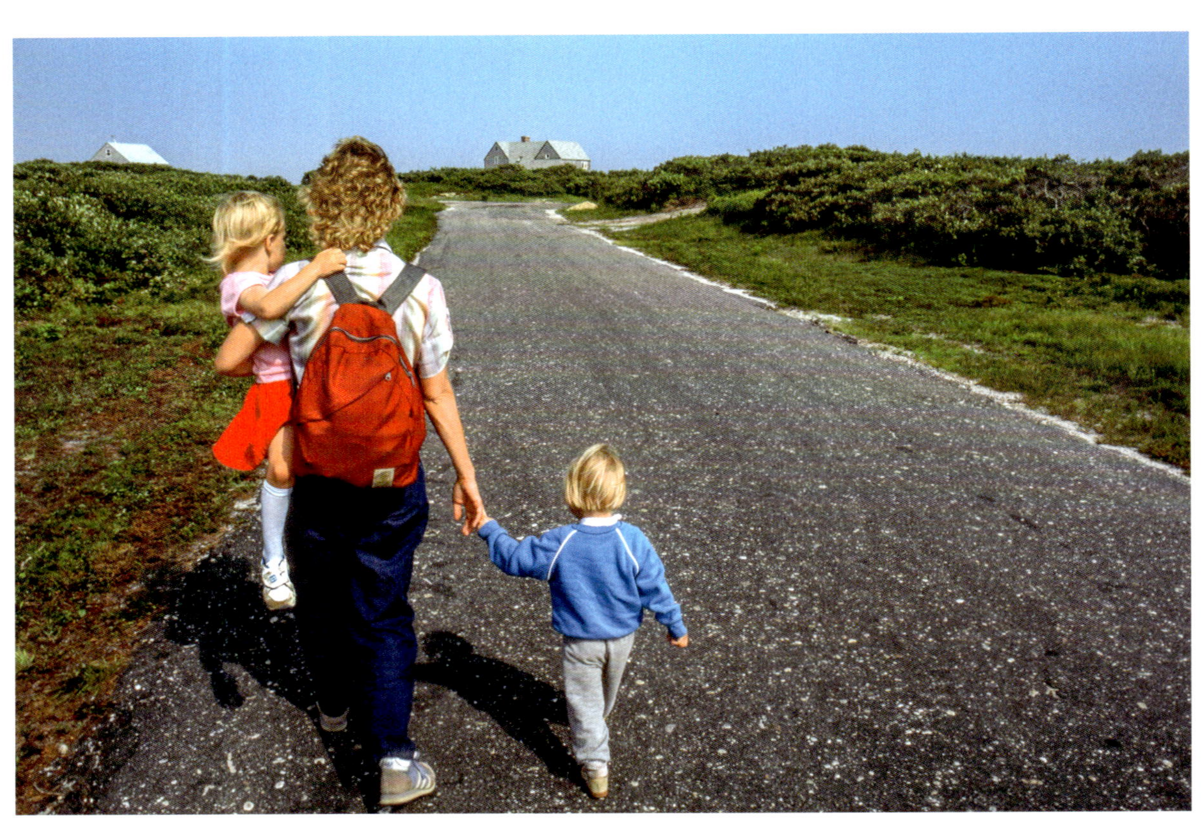

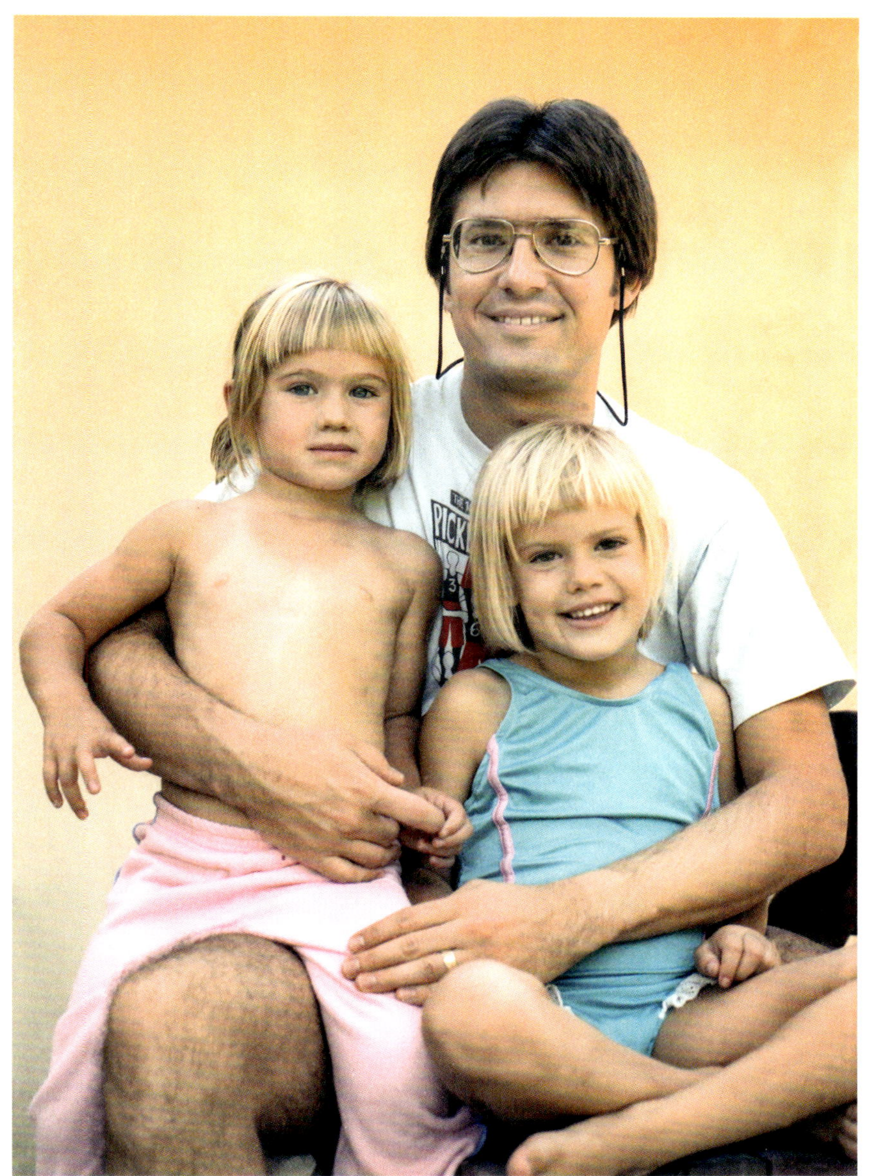

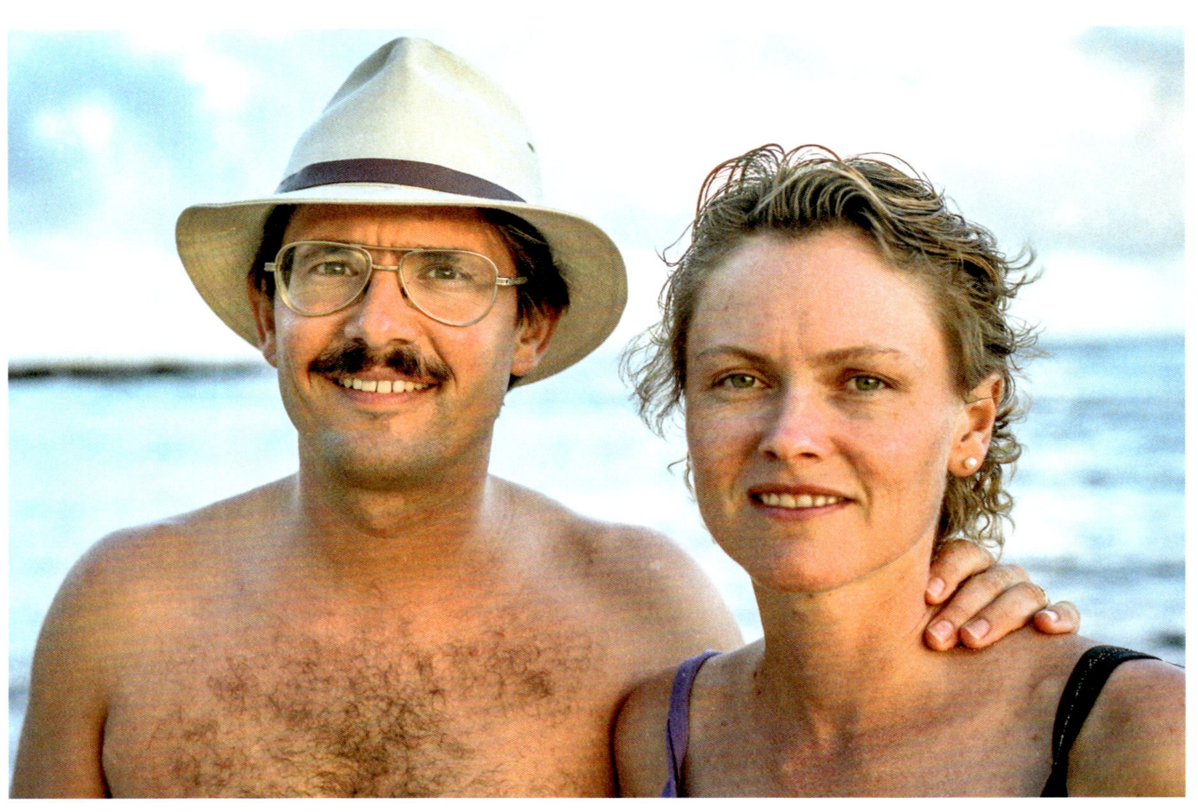

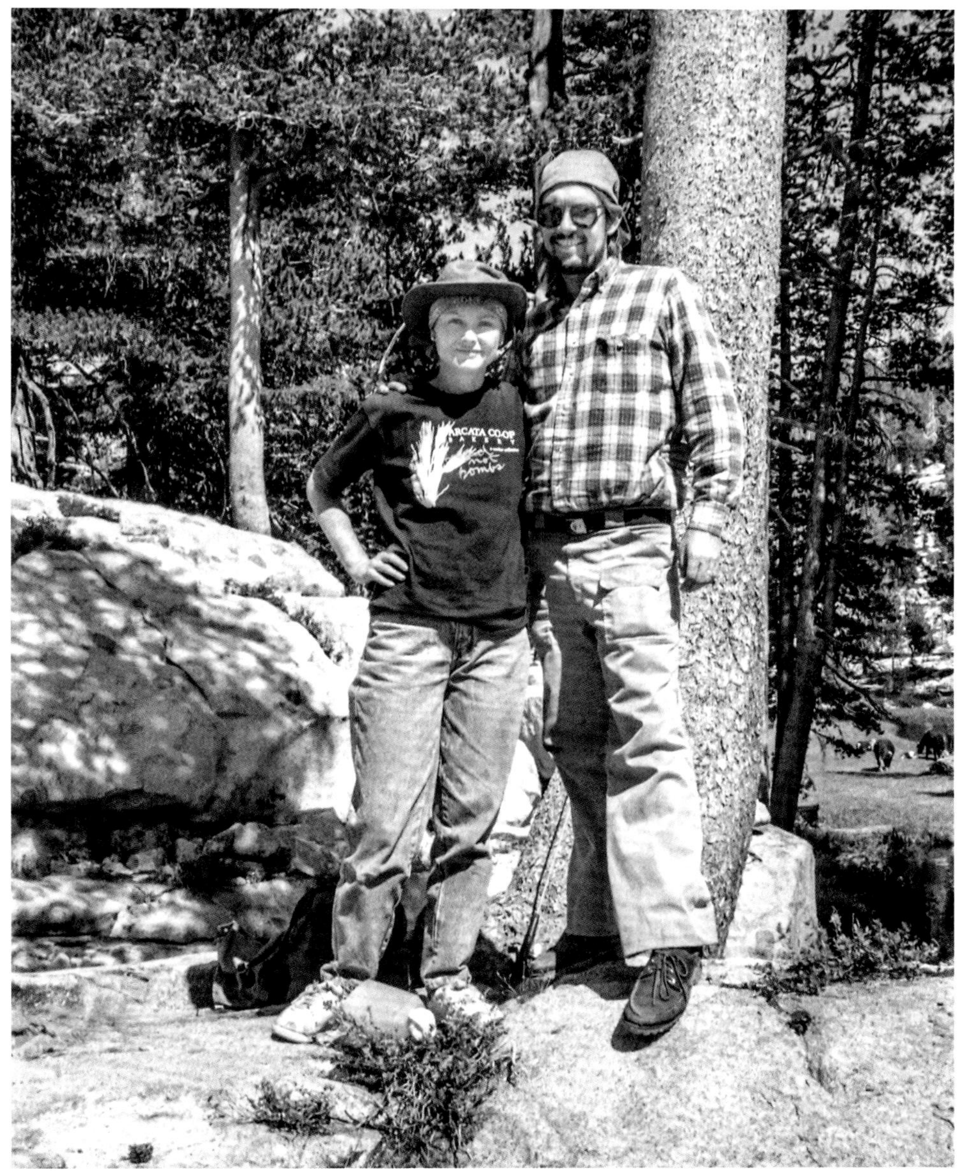

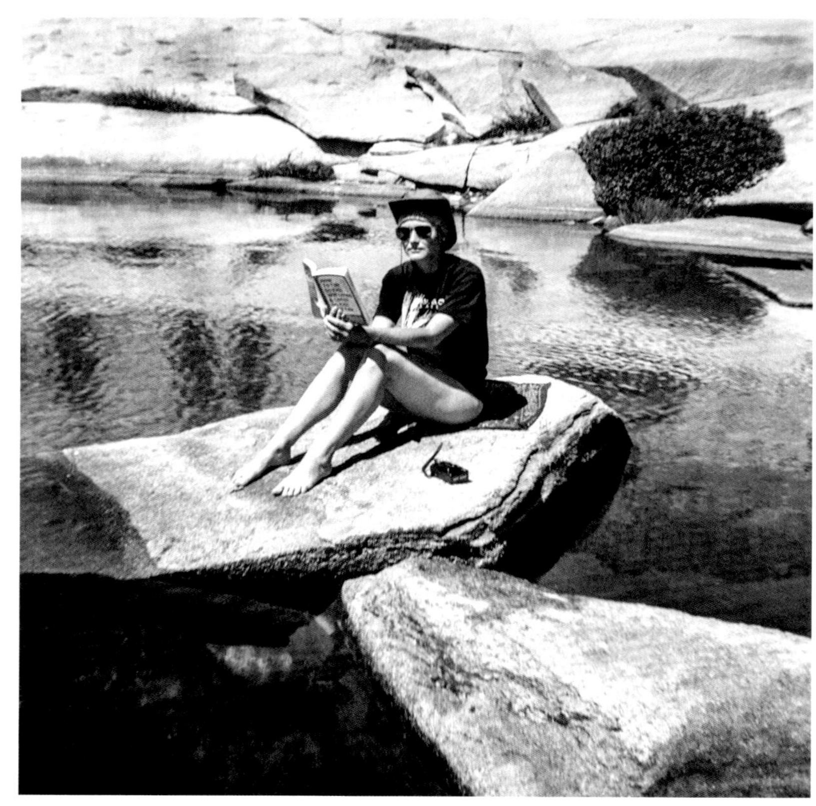

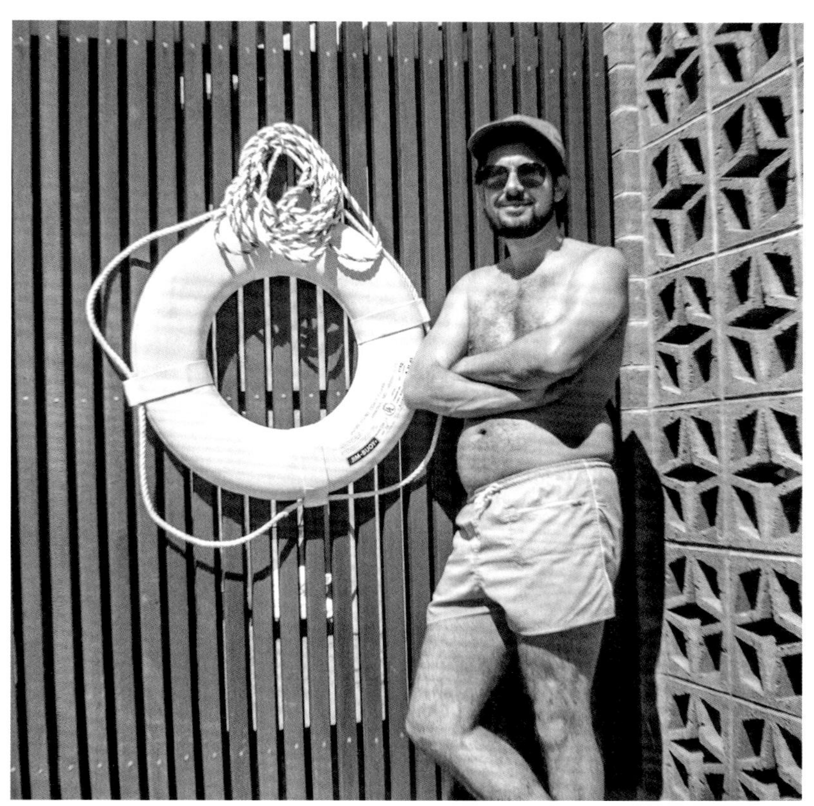

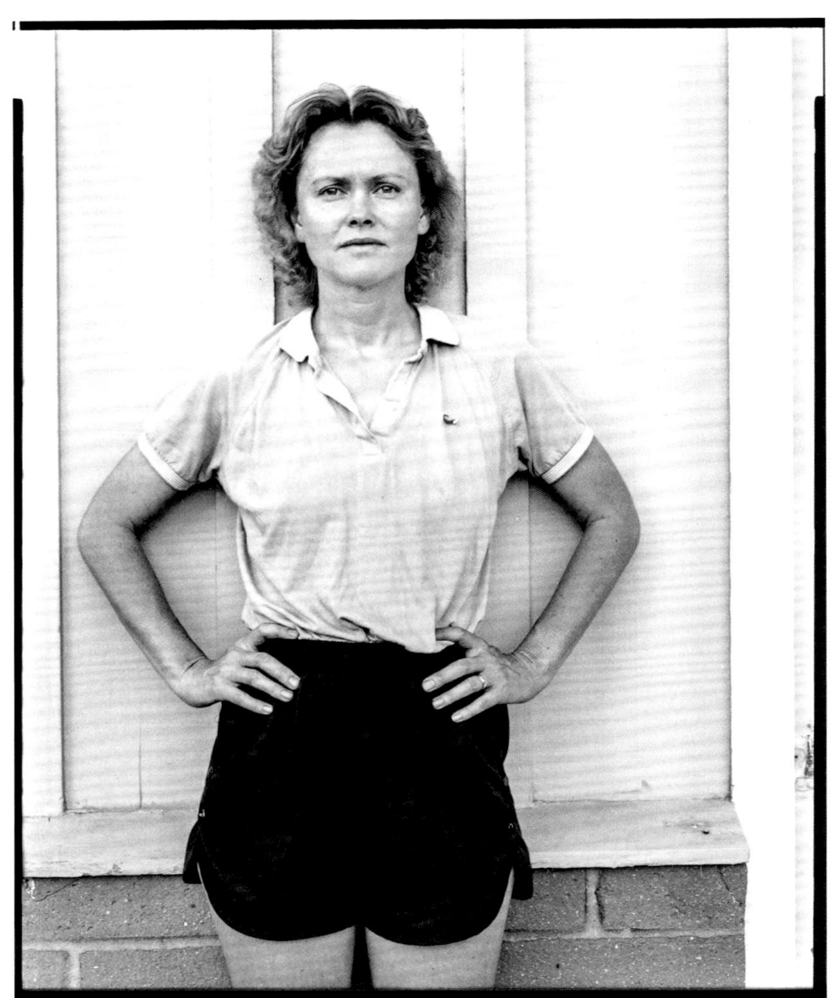

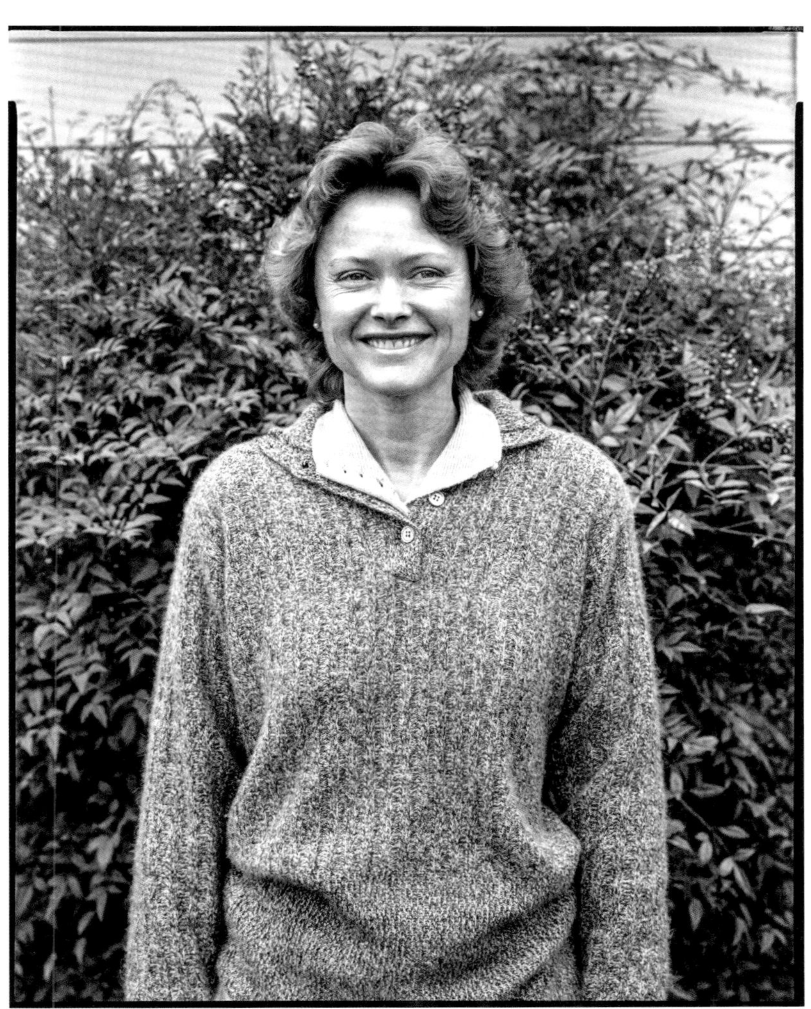

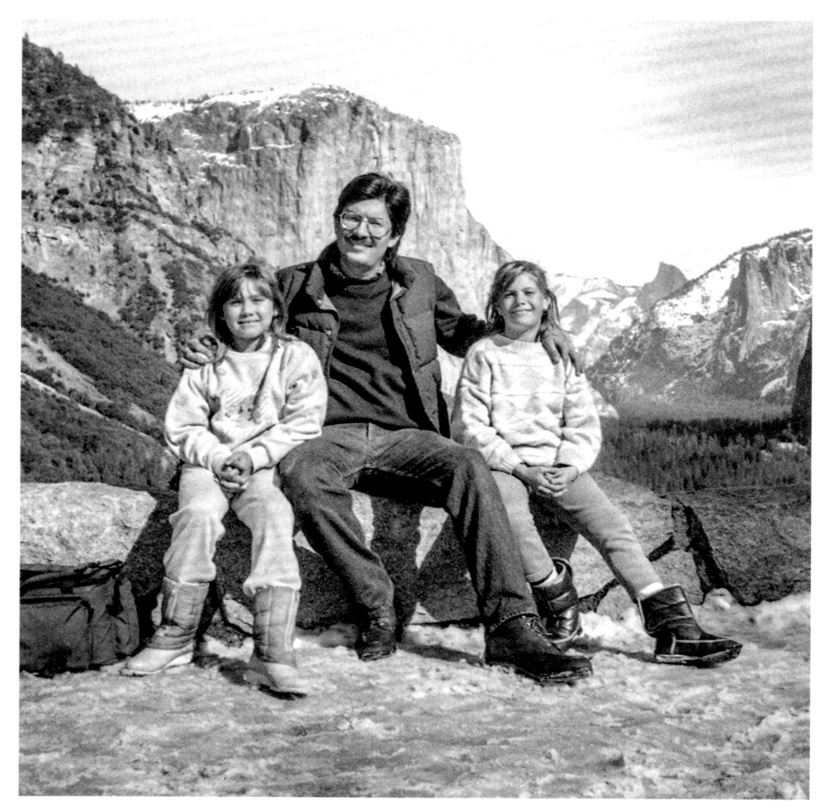

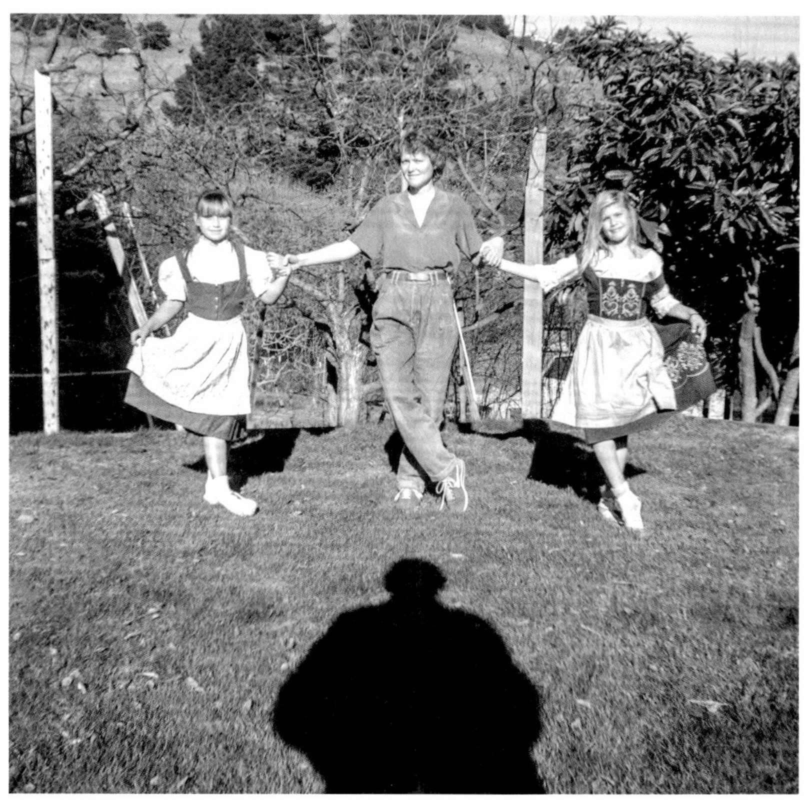

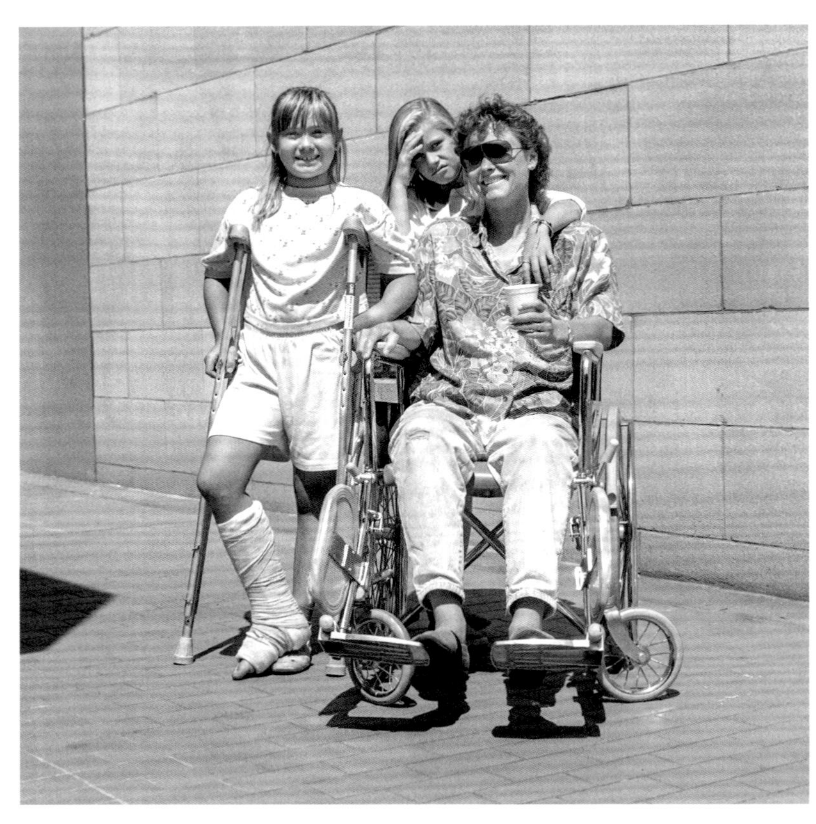

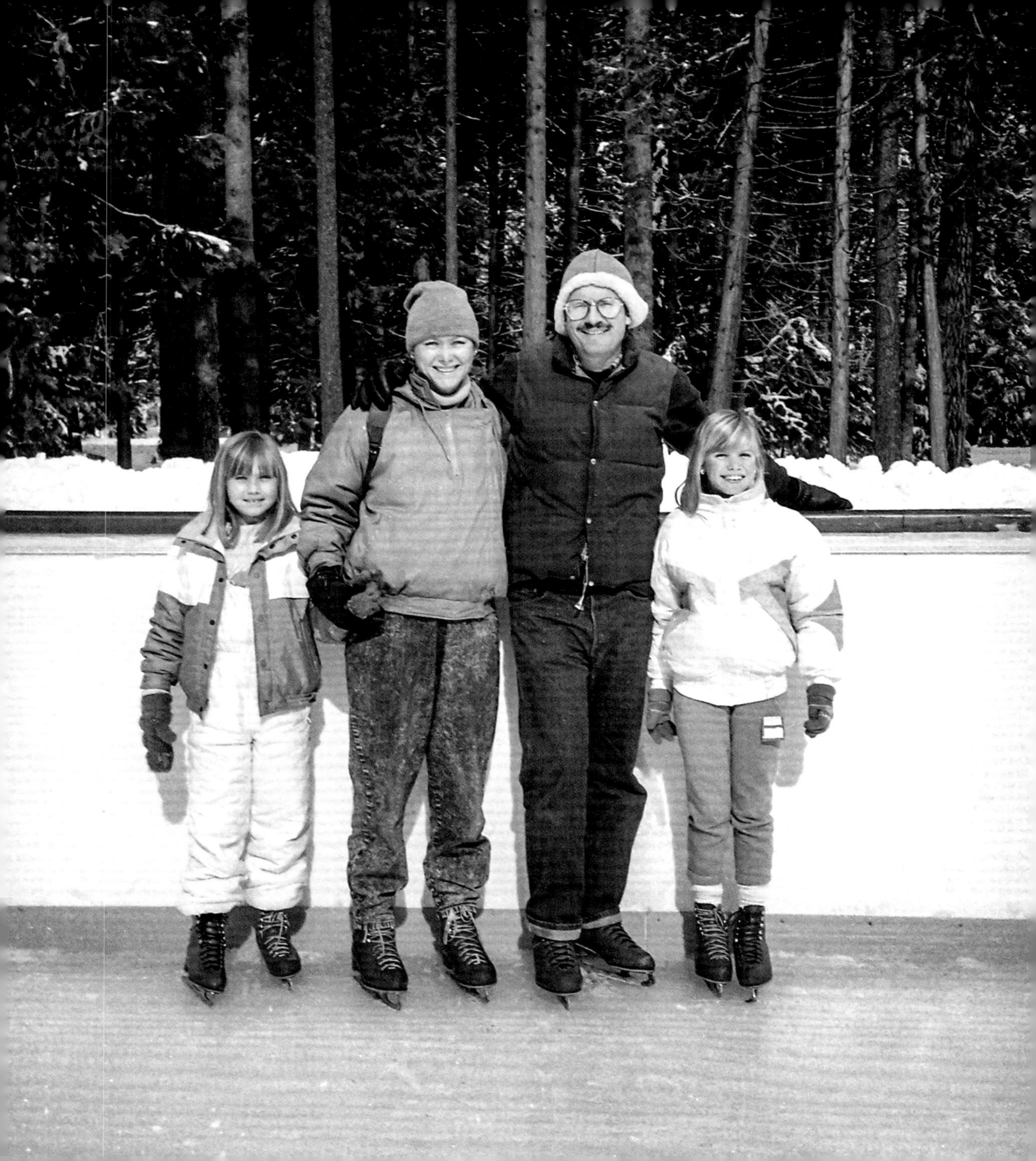

I'll interpret the rocks,
learn the language of flood,
storm, and avalanche.
I'll acquaint myself with
the glaciers and wild
gardens, and get as near
the heart of the world as
I can.

– John Muir, Journals

My sense of self and place are strongly shaped by my family constellation and my experiences in the California wilderness. I am the oldest of six sisters, some of whom are shown in these photographs. My family's interactions and sense of identity were deeply influenced by our annual backpack trips in the rugged mountains of California's Sierra Nevada range, and by my father's love of the writings of John Muir. In the early years of our relationship, David joined my family on several trips to the Sierras. Later I took David and our young children to other locations my family had visited – Tuolumne Meadows, Fordyce Creek, and Mineral King; Scottie's Castle and Furnace Creek in Death Valley; and the ghost towns of the Mojave Desert.

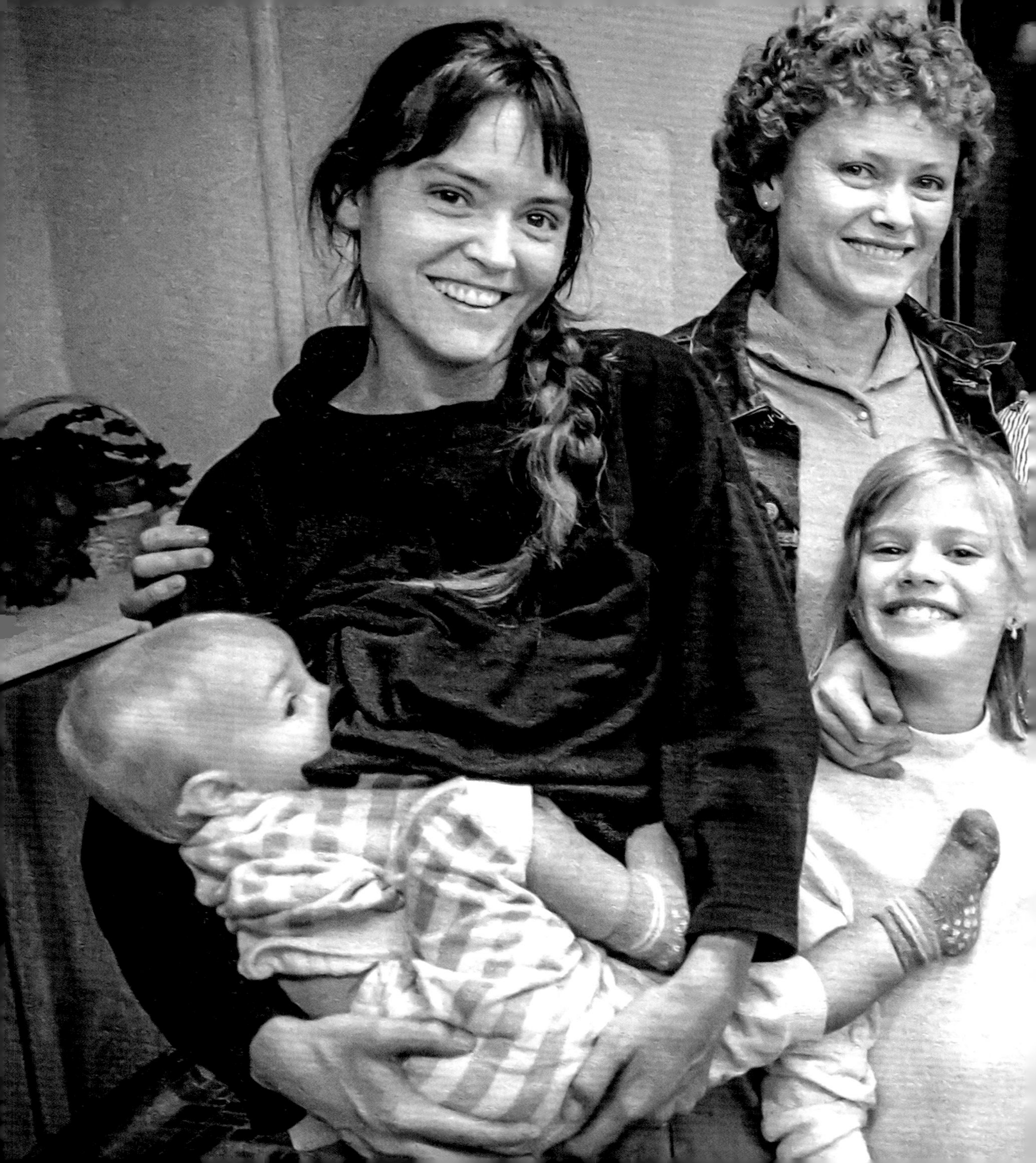

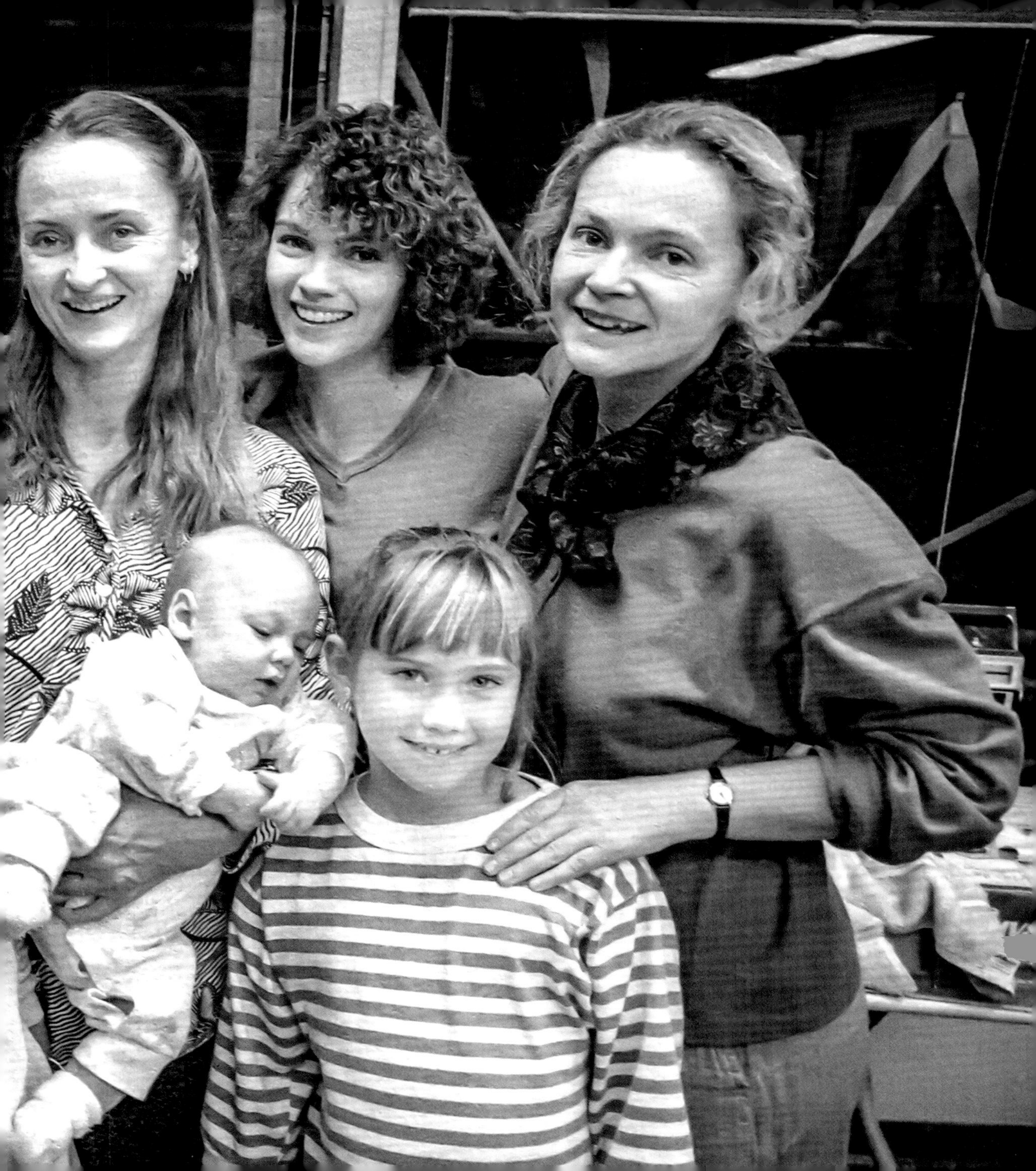

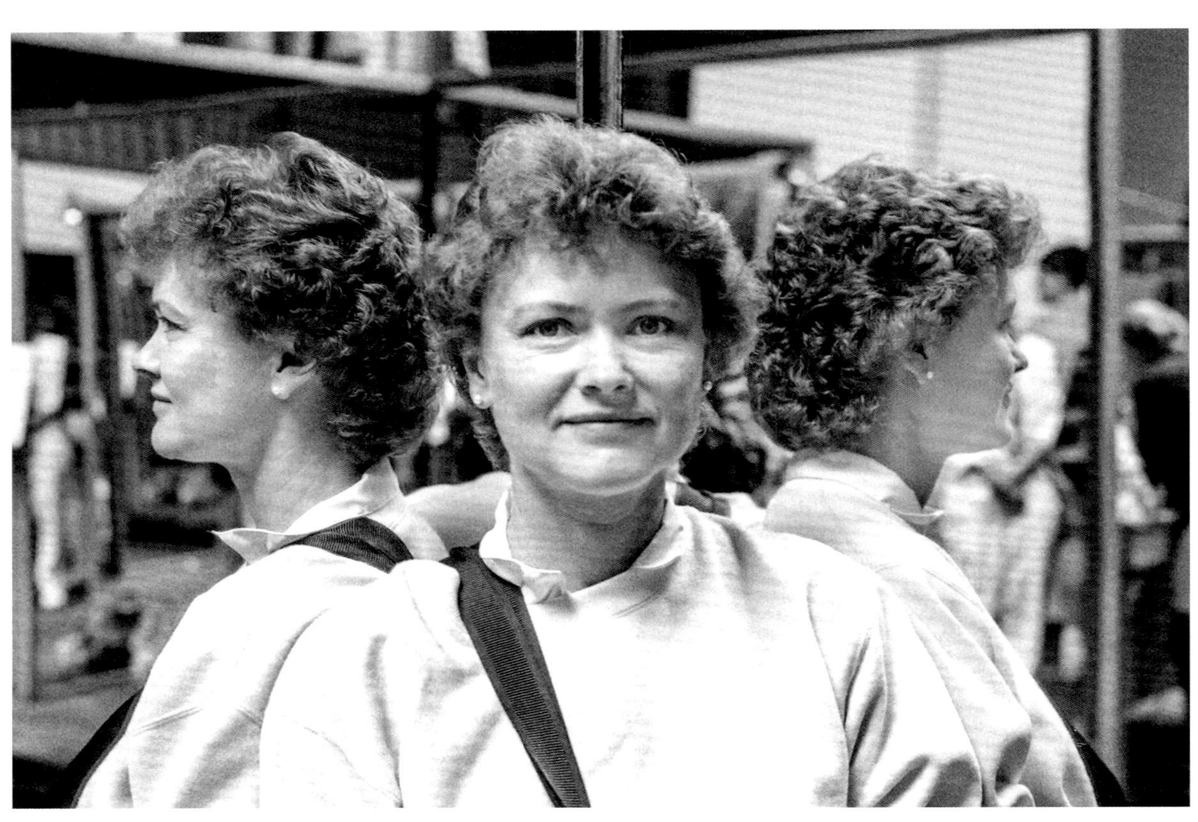

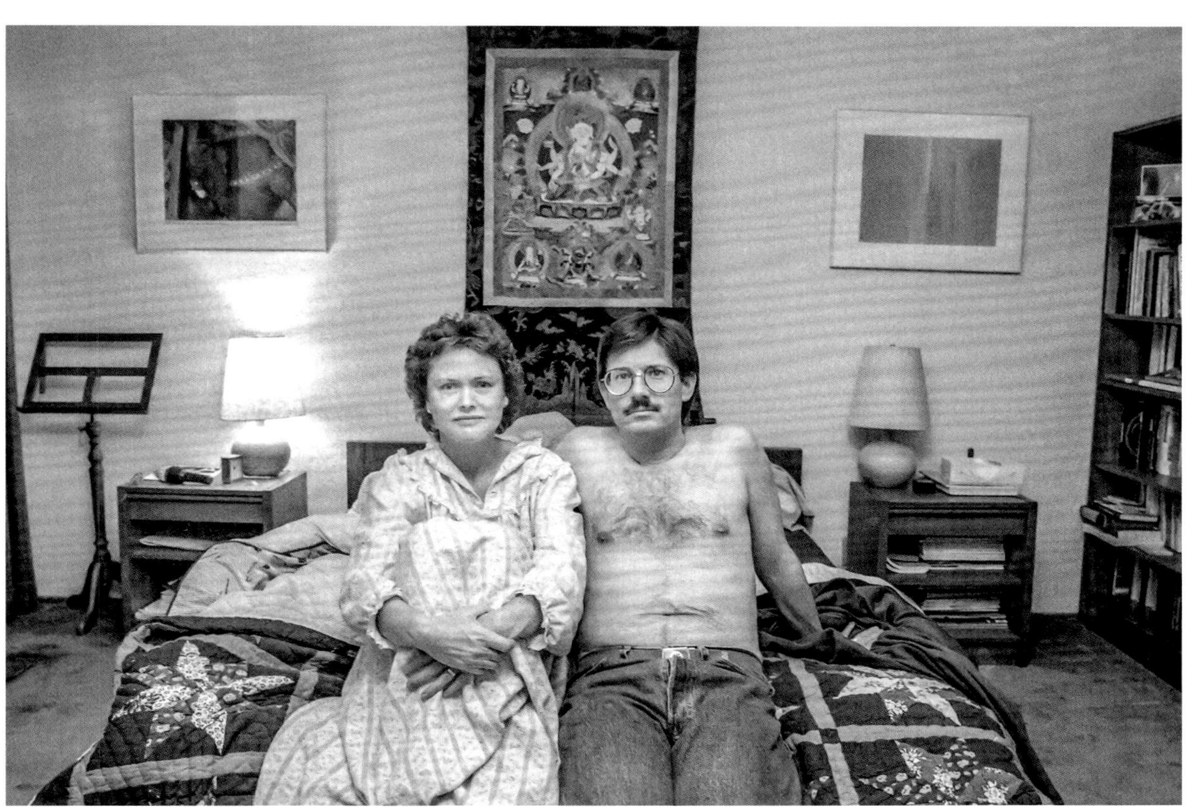

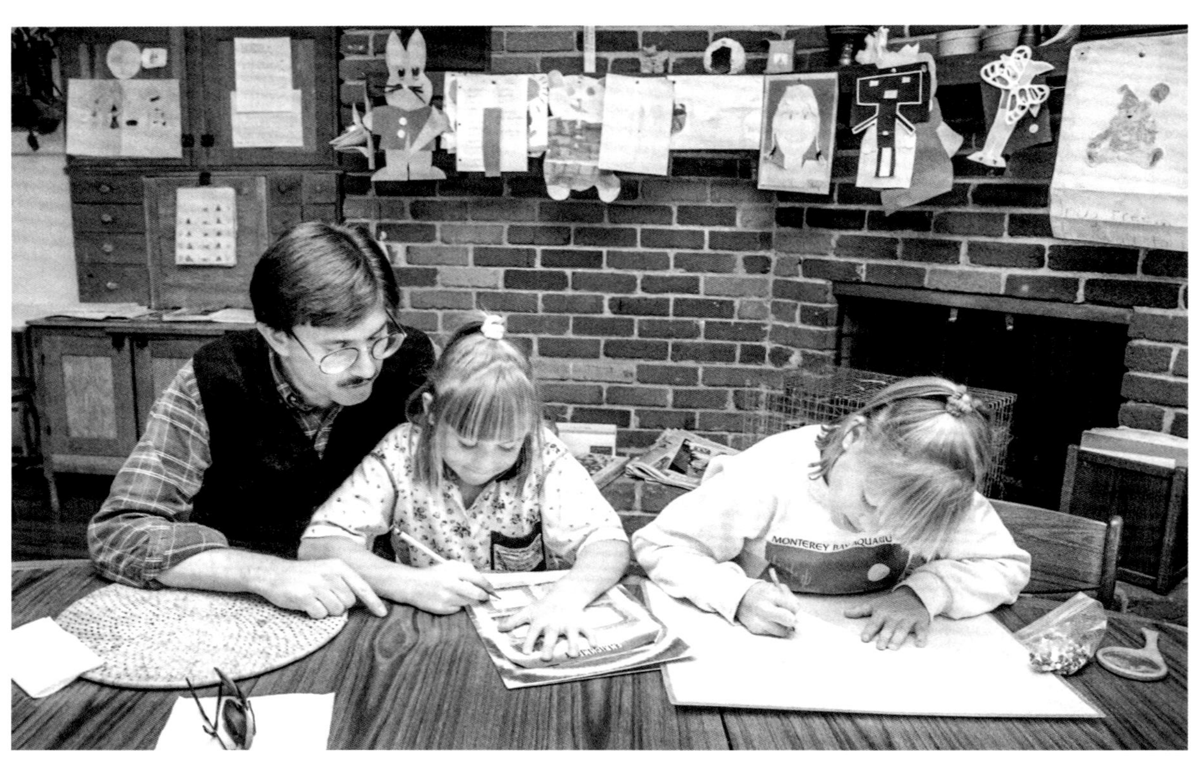

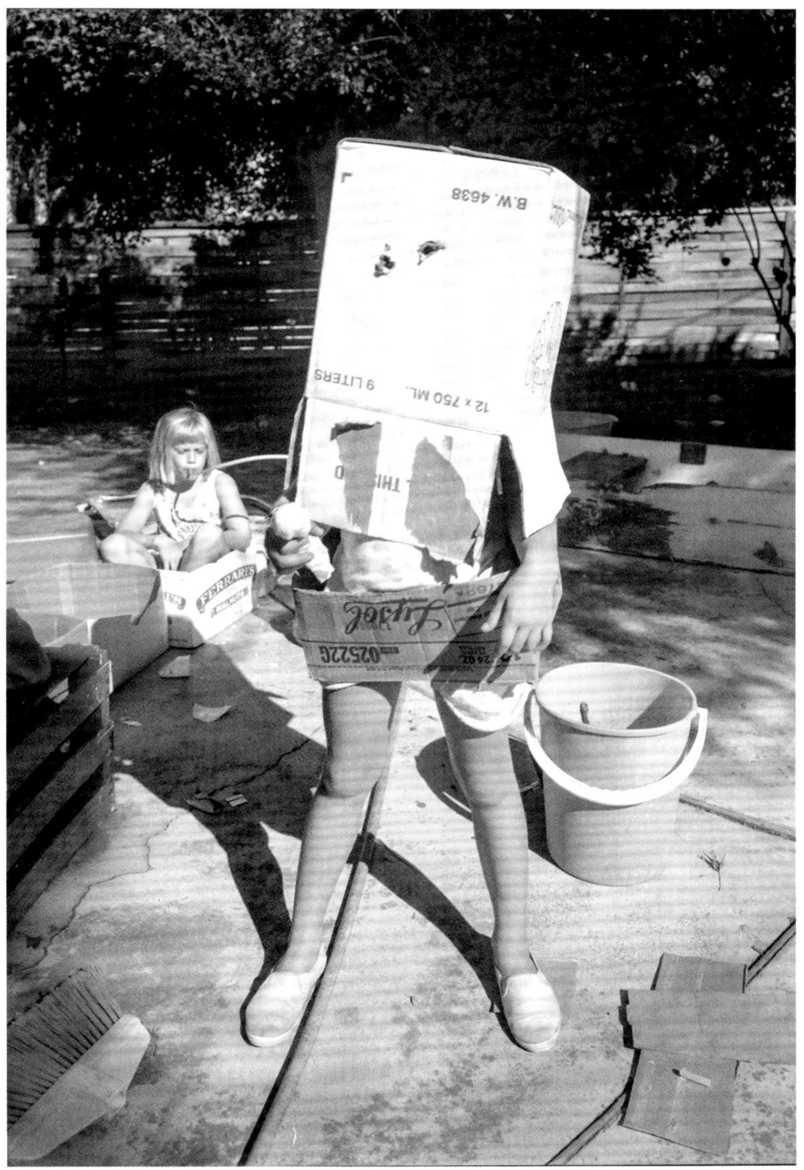

B.W. 4638
12 x 750 ML.   9 LITERS
FERRARIS
Jujol
025220

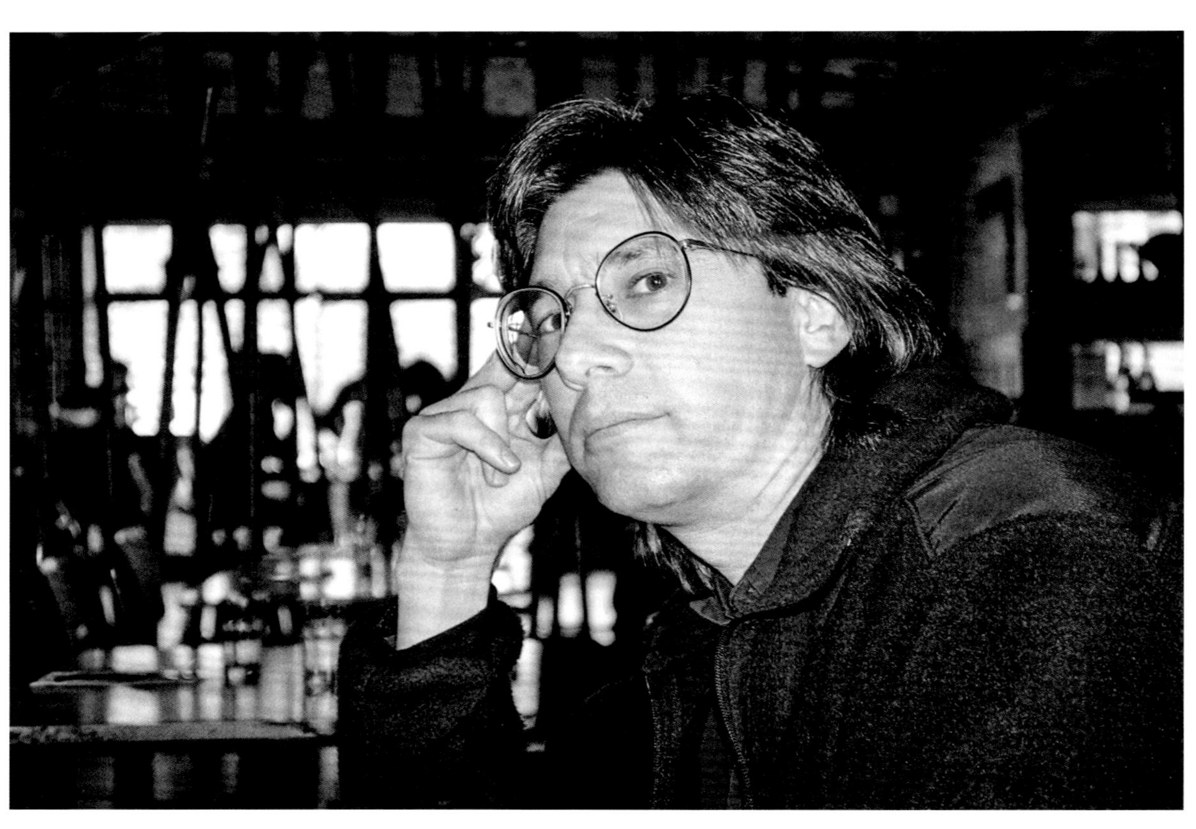

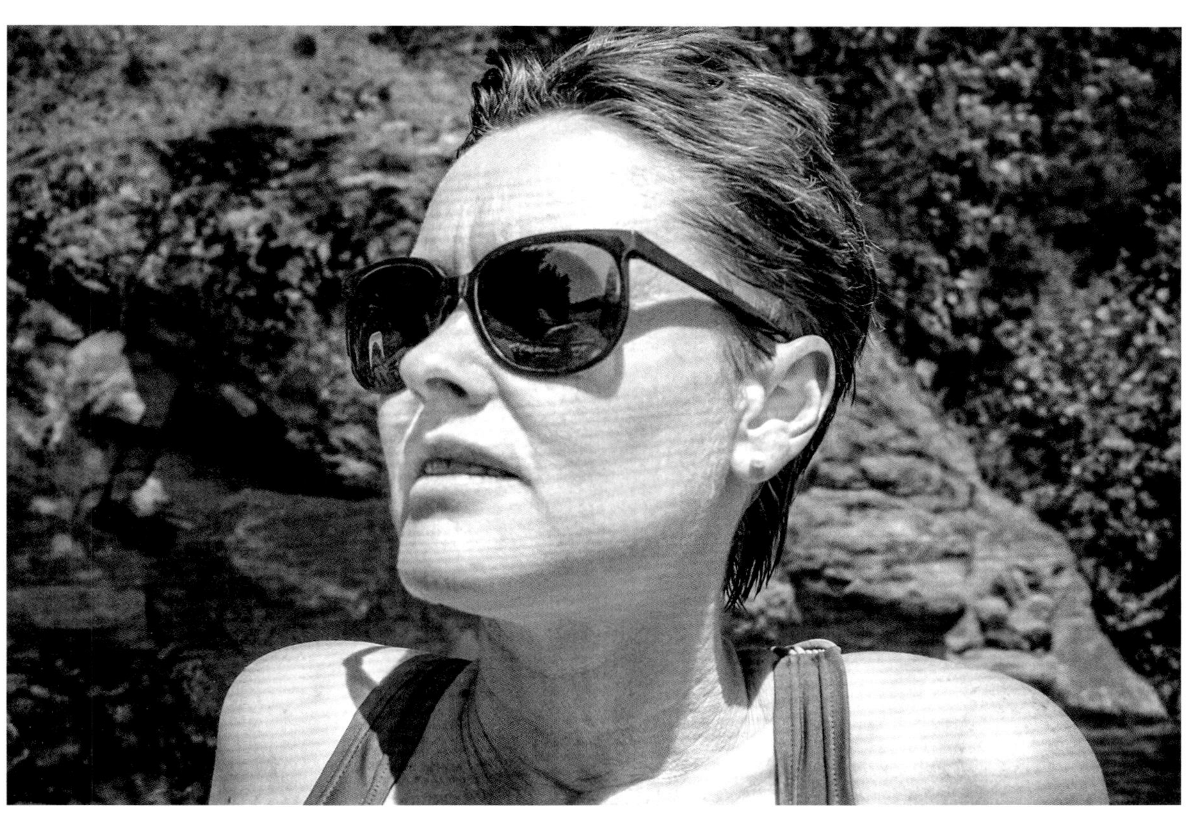

COEUR D'ALENE, IDAHO 1992 | 91

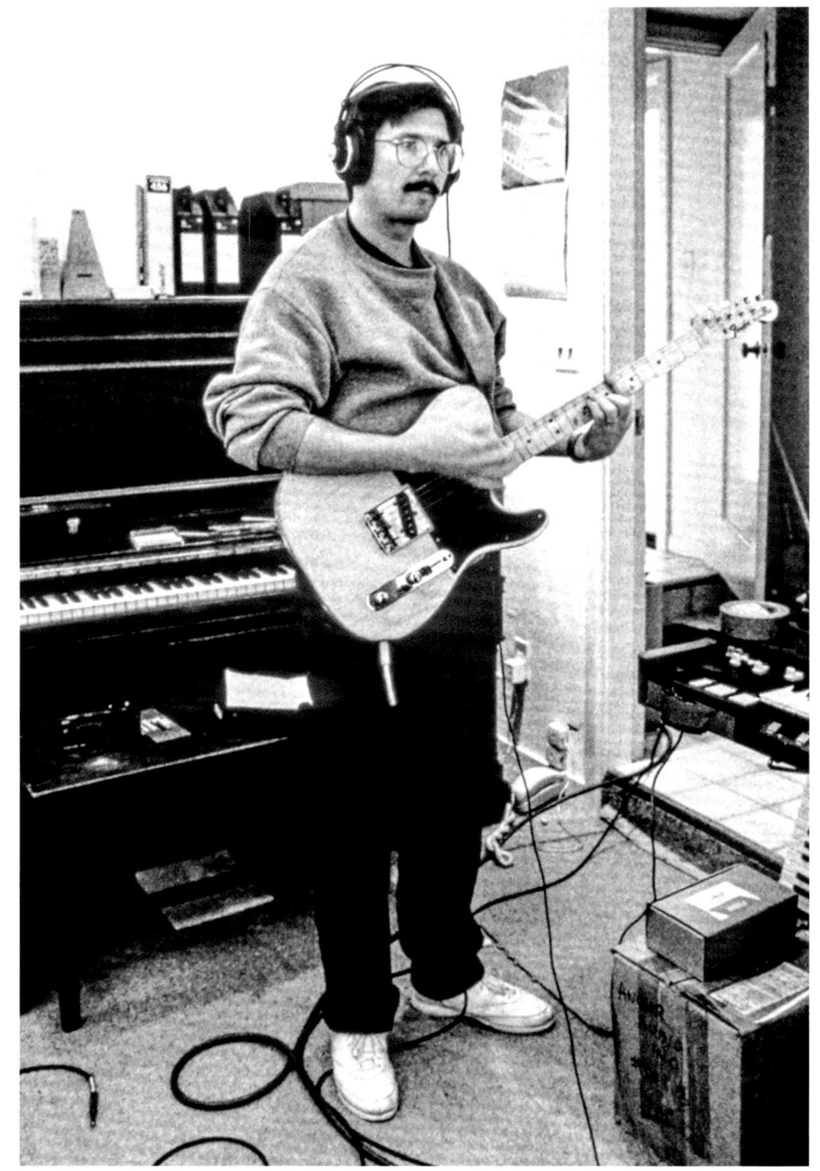

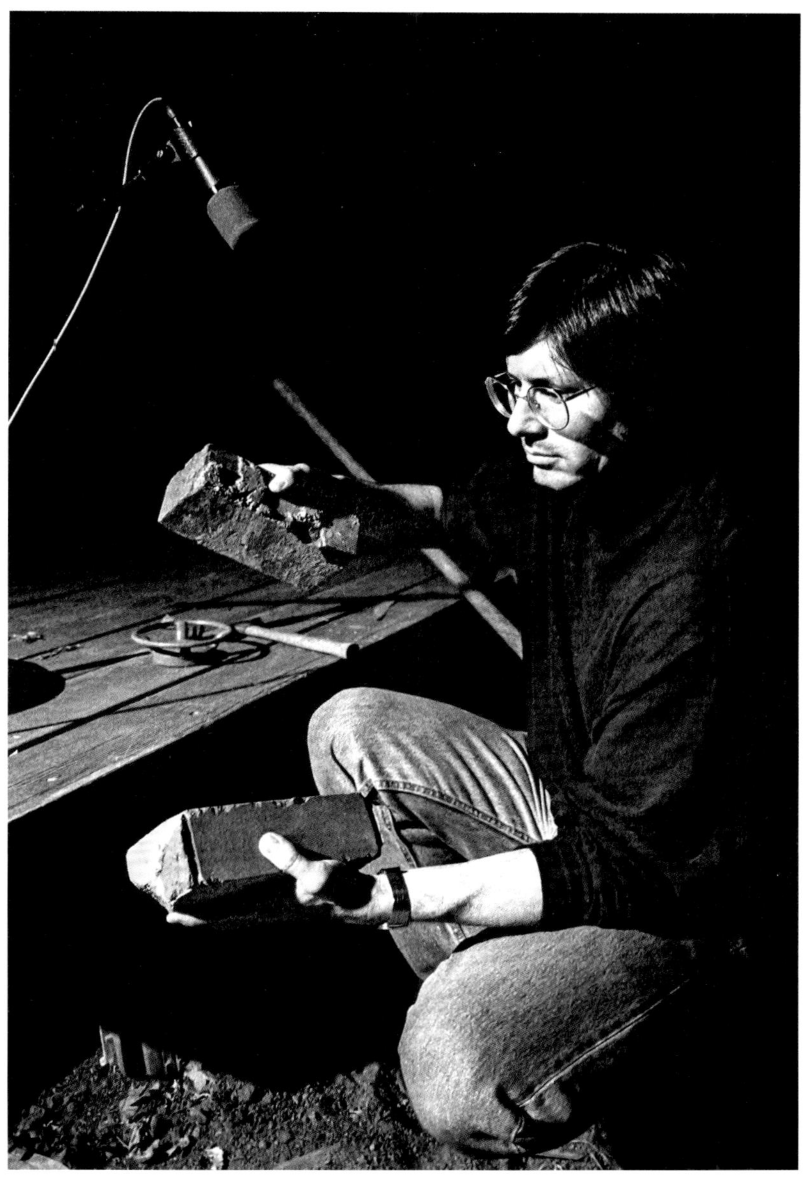

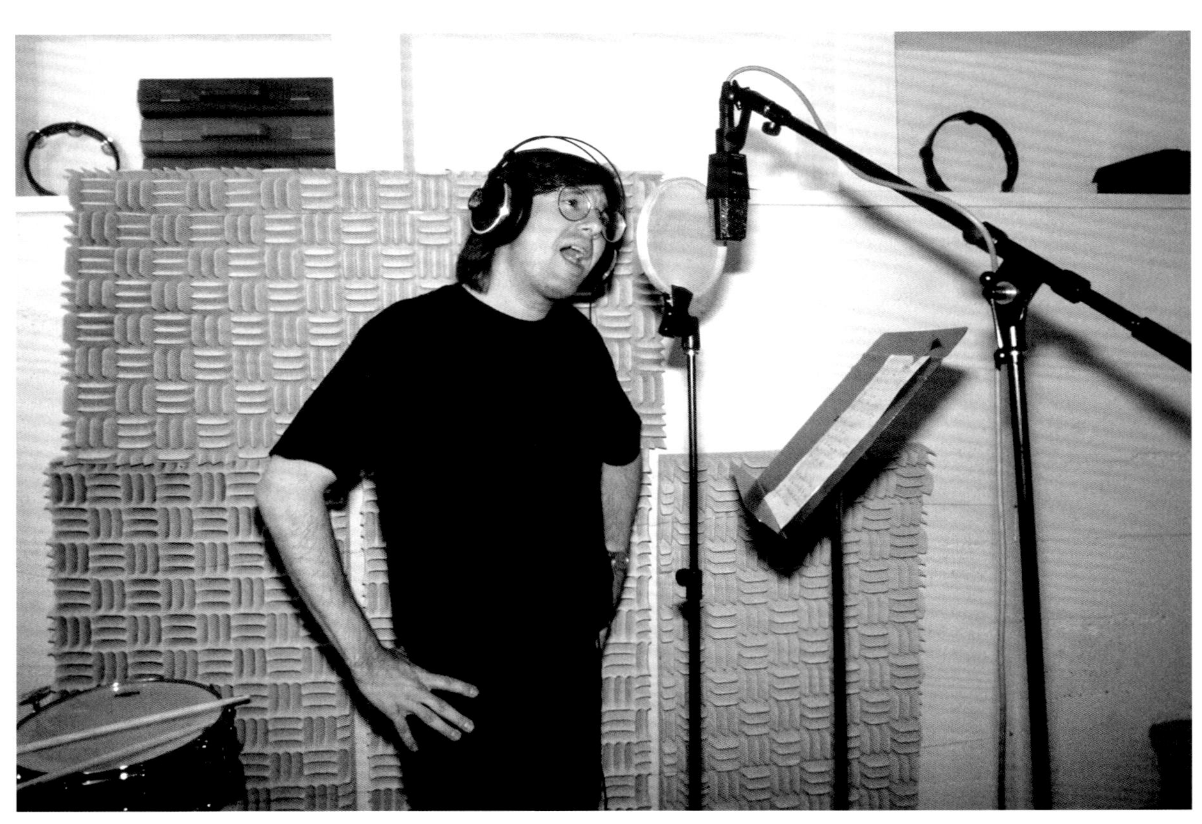

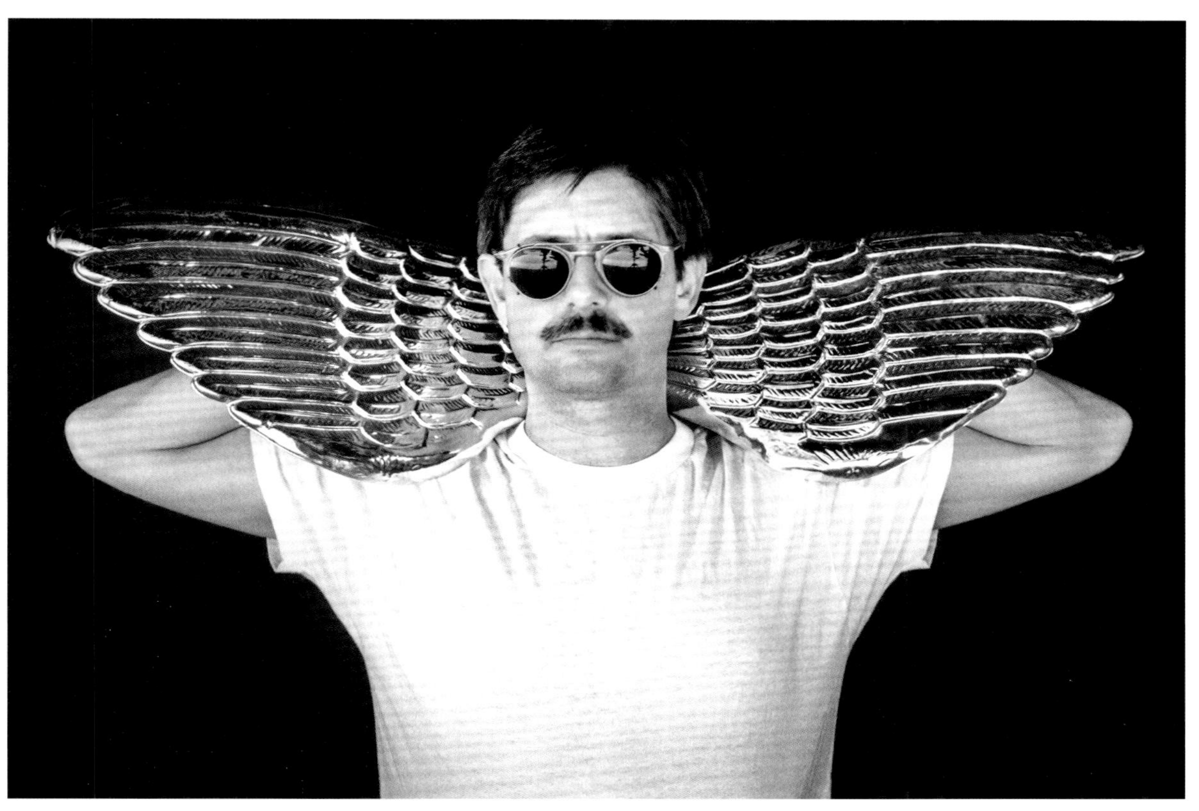

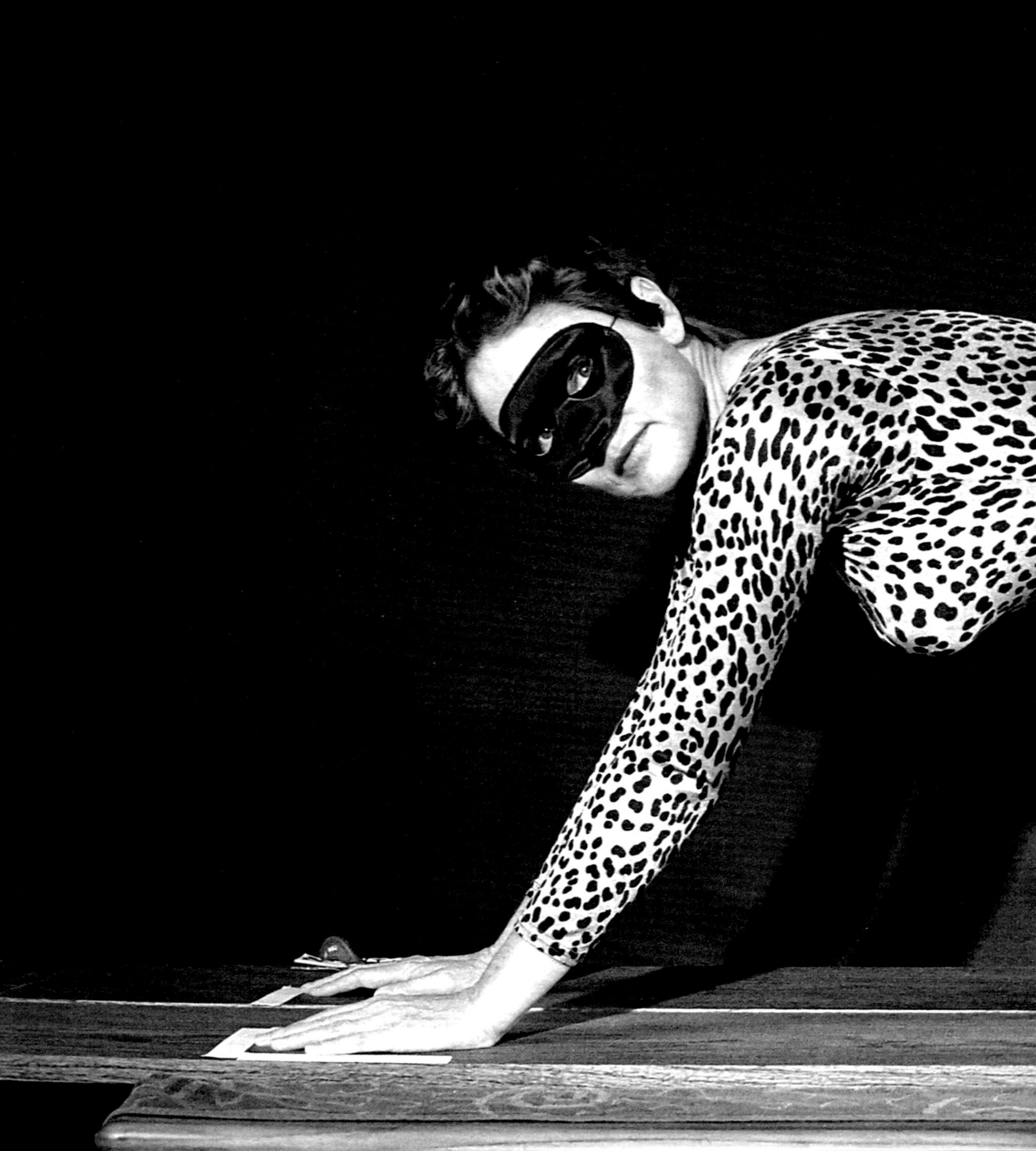

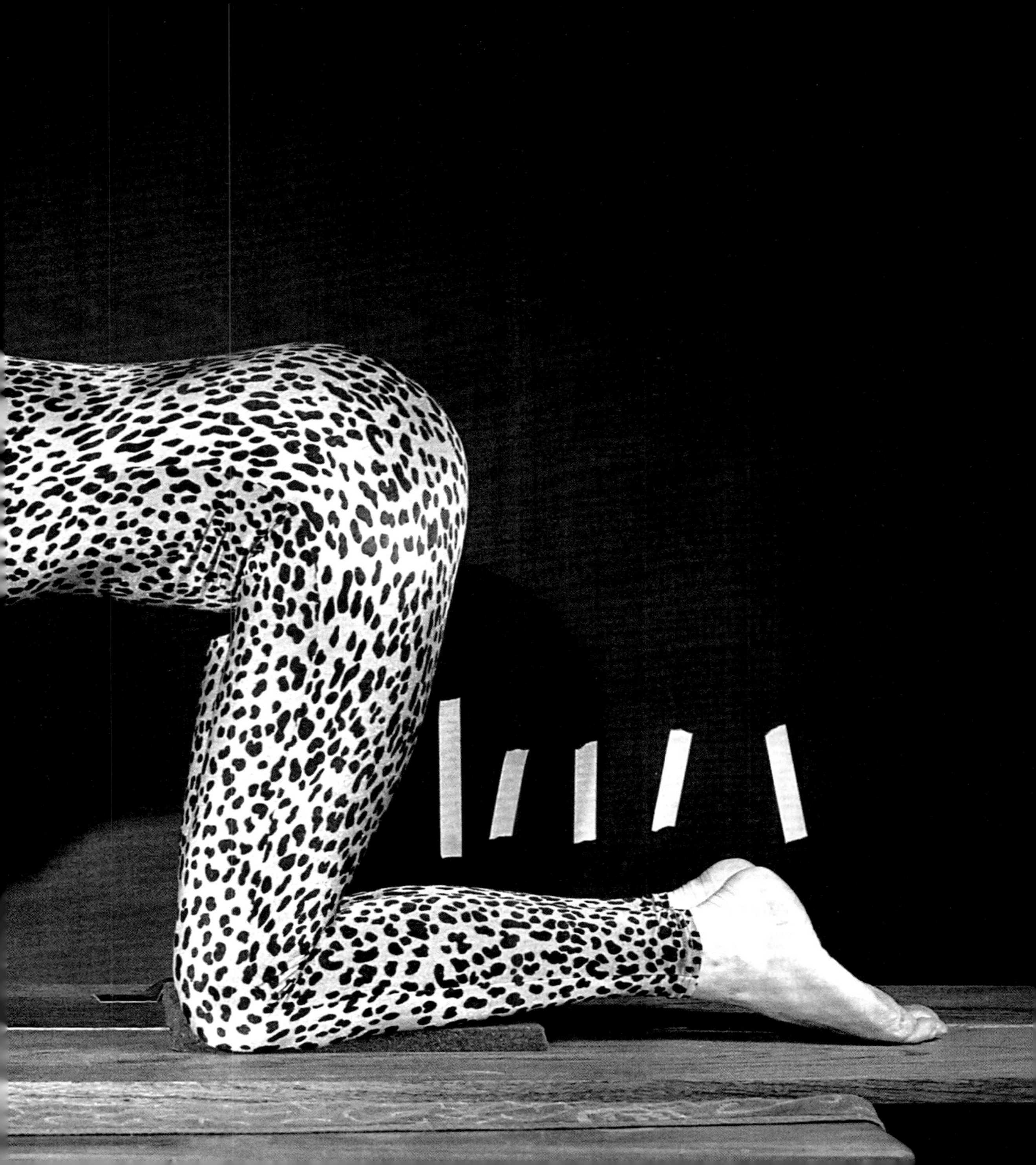

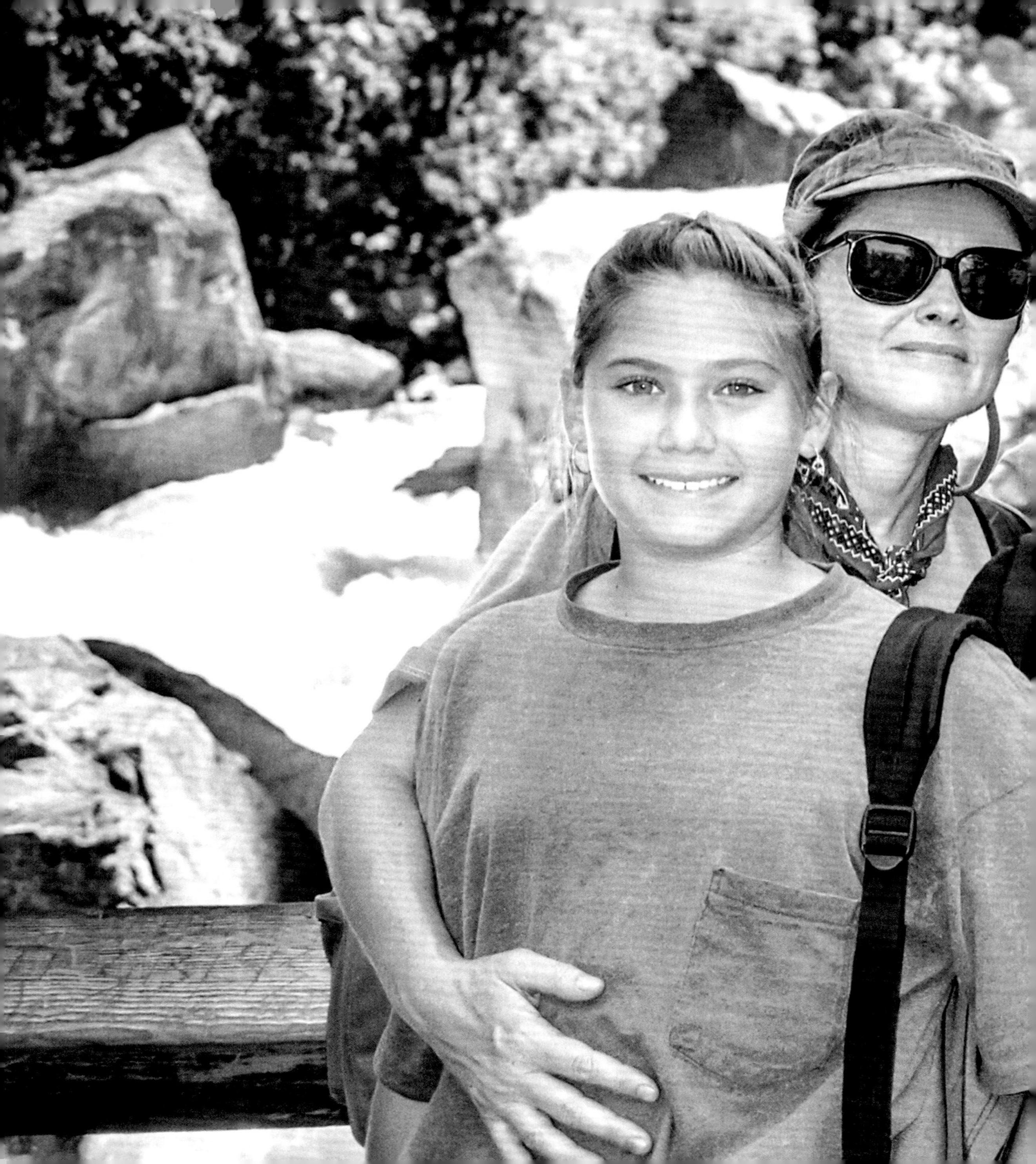

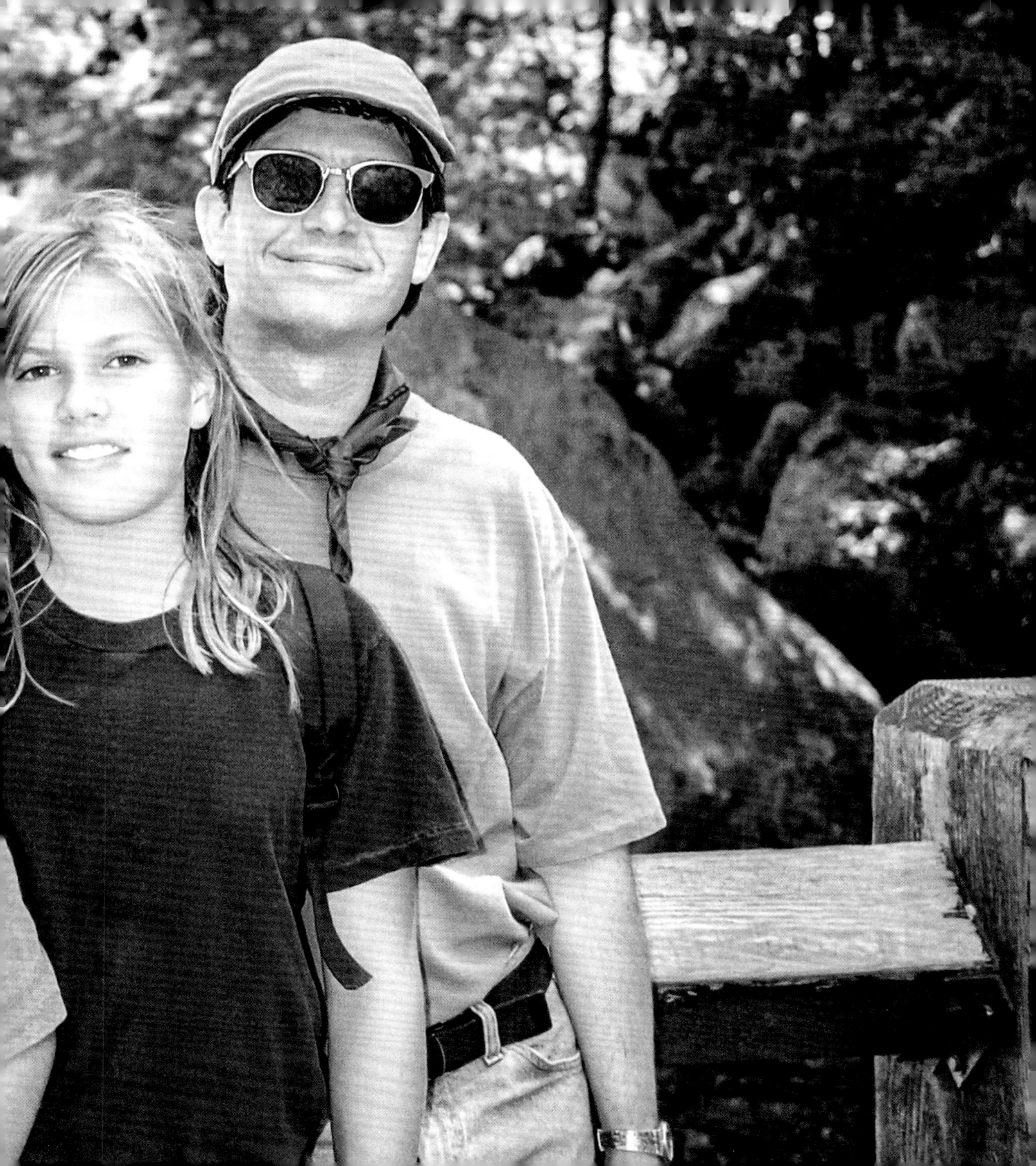

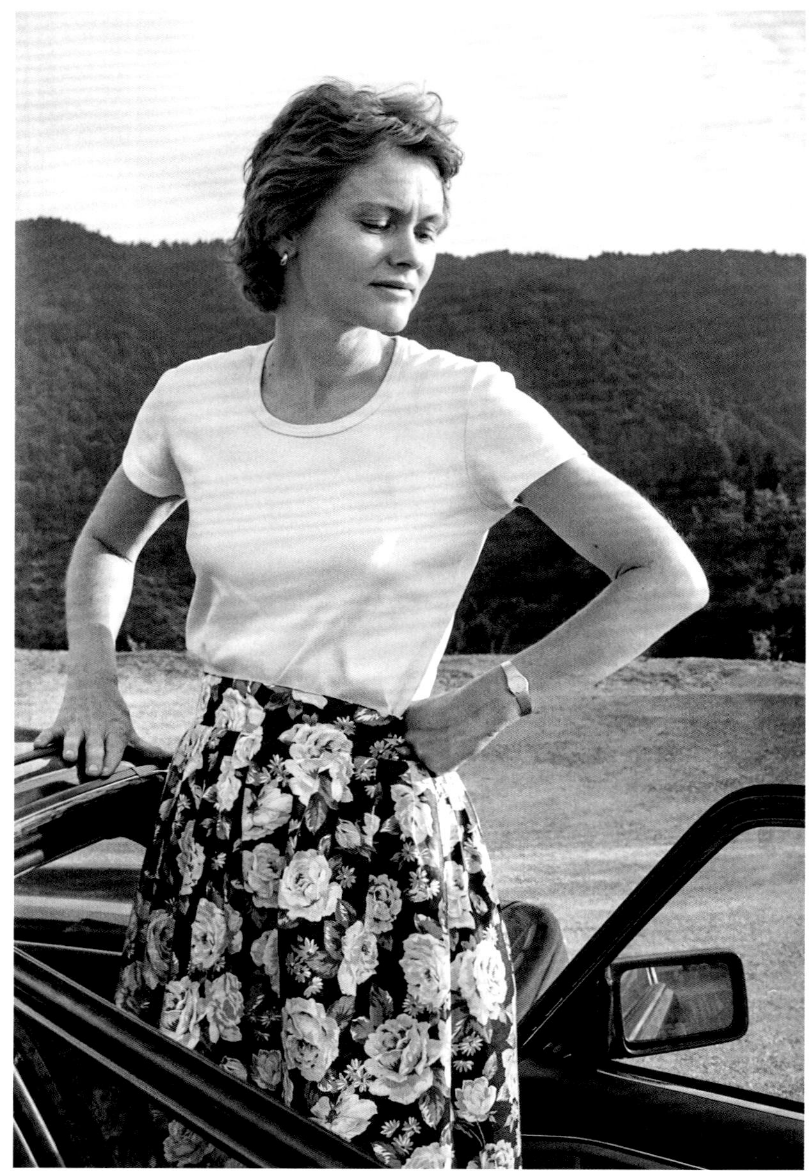

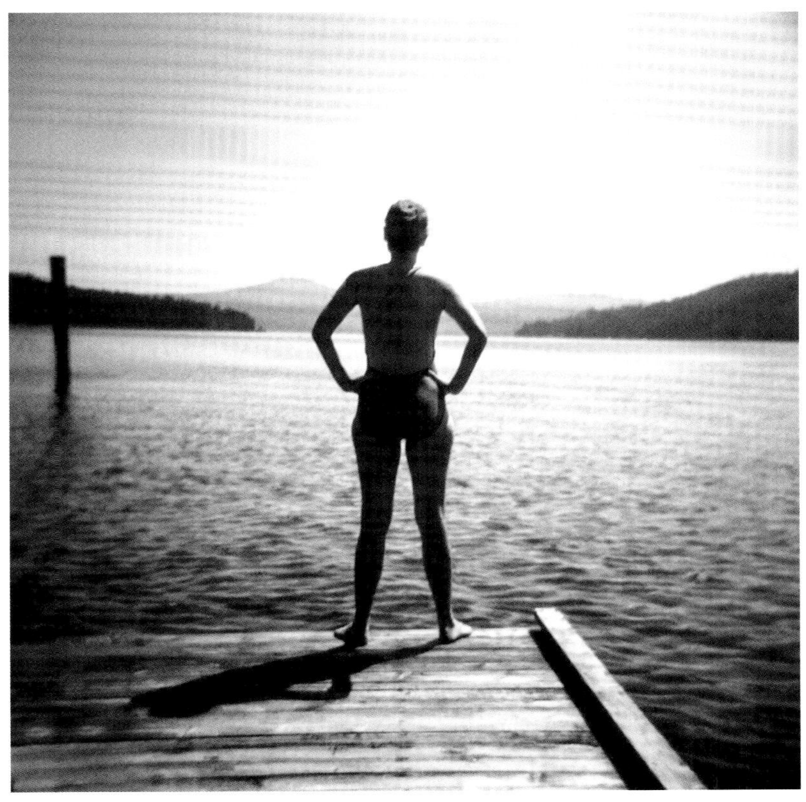

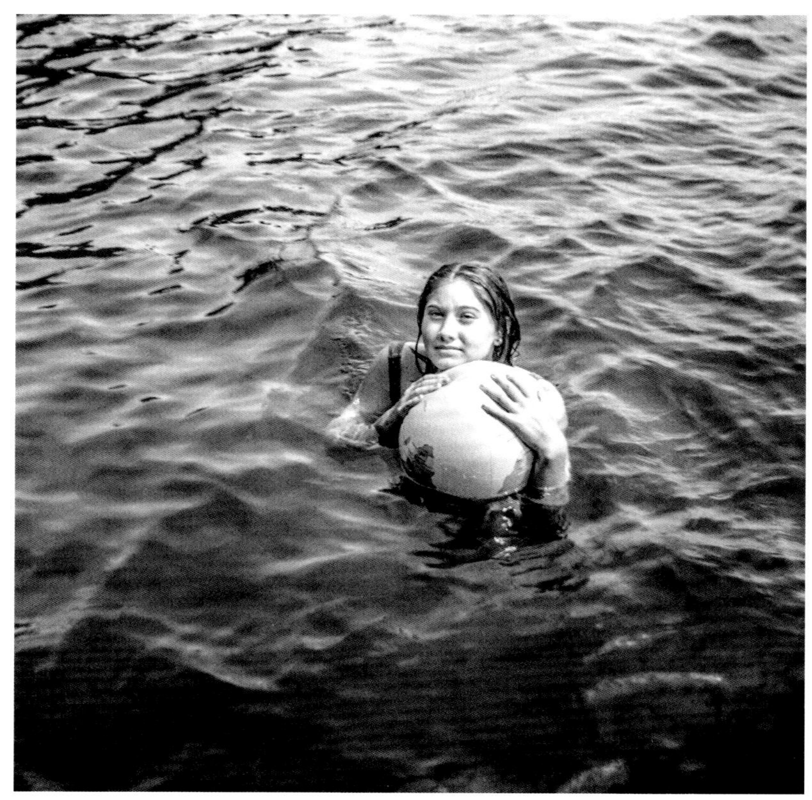

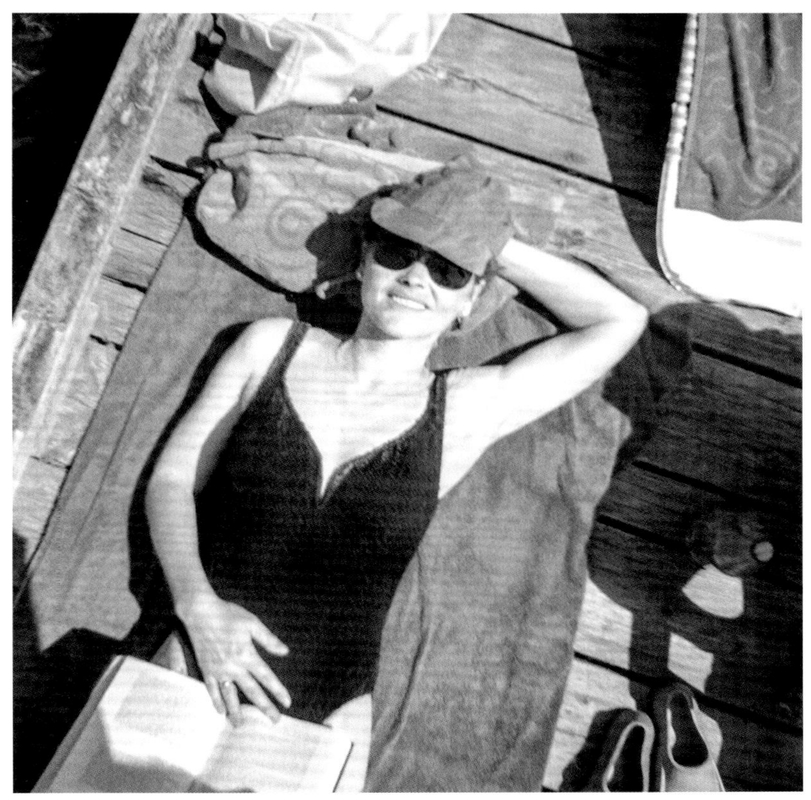

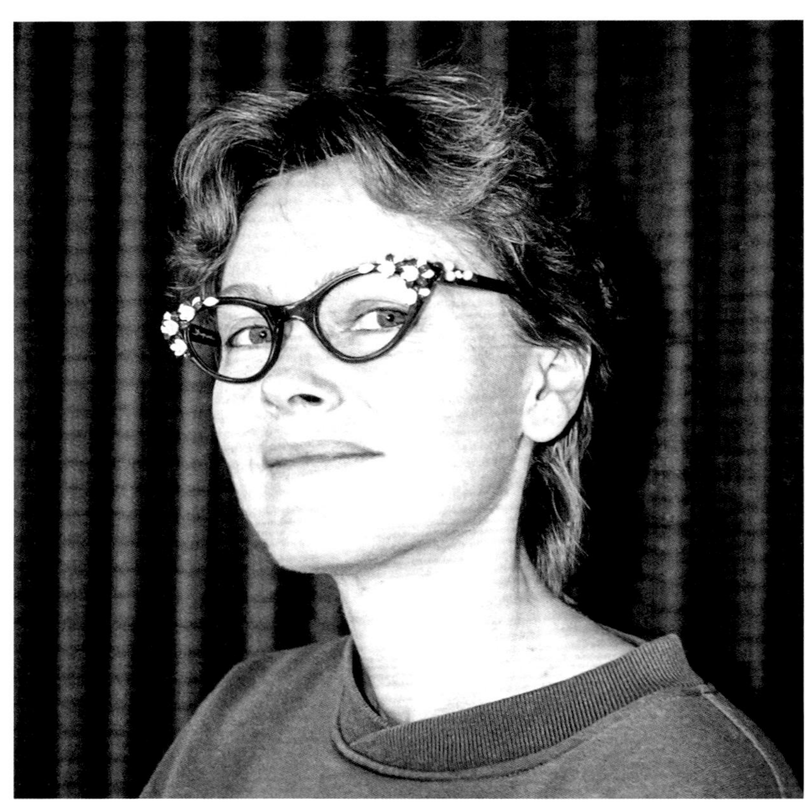

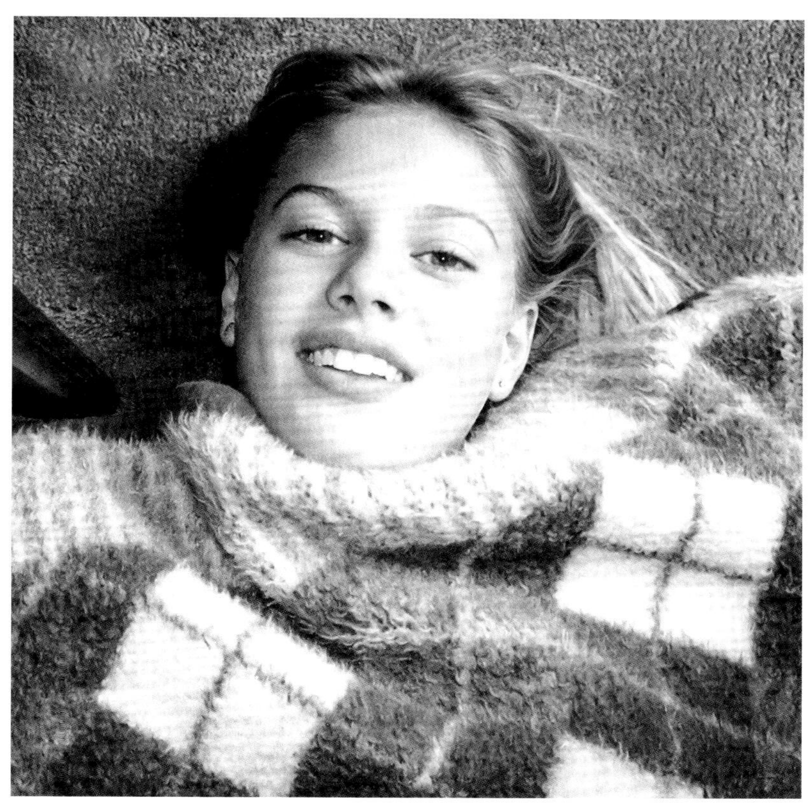

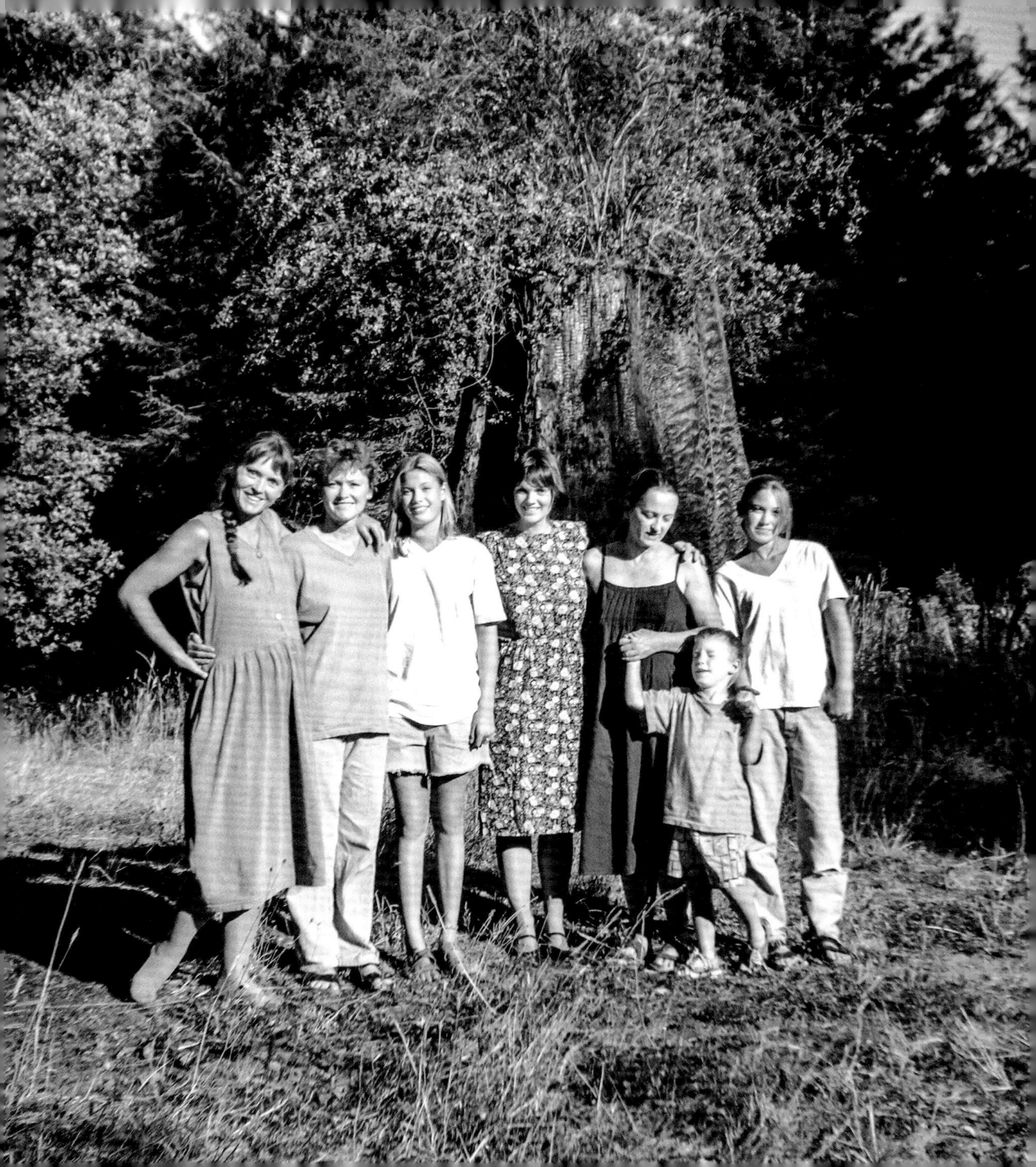

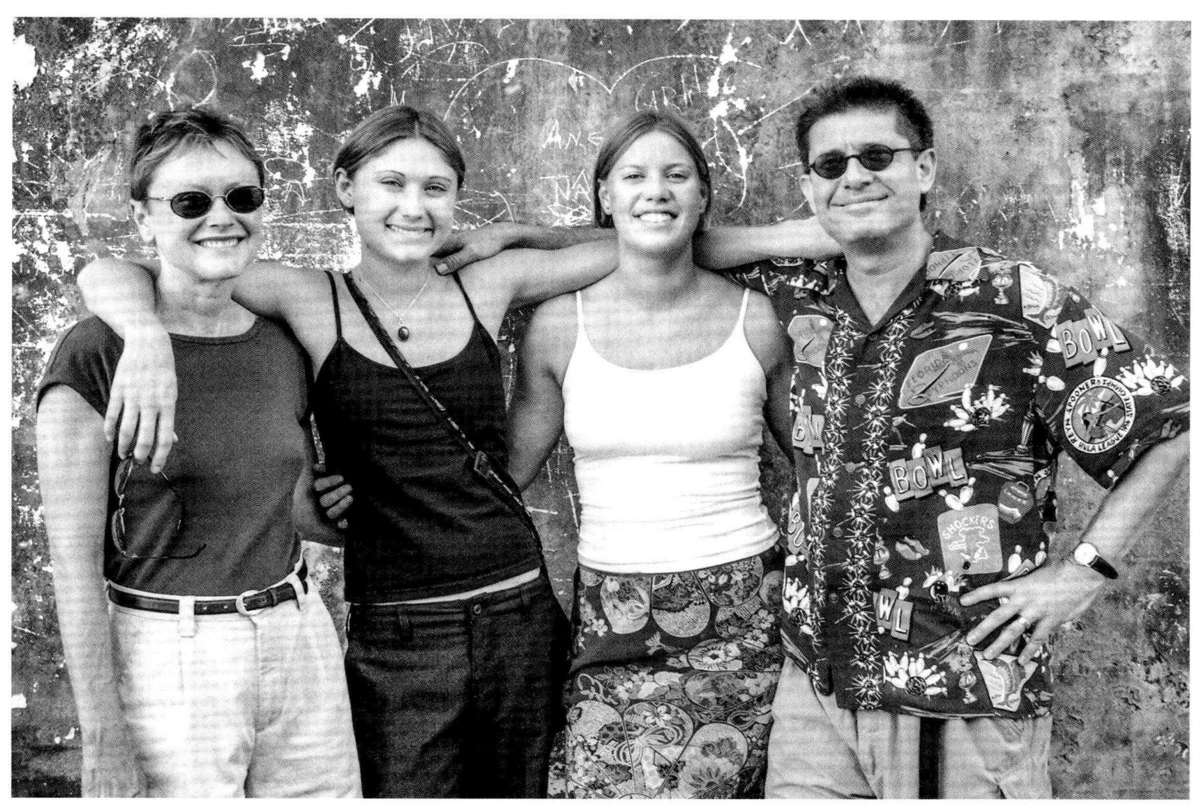

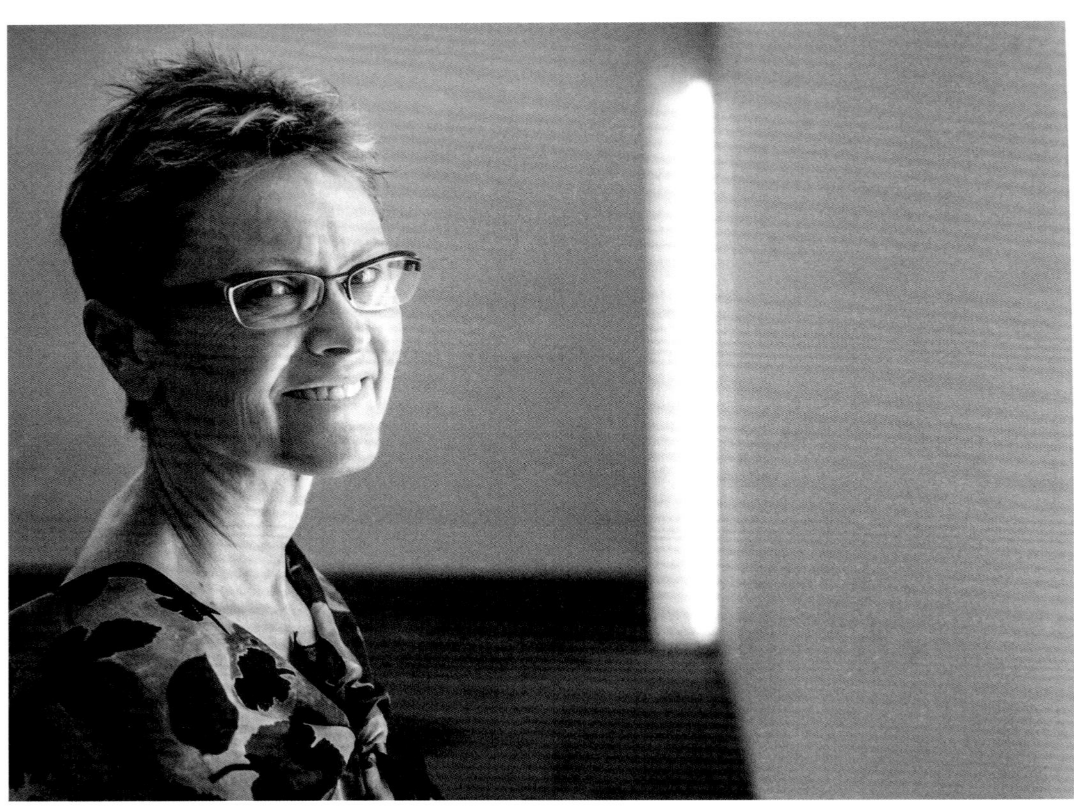

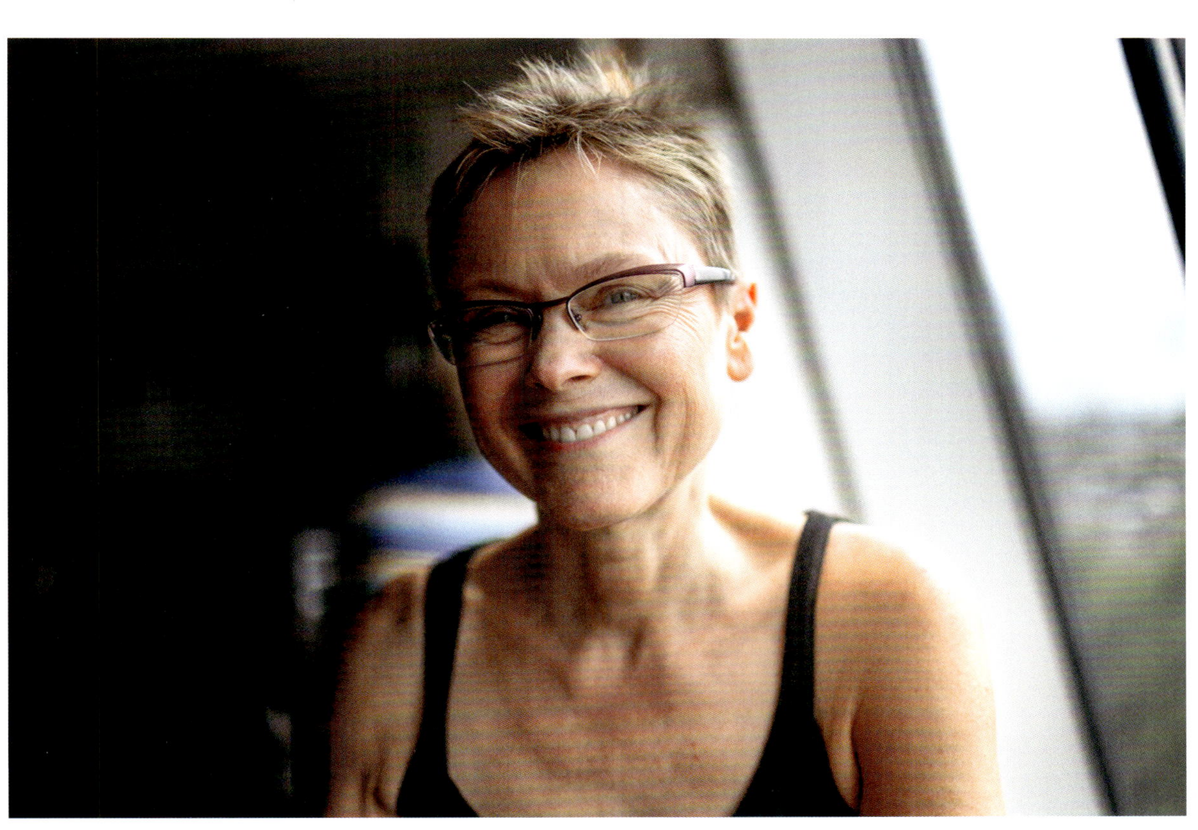

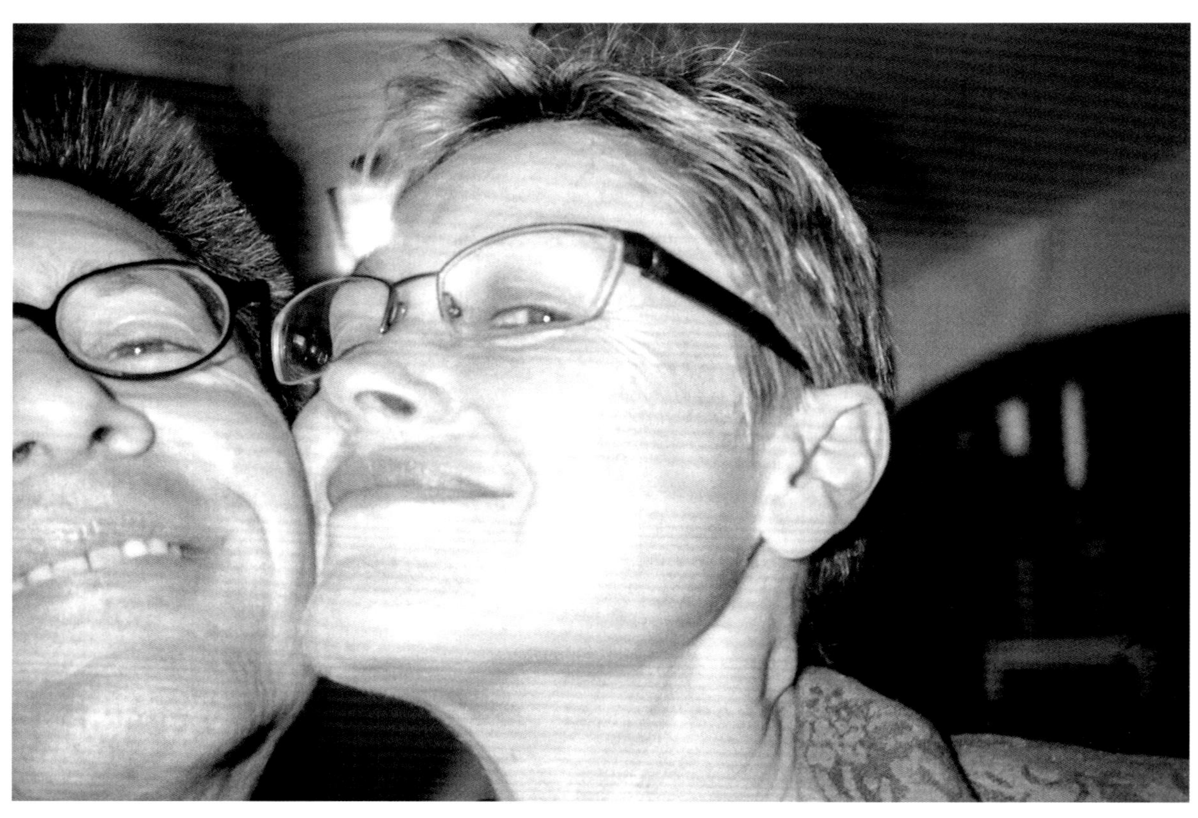

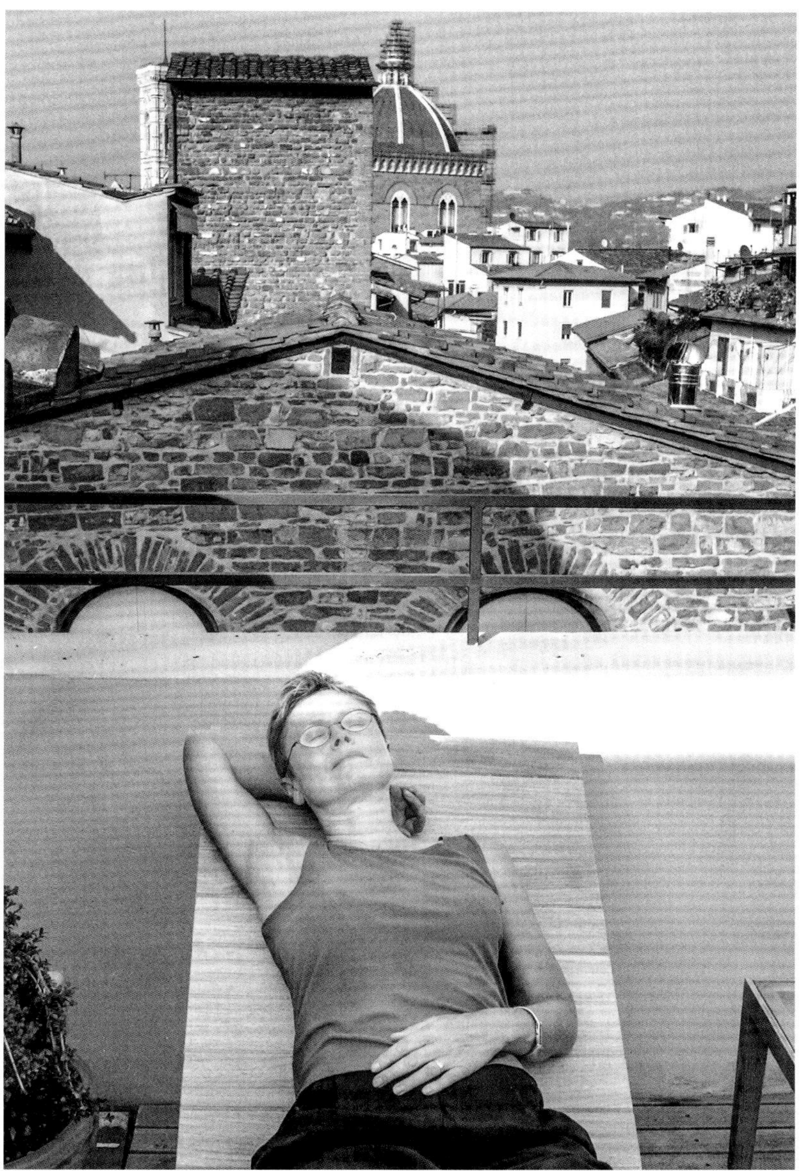

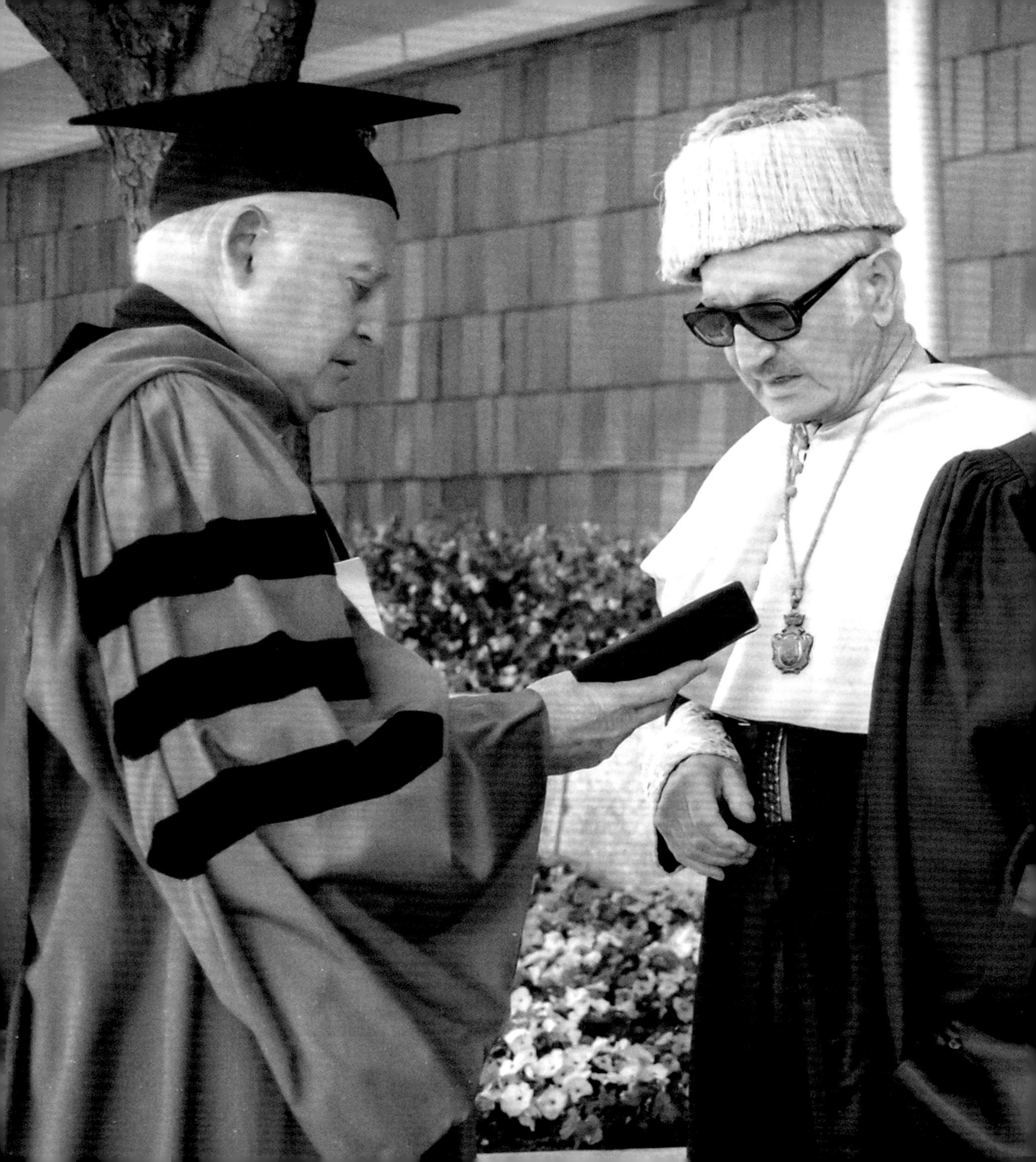

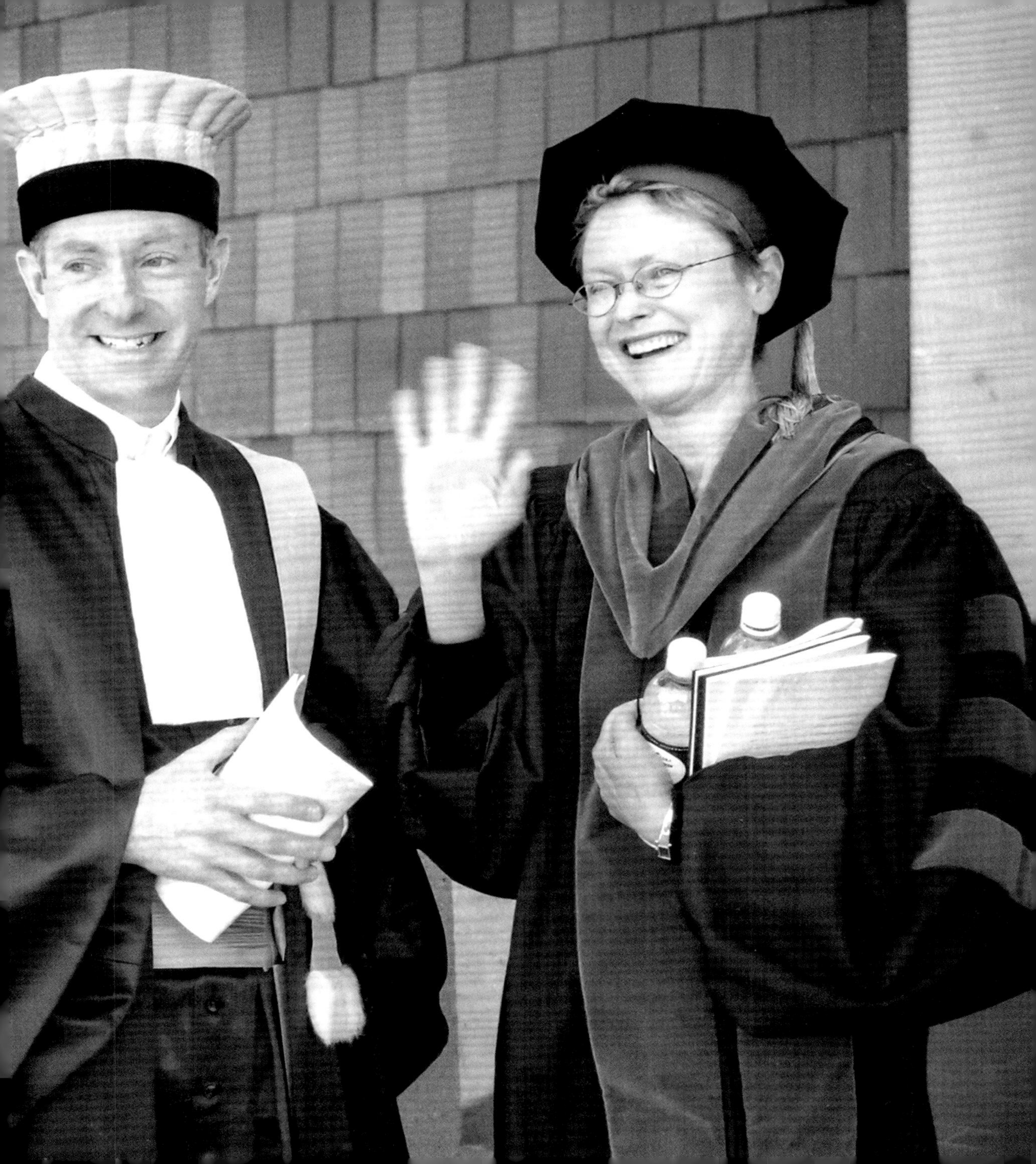

Instructions for
living a life –
Pay attention.
Be astonished.
Tell about it.

– Mary Oliver, Red Bird

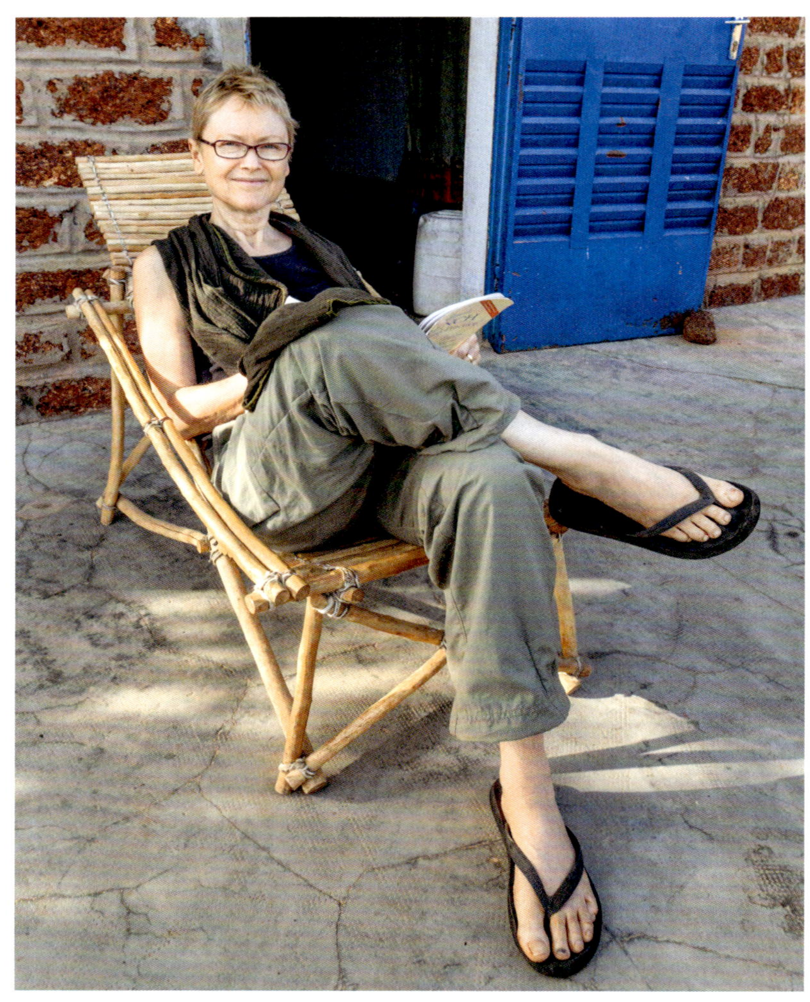

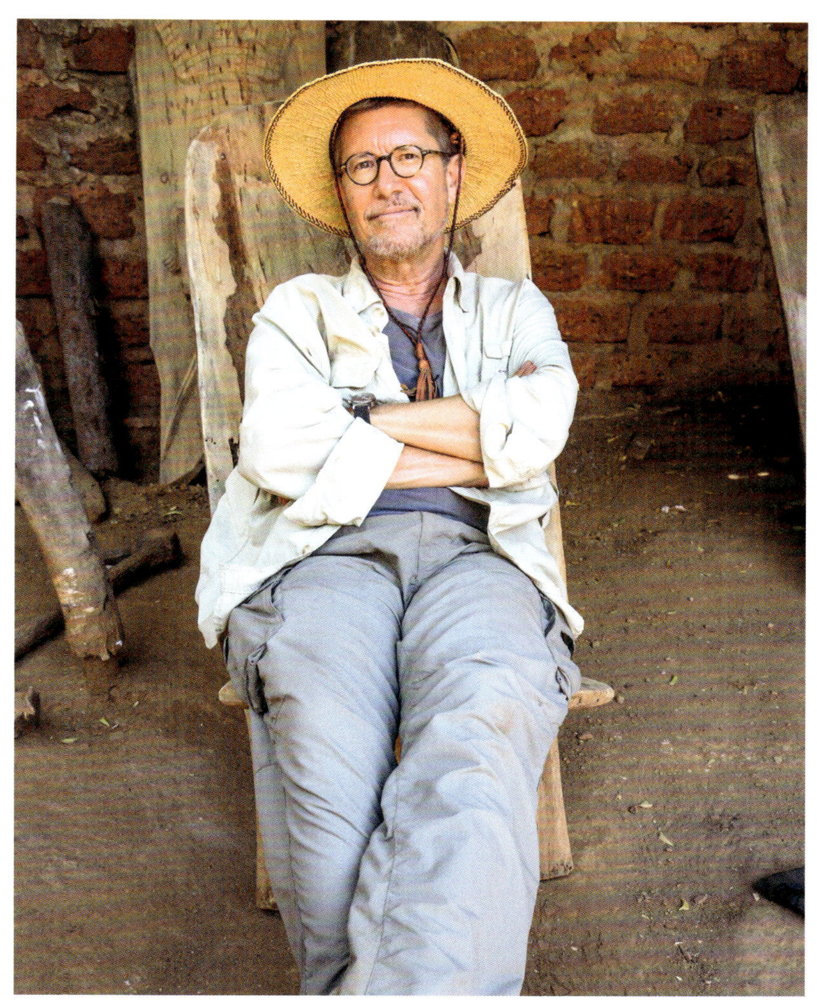

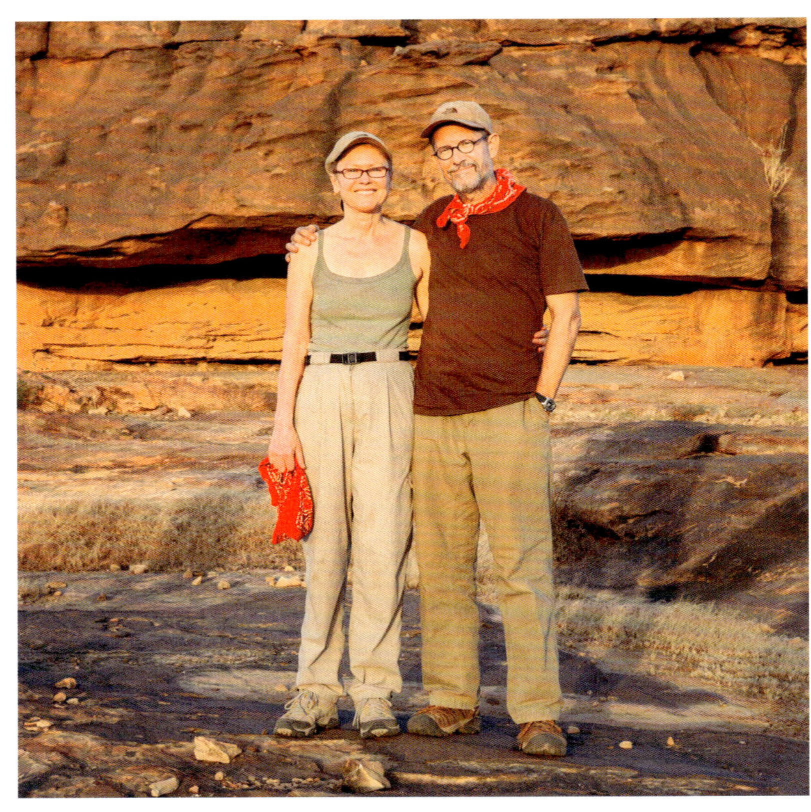

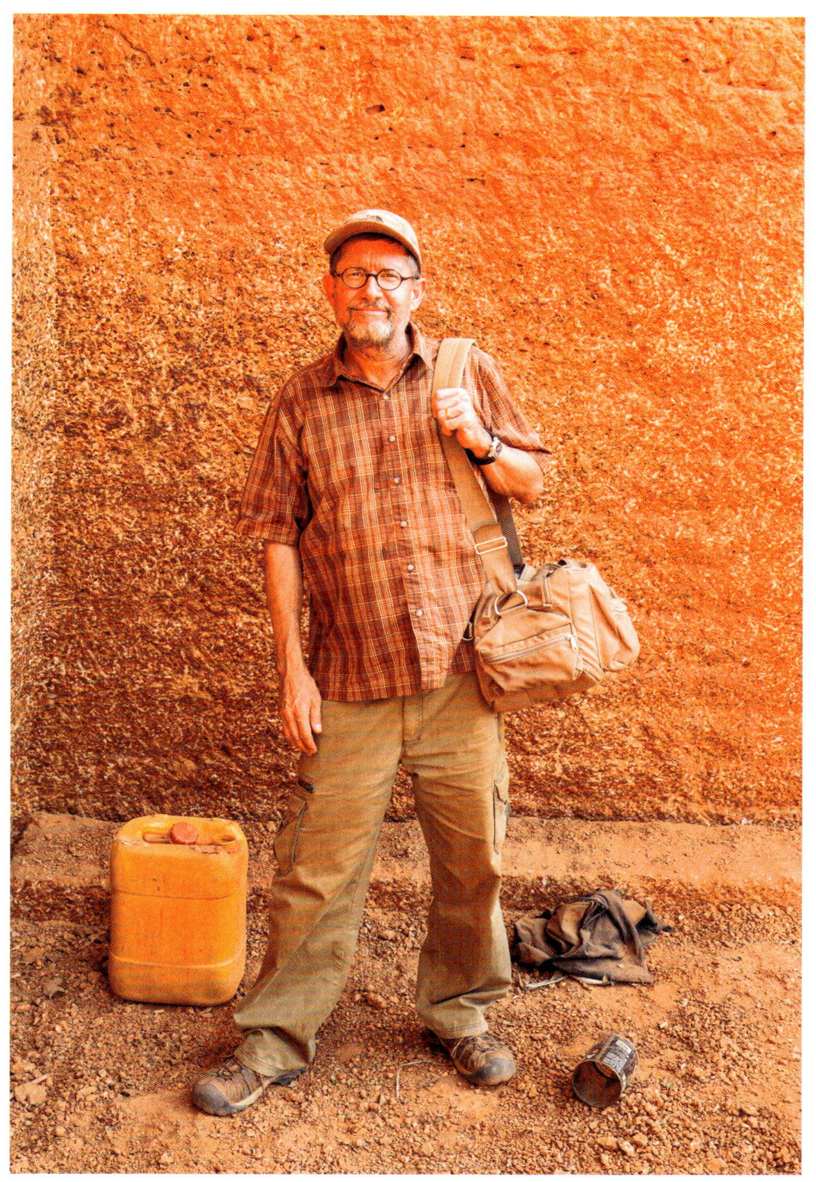

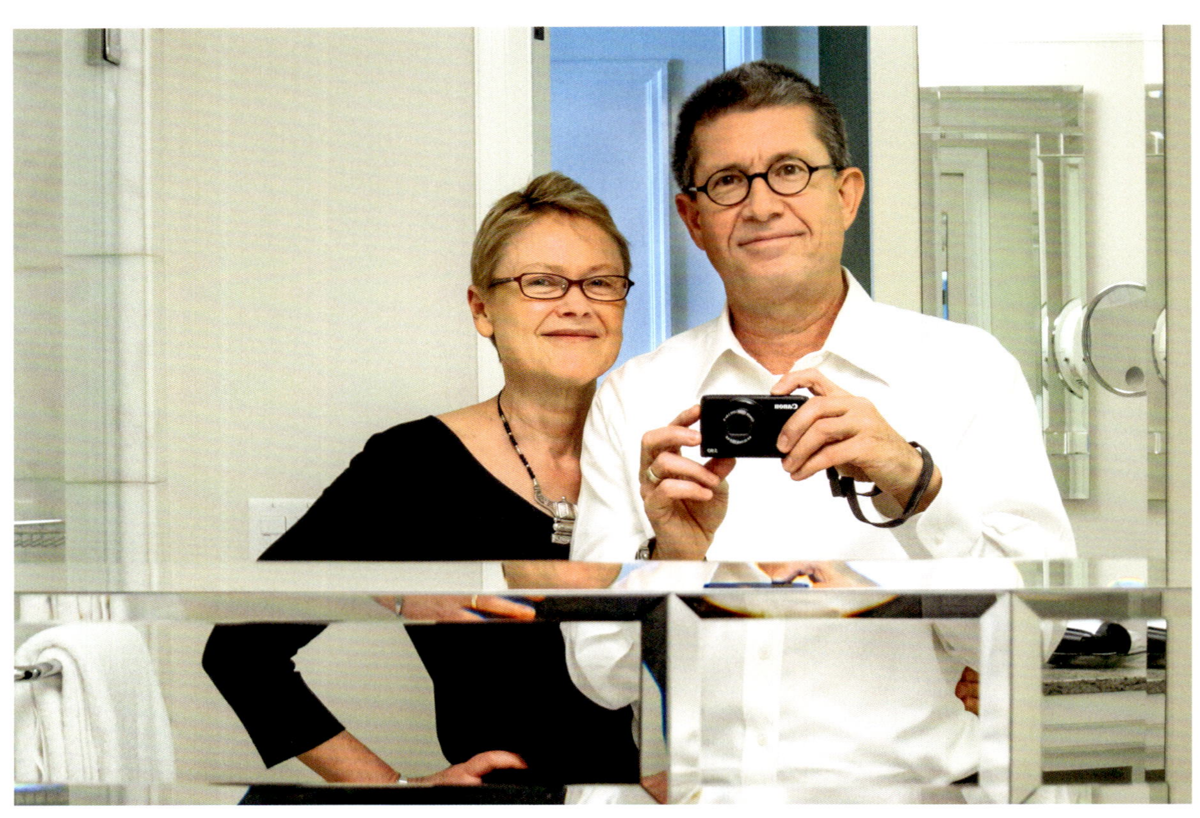

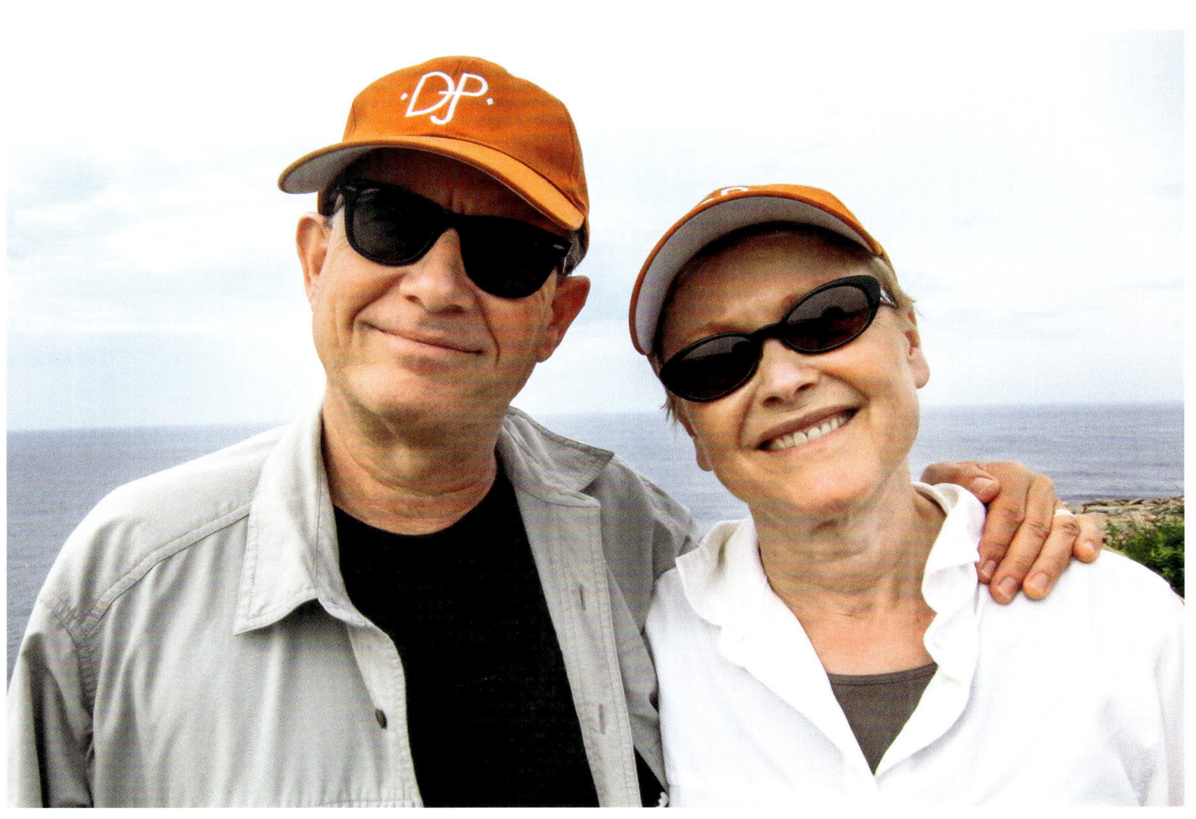

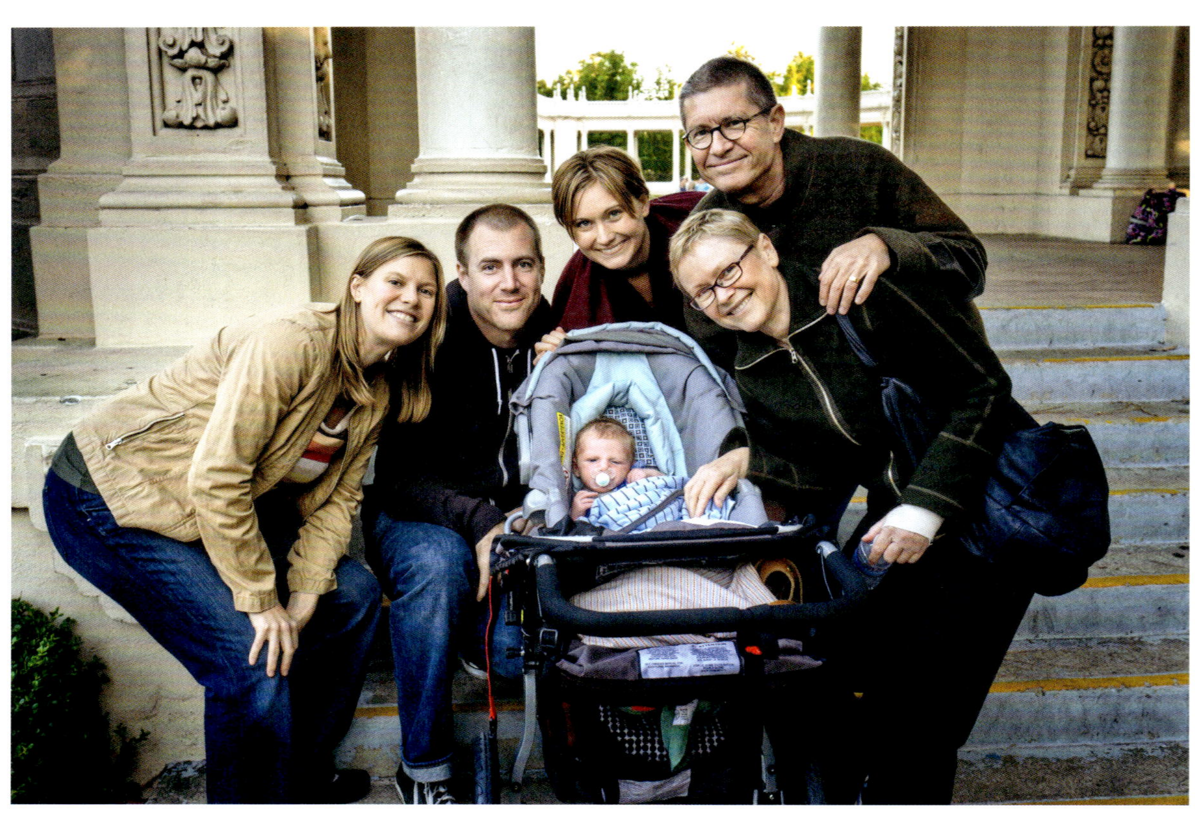

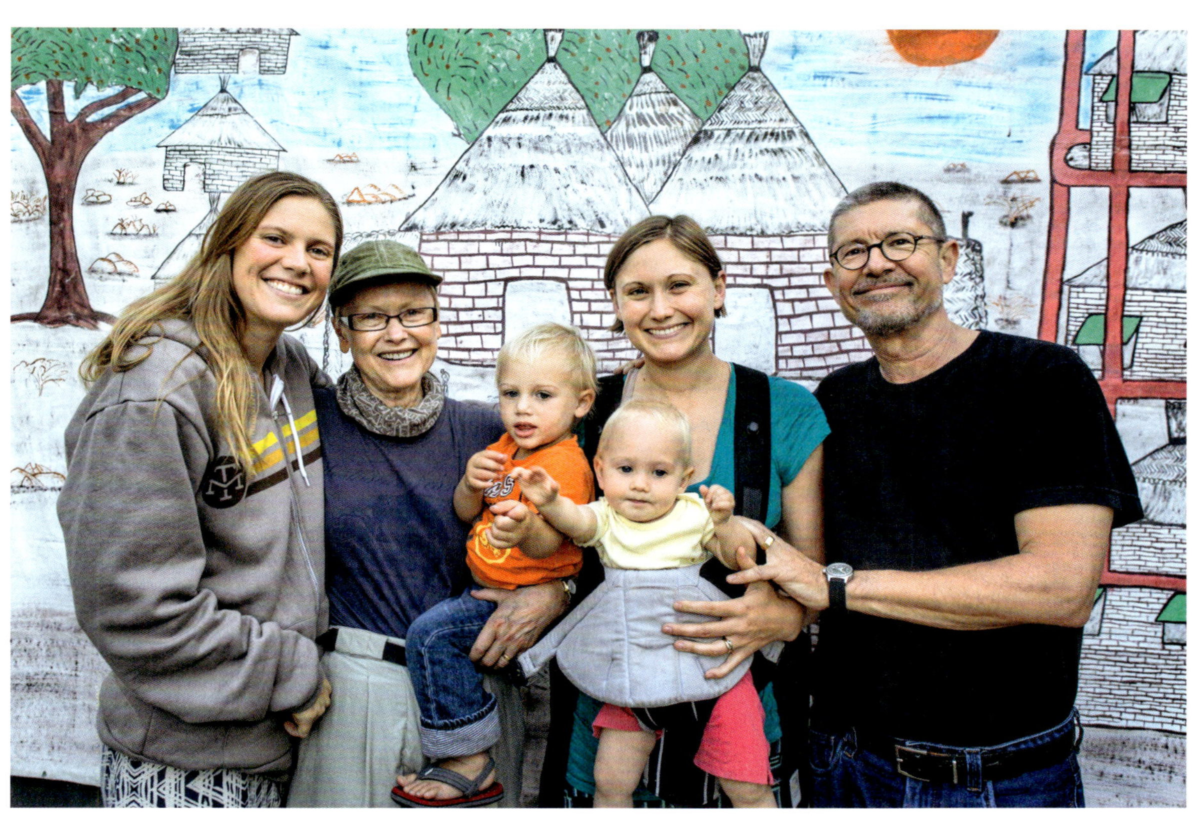

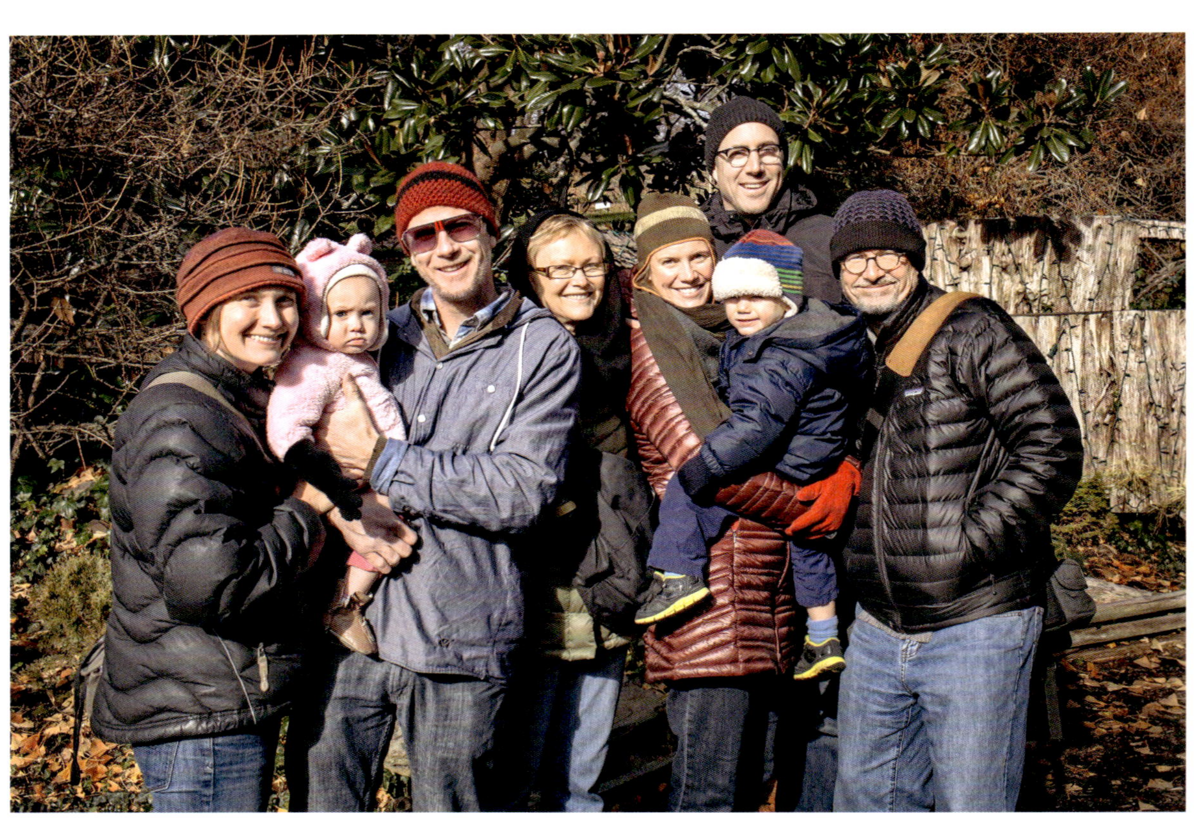

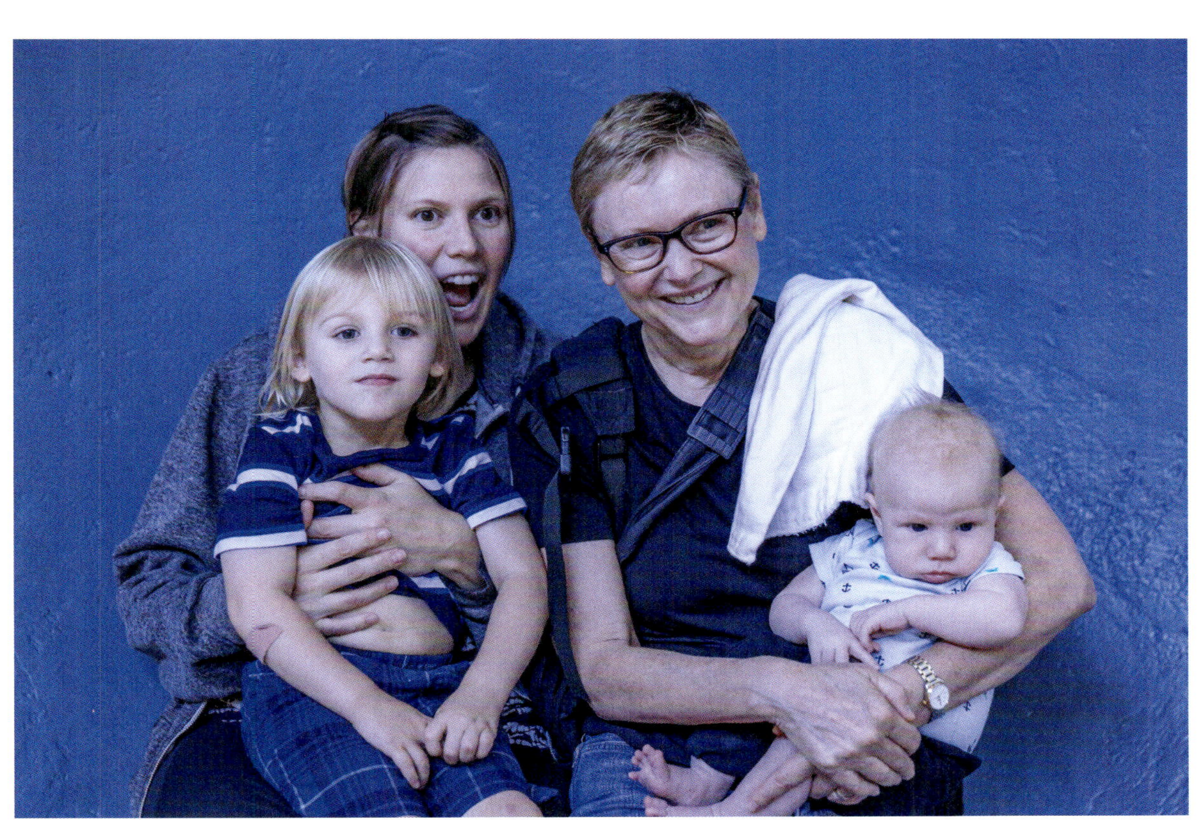

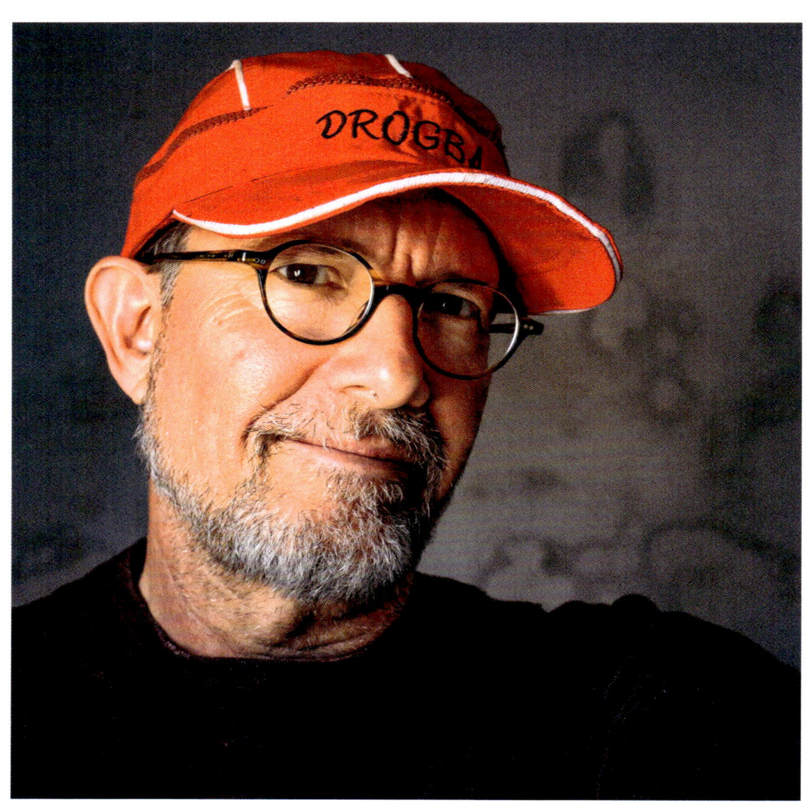

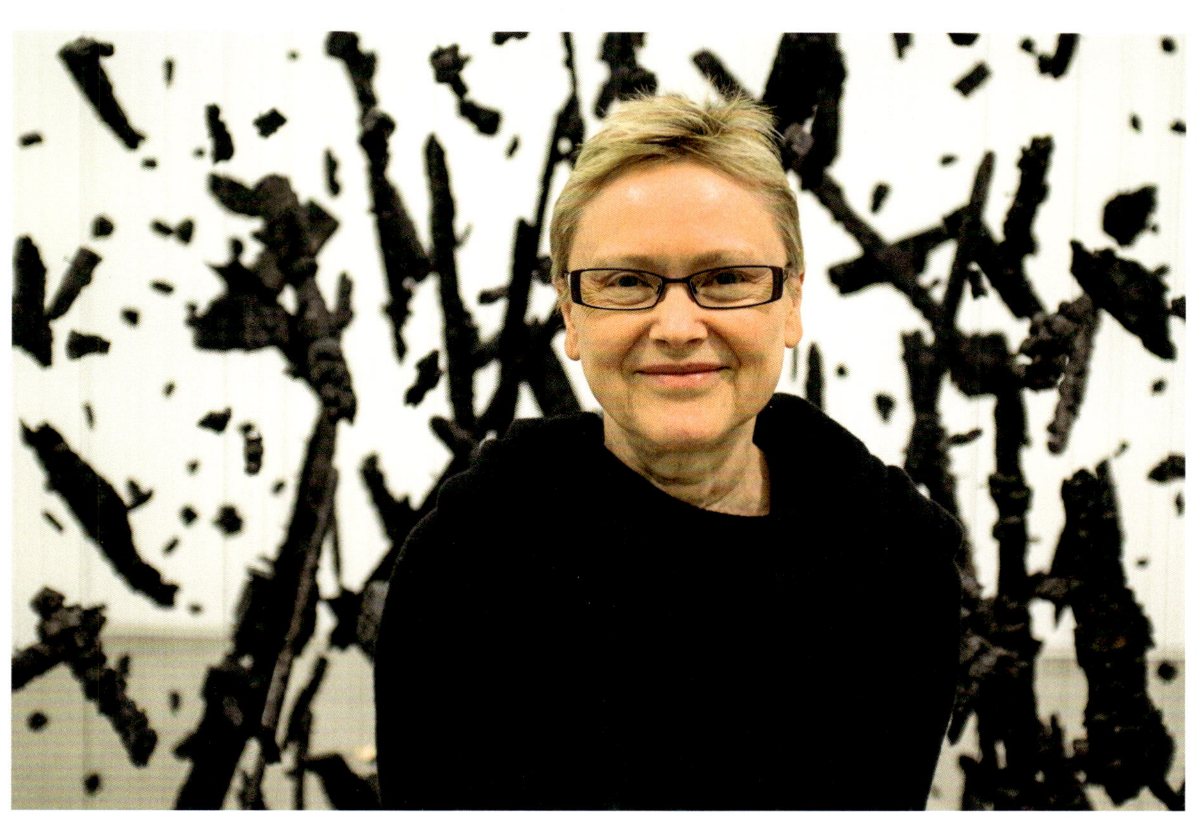

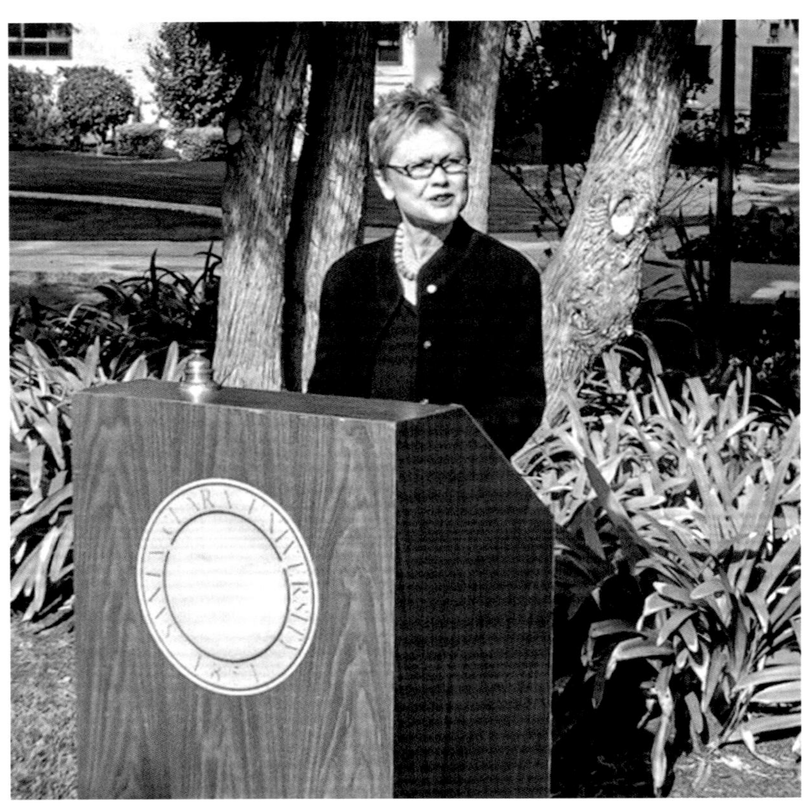

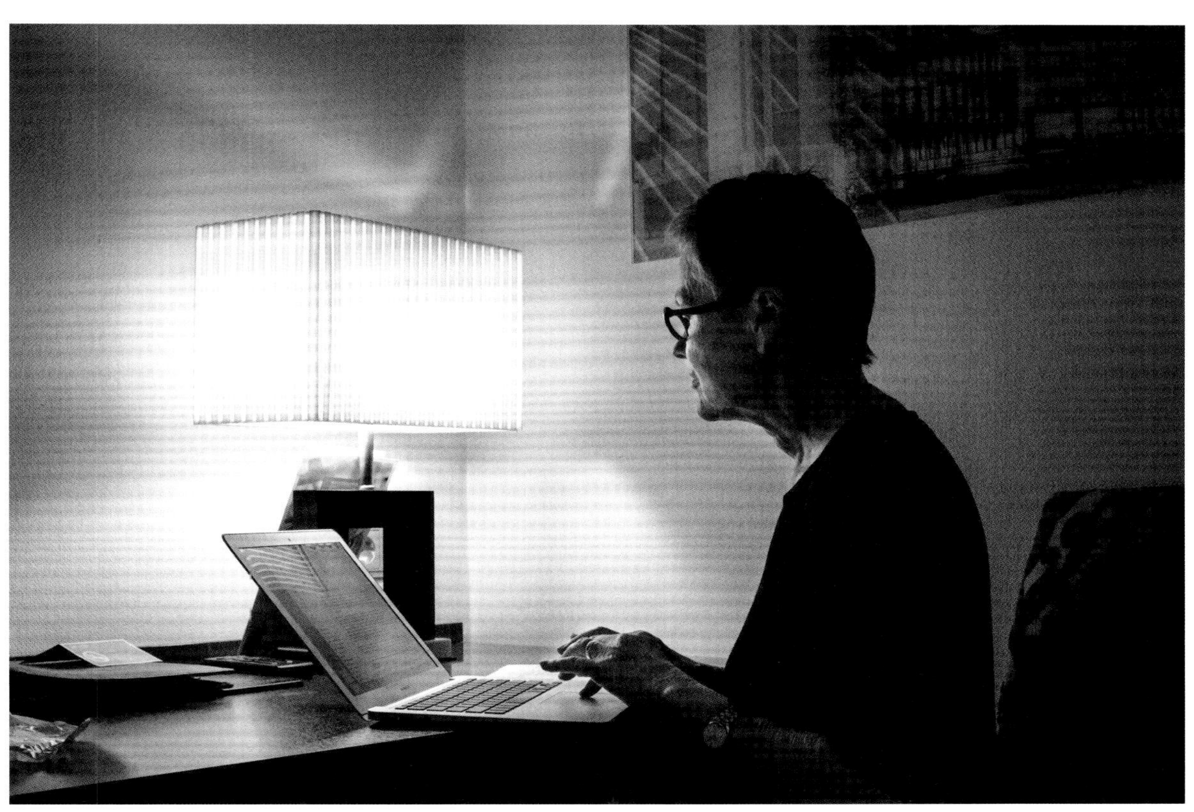

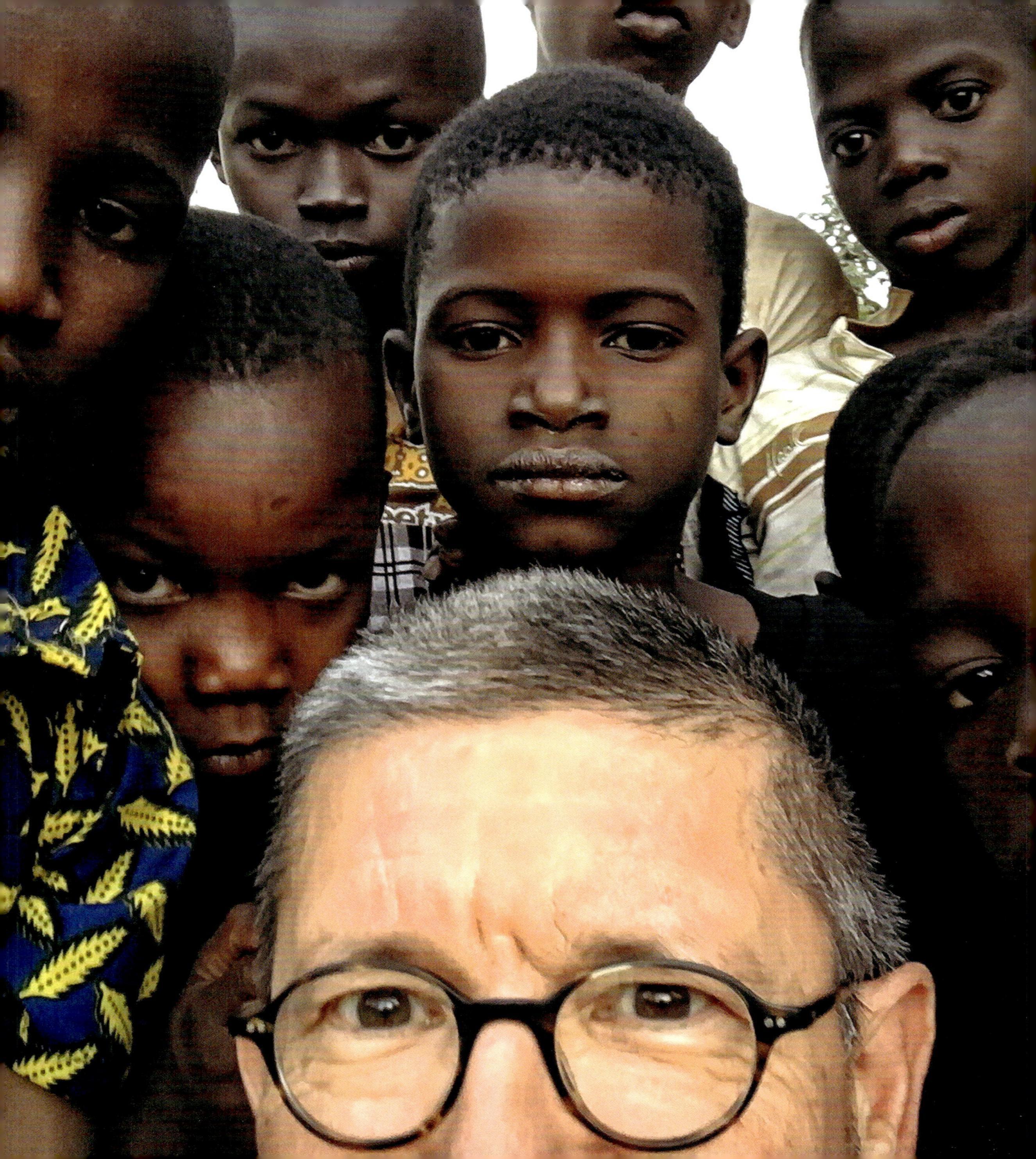

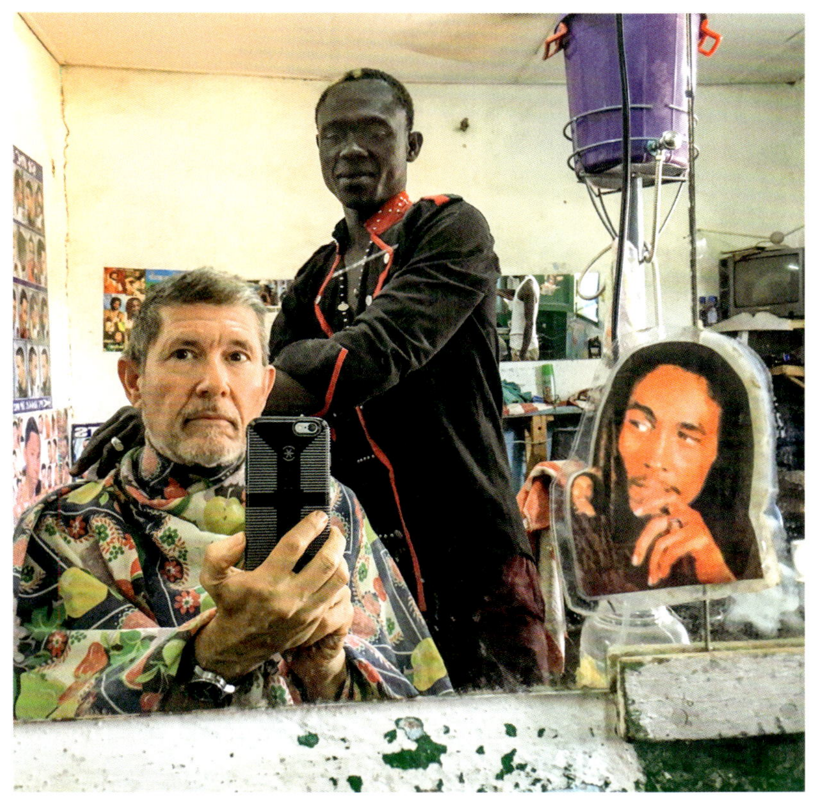

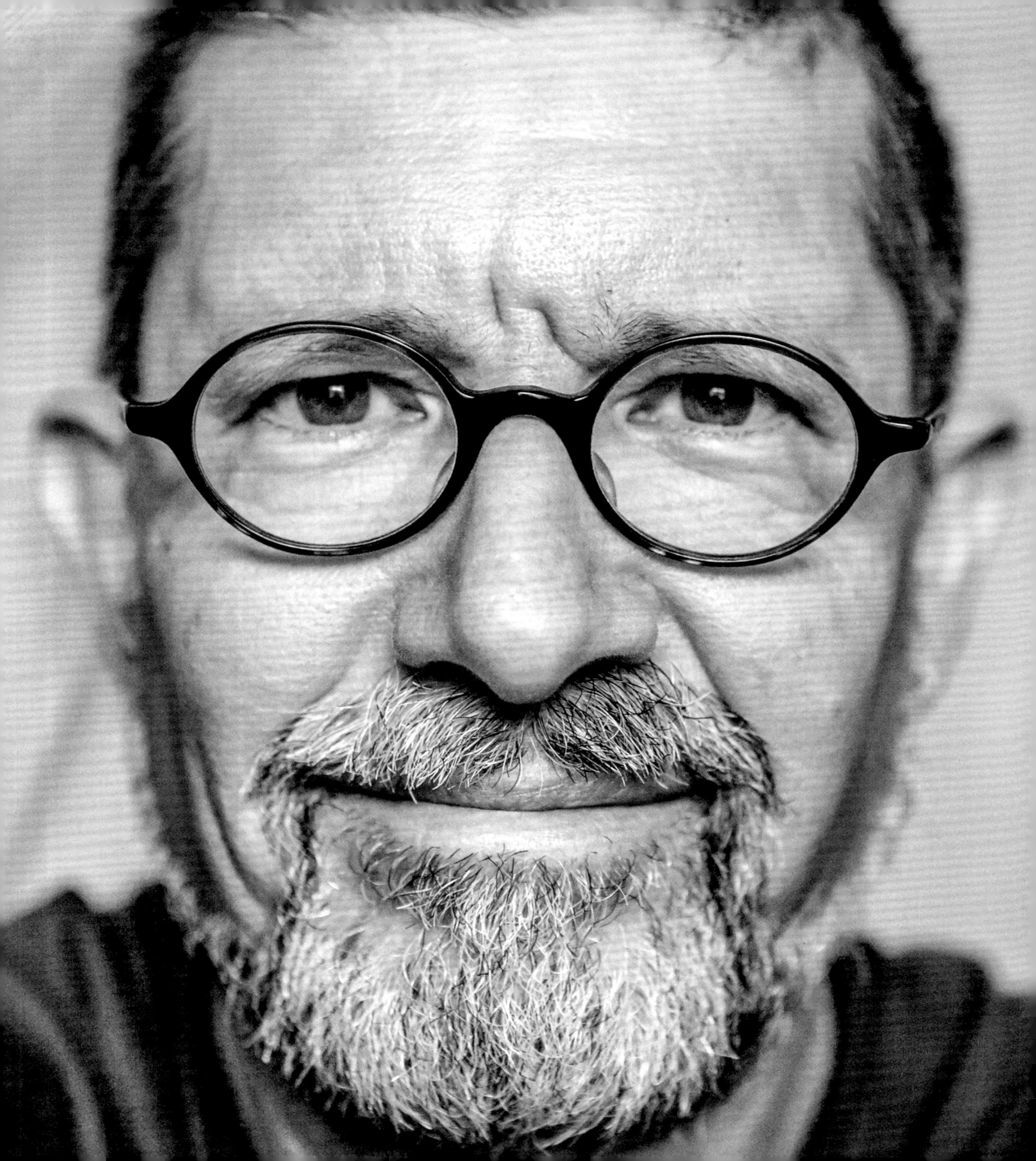

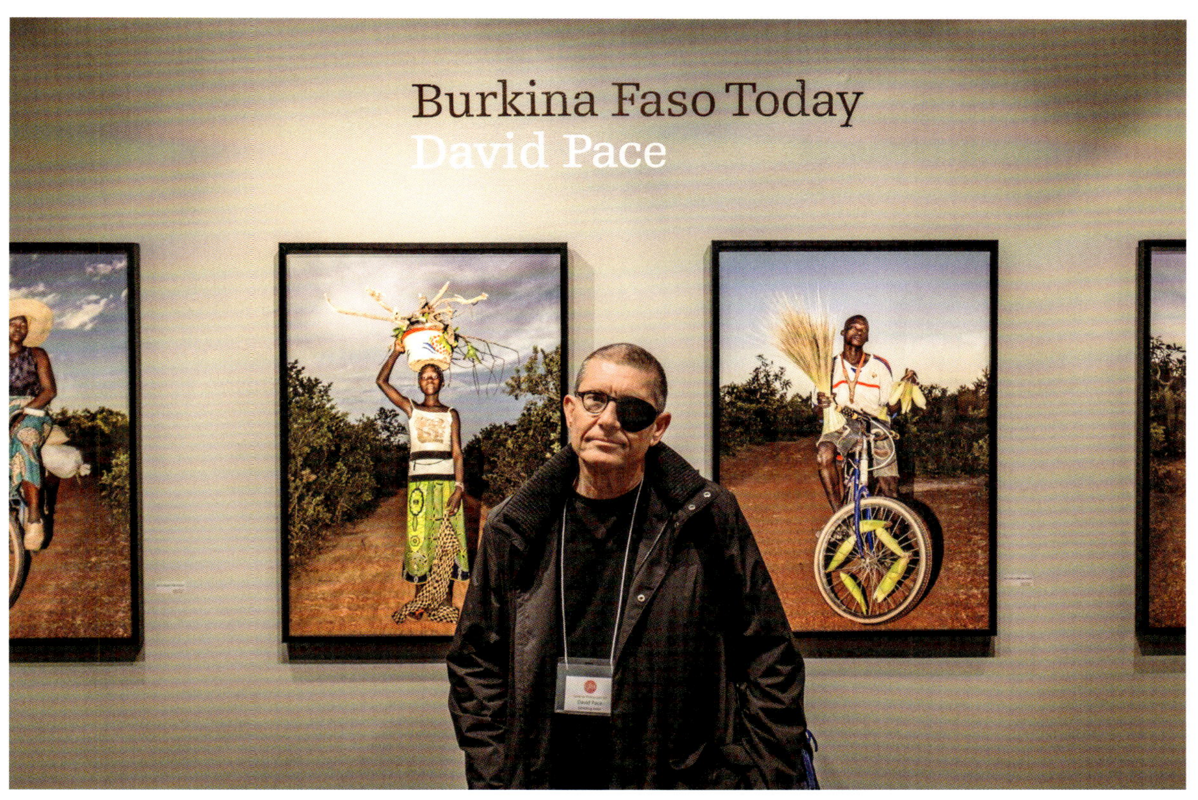

Burkina Faso Today
David Pace

The world is a beautiful place
to be born into
if you don't mind happiness
not always being
so very much fun

– Lawrence Ferlinghetti, Greatest Poems

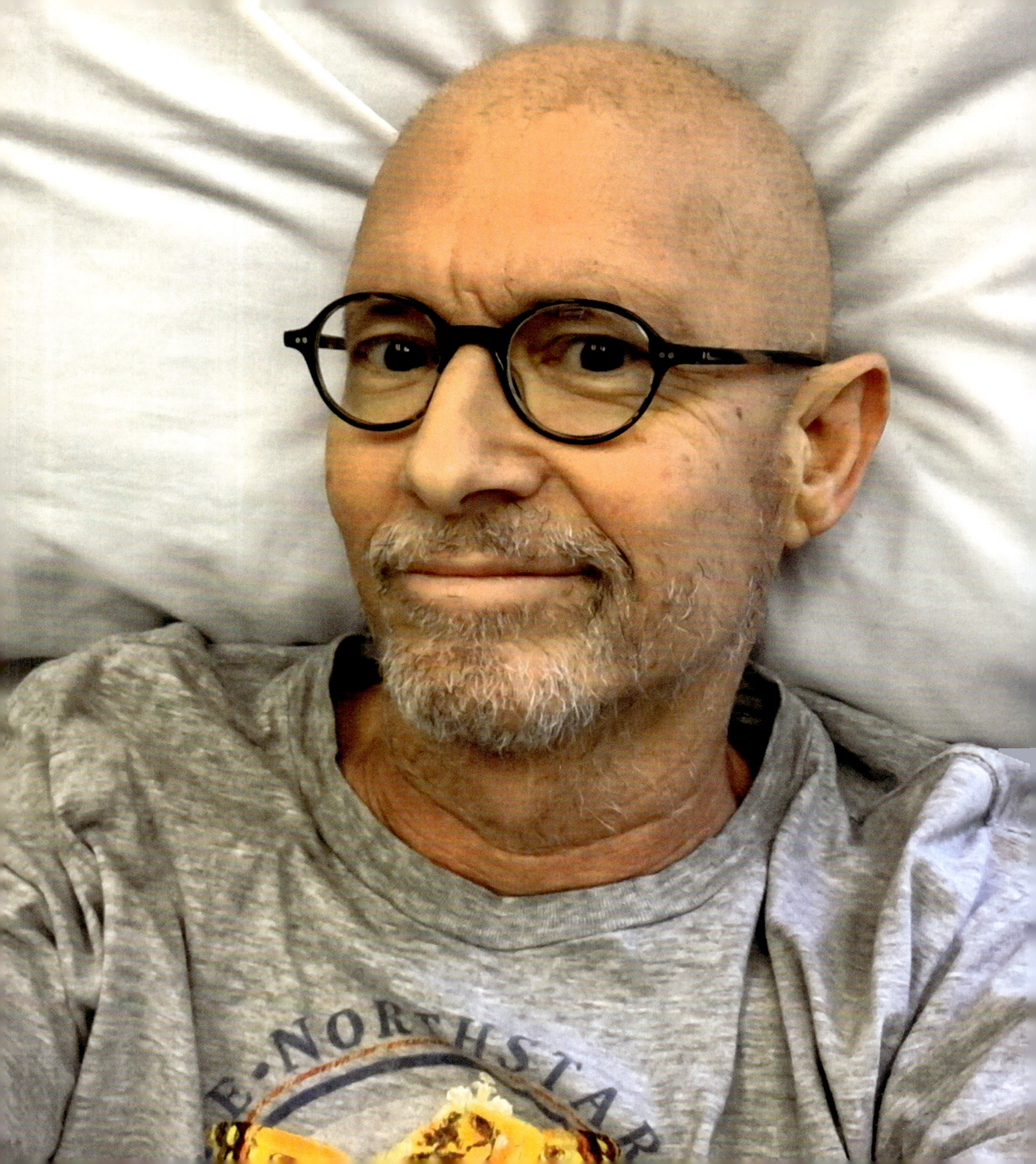

E·NORTHSTAR

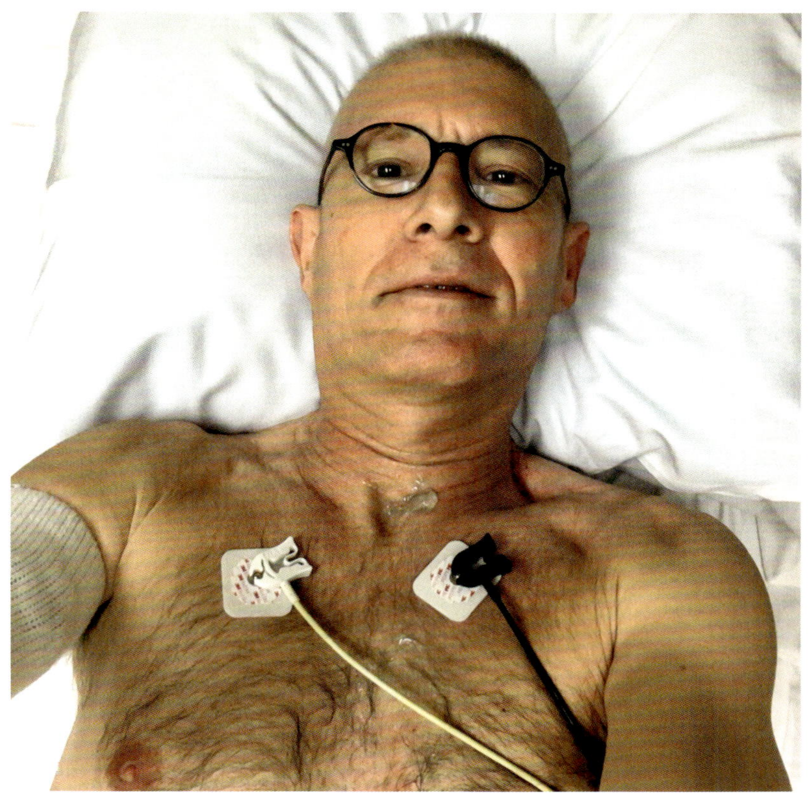

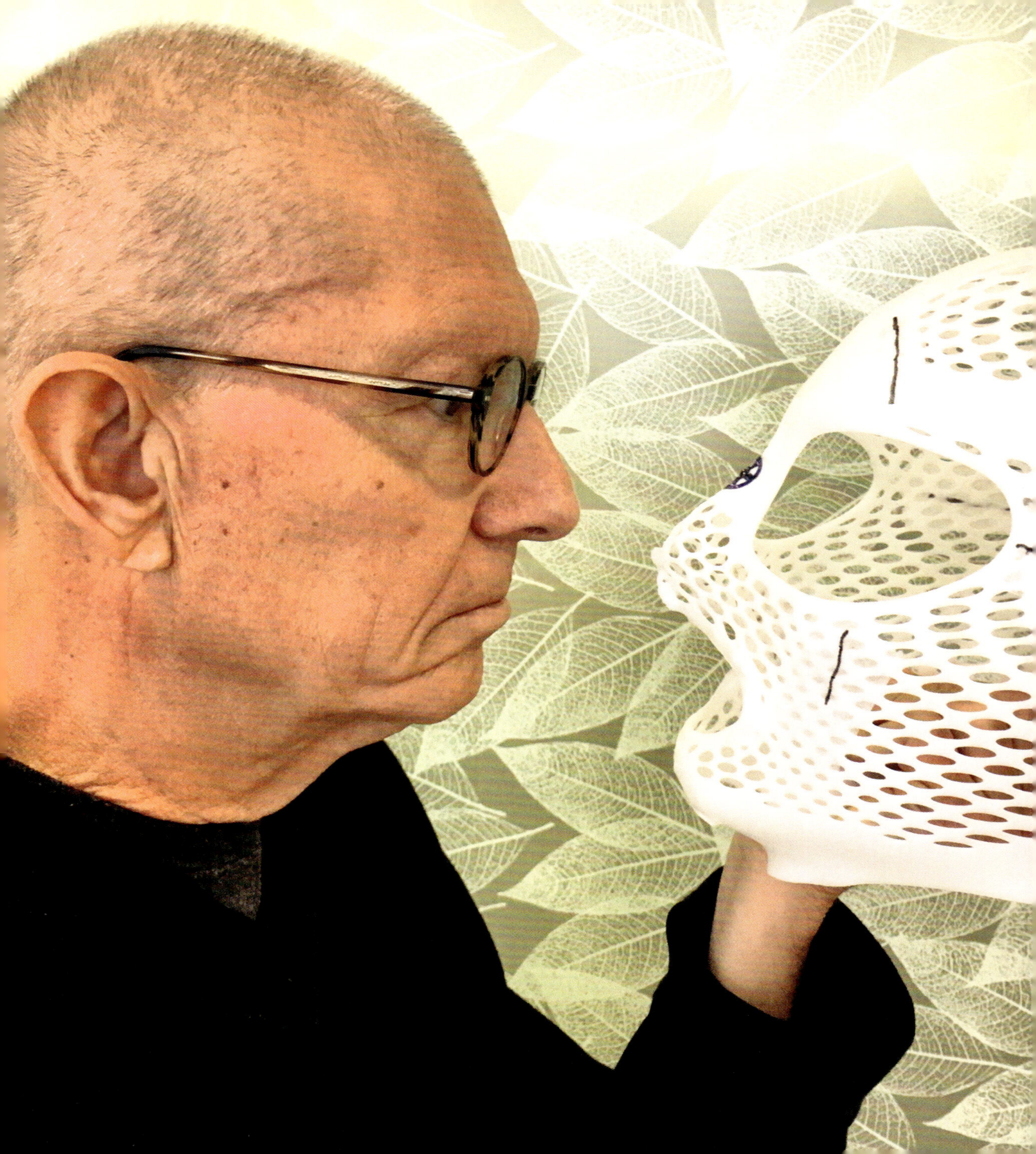

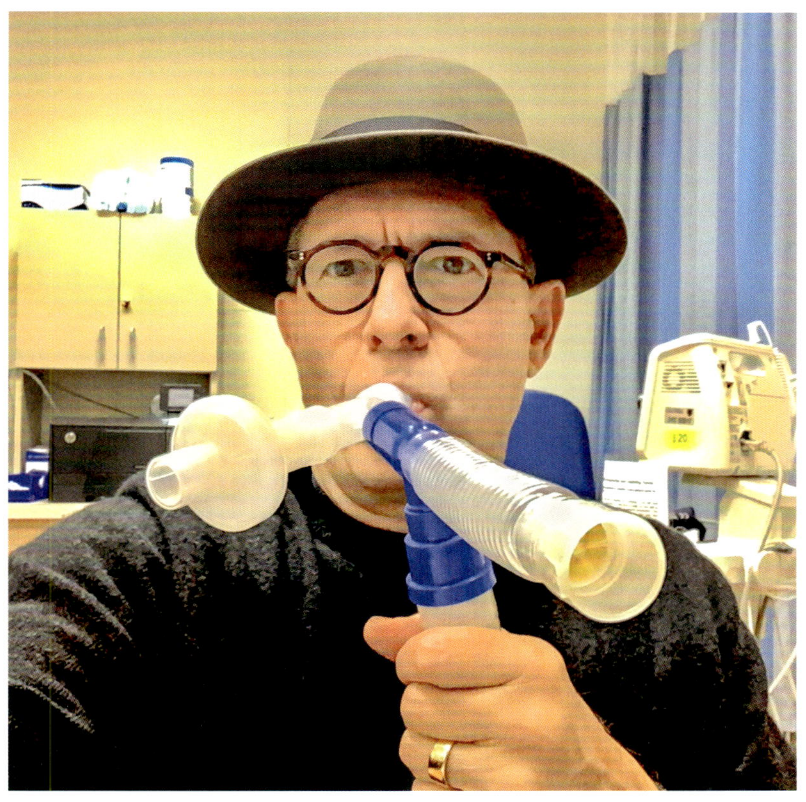

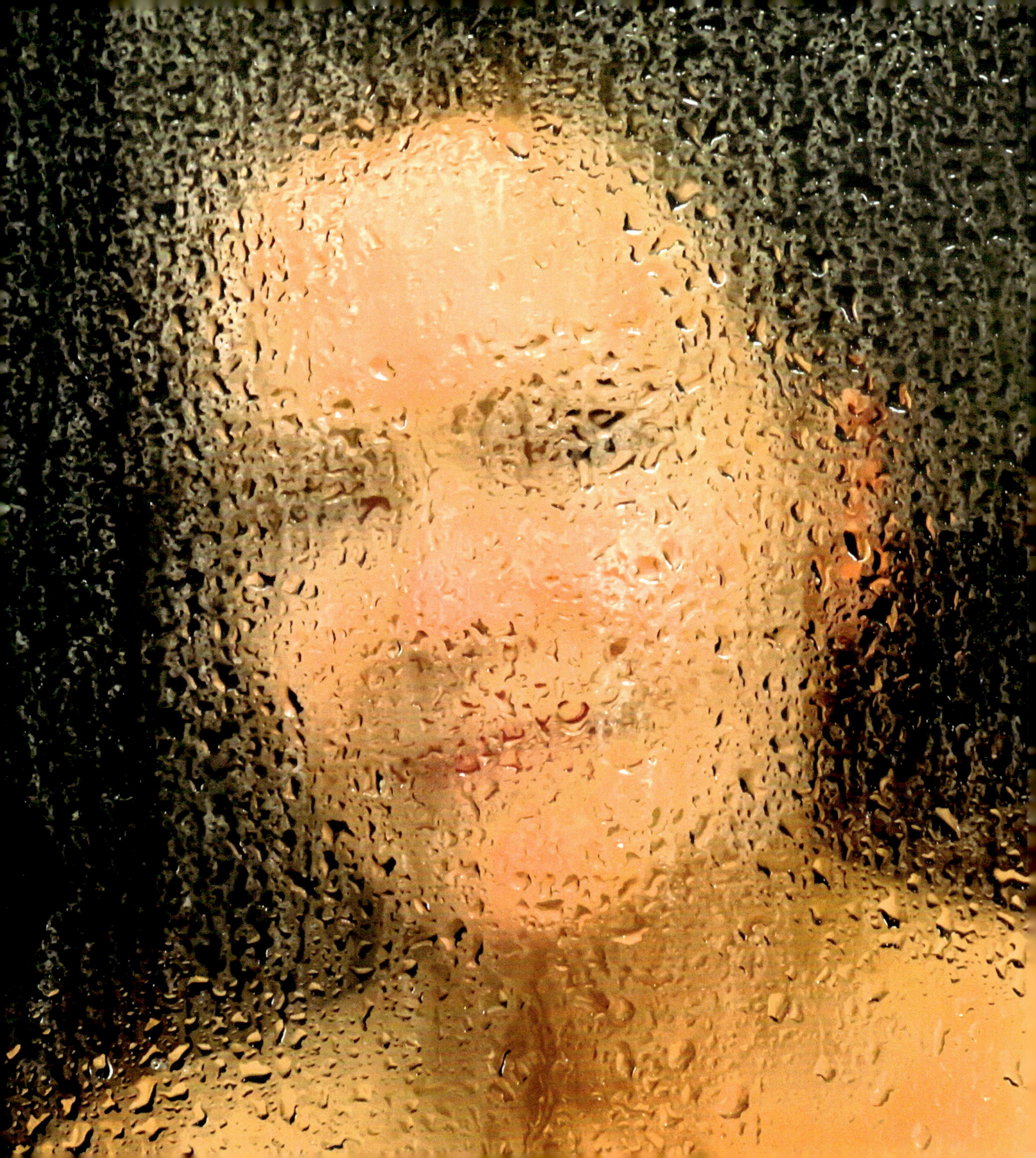

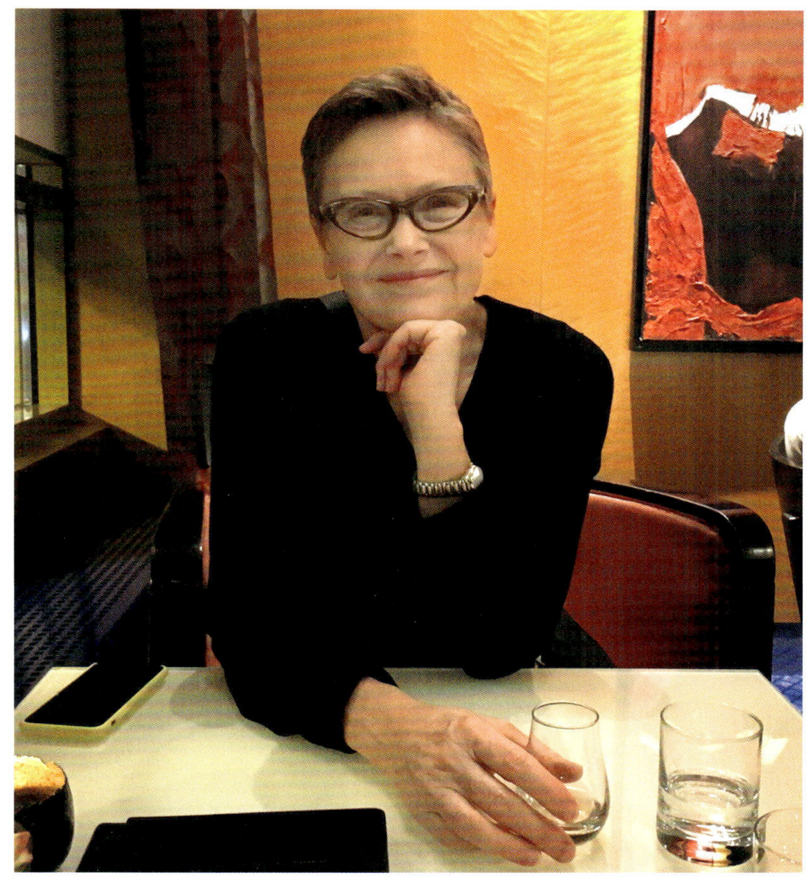

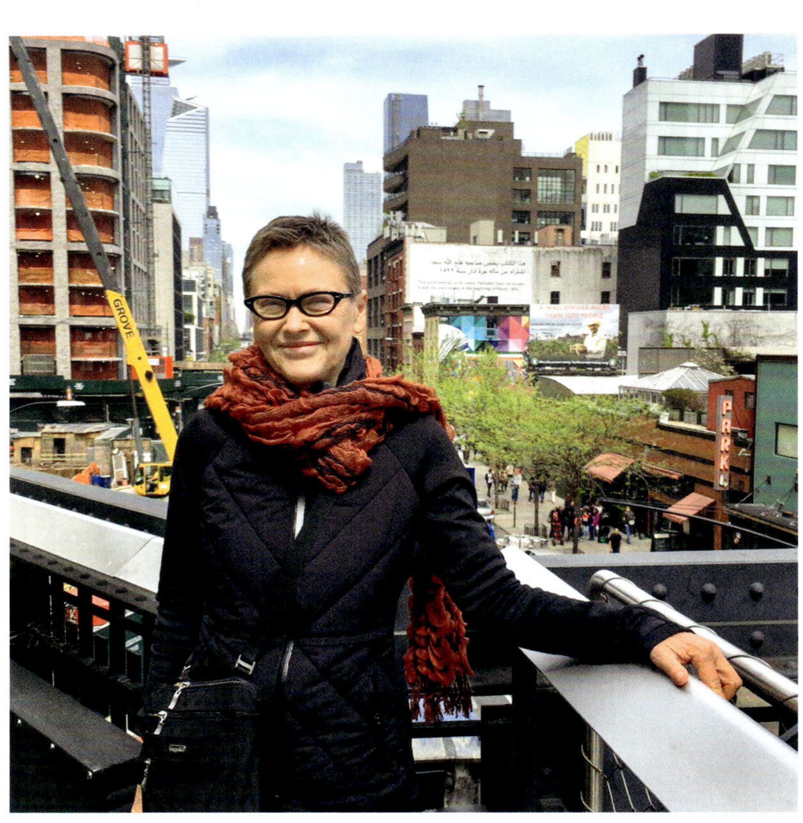

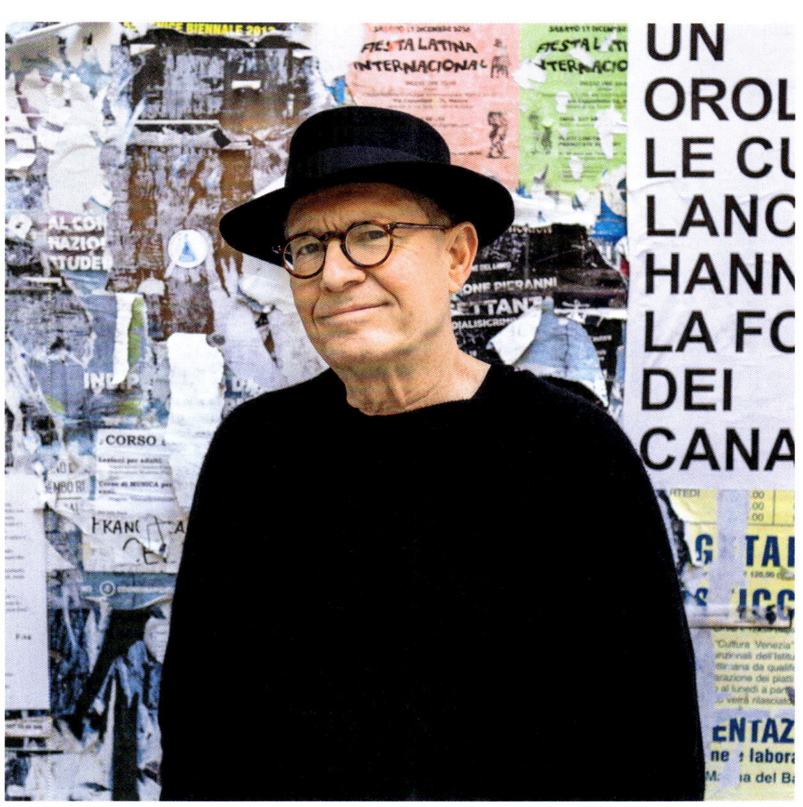
FIESTA LATINA
INTERNACIONAL
FIESTA LATINA
INTERNACIO
UN
OROL
LE CU
LANC
HANN
LA FO
DEI
CANA
CORSO
FRANC

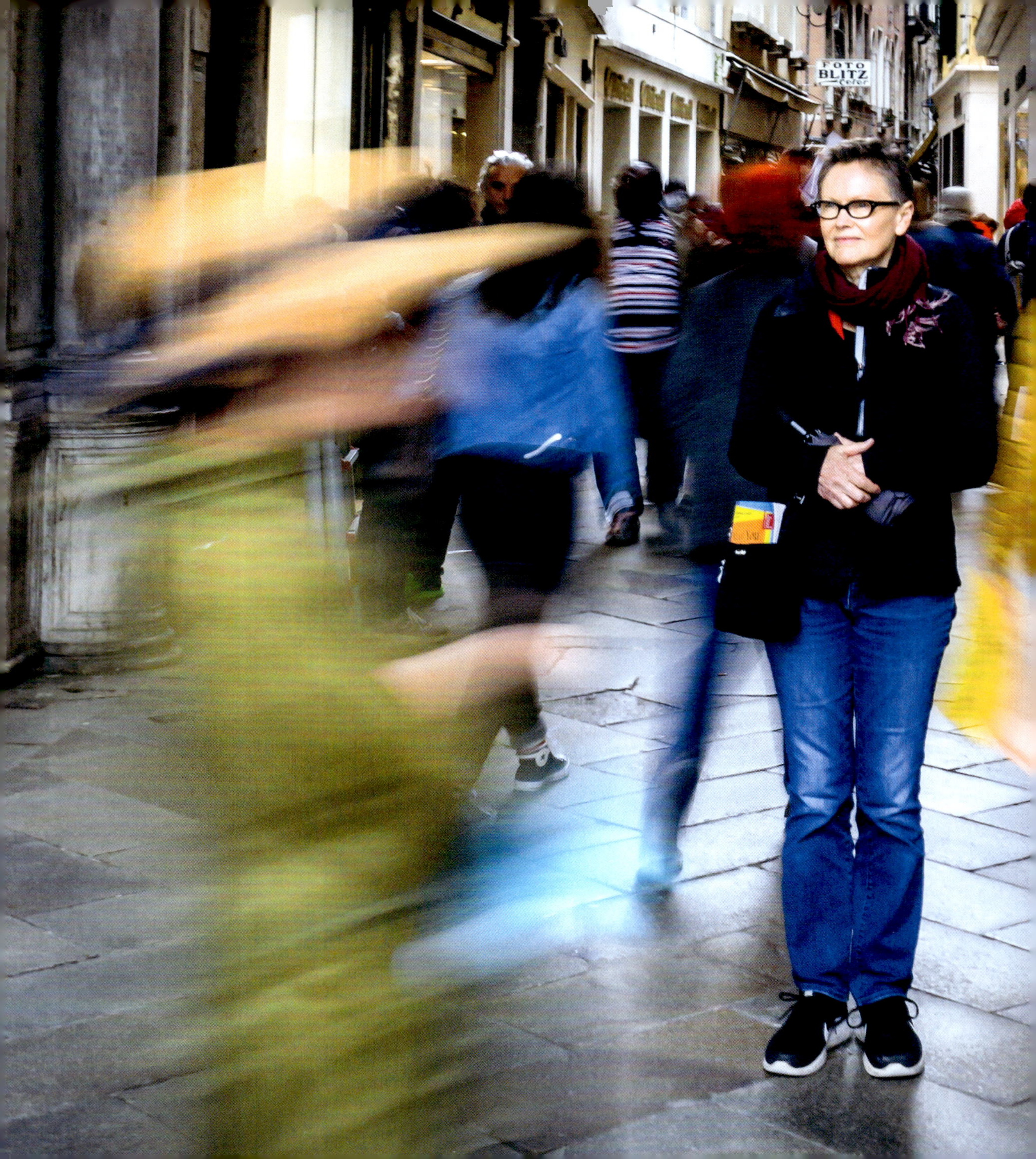
FOTO
BLITZ
color

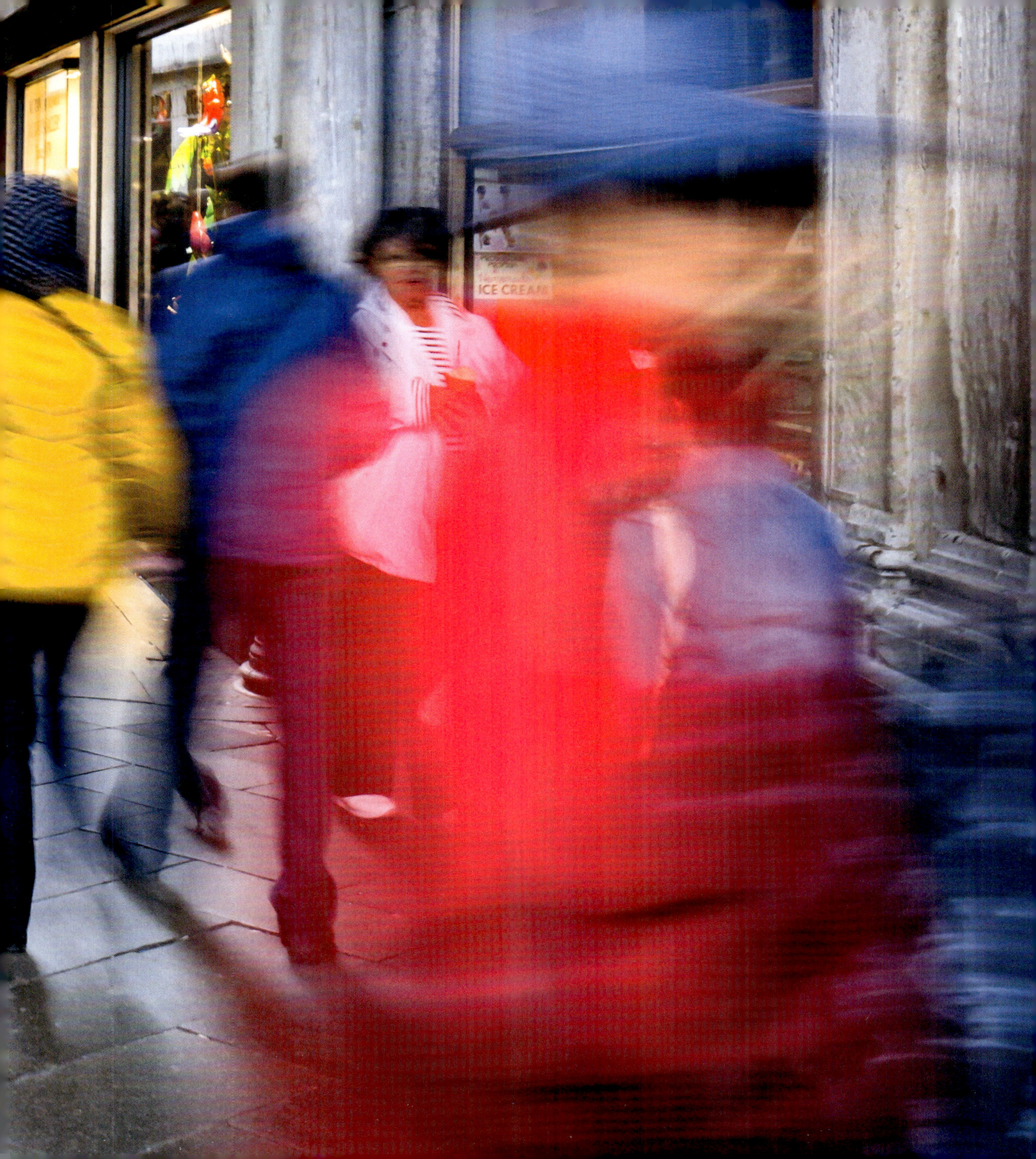

ICE CREAM

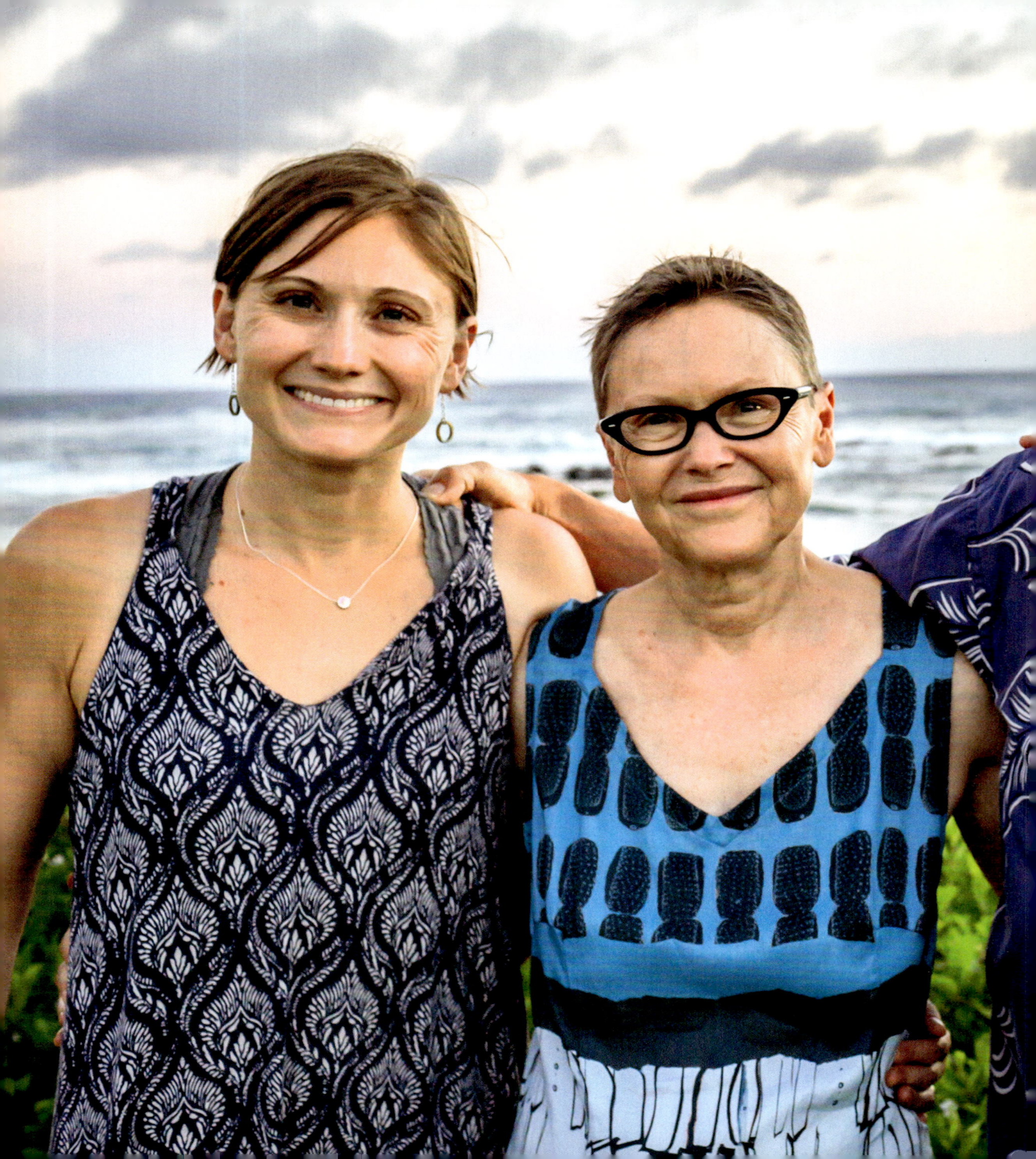

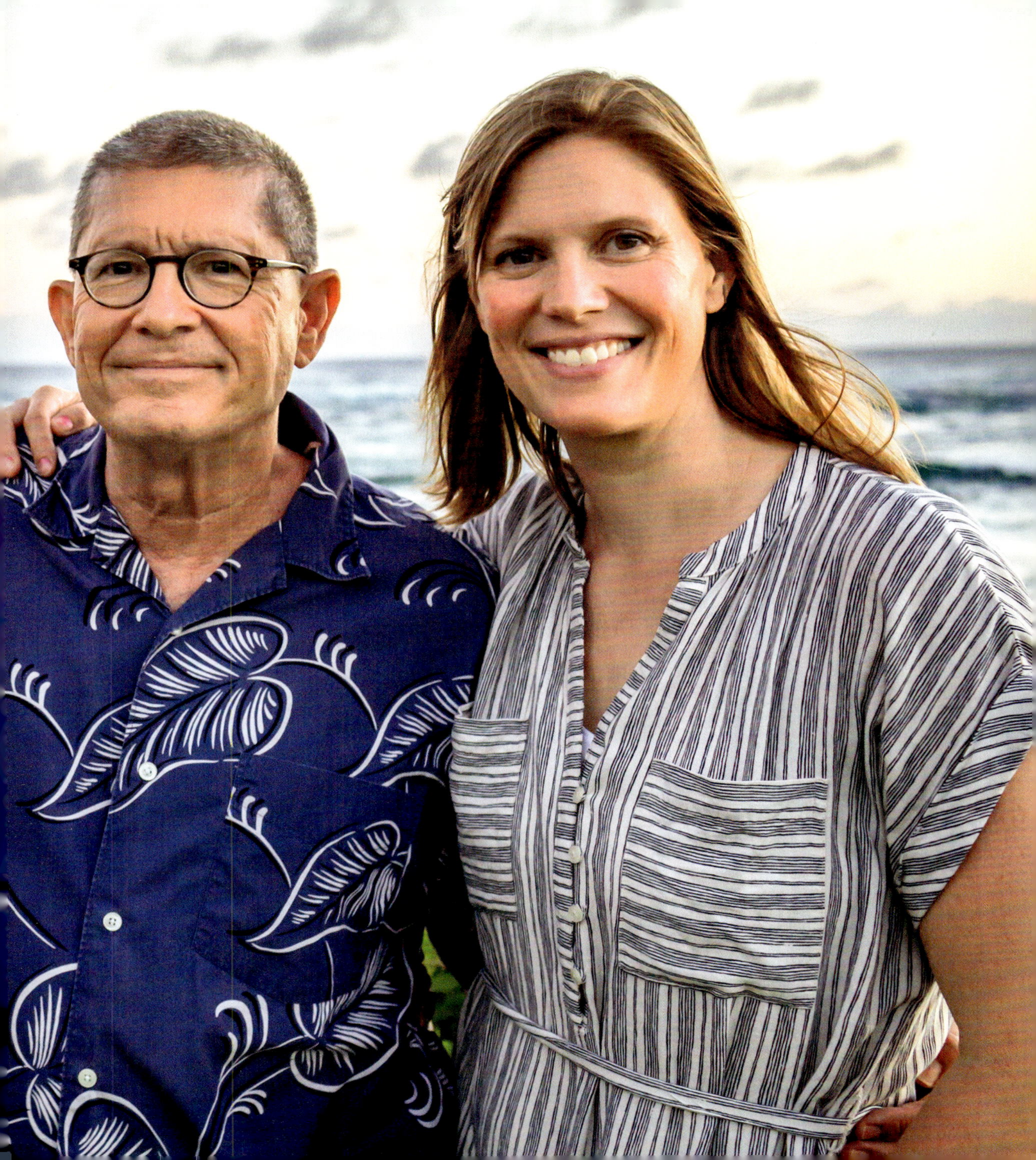

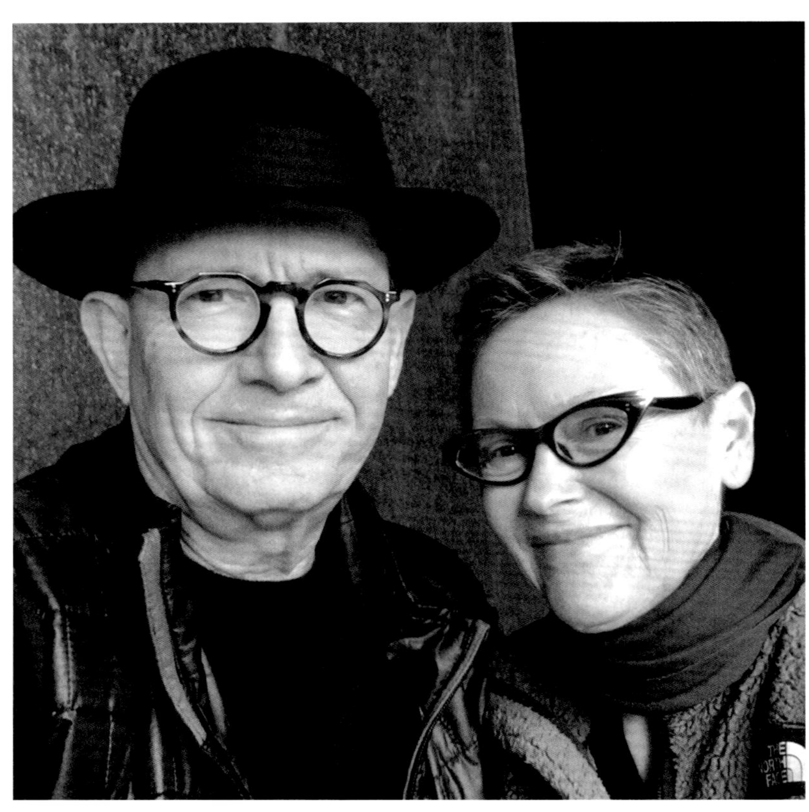

Where the Time Goes   Diane Jonte-Pace and David Pace   July 2019

This book would not exist if David hadn't come so close to death. In December 2016 David was diagnosed with a rare and aggressive form of lymphoma. The oncologist gave him a thirty percent chance of survival. I didn't expect him to live. I took a leave from my job as vice provost at Santa Clara University and became caregiver and manager of medications and medical appointments. A month-long hospitalization was followed by a two-year regimen of chemotherapy and radiation.

For several months David lay in bed at home, unable to walk without a walker, eat without choking, or talk above a whisper, needing my assistance with almost everything. During that time, I turned, in free moments, to a long-postponed household project. Our closets and cupboards contained many shoeboxes full of old photographs, all unlabeled and unsorted. I bought a dozen large archival photo boxes and began a rough sort. I found prints and slides, some from our earliest years together taken with the 35mm Canon I brought with me when I moved into David's house in 1972.

Finding and sorting these decades-old images became a kind of meditation, a reconnection to, and an acknowledgement of, the loss of the past. In some sense the project was an attempt to work through or control the emotional chaos that came with David's cancer diagnosis. I couldn't control the progress of his illness or the effects of the chemotherapy, but I could organize the photos in the closets. And almost miraculously, my organizational project gave me an opportunity to view – and review – our shared past. It was a kind of grieving or mourning of what we once had – health and youth and love – and what I feared we were losing – our life together. Roland Barthes says that we interrogate photographs in relation to love and death. This project did, in fact, begin with the expectation of death, and it led to the collection of photographs in this book that weave a story of aging and change, love and life, through many decades and in many places. It's a story that asks "where does the time go?"

As David slowly regained strength and health, he became interested in the project. Together we began to look more carefully at the photographs I had organized. And we began to examine negatives and proof sheets stored in David's darkroom, as well as digital images stored on his computer.

Photographs are always portals to the past. They tell a story of what's
gone, what *was* in the past, but no longer exists, sometimes reminding us
of what can be reclaimed, if only through memory. These photos provided
keys to our memories, reminders of who and where we had been. They kept
our memories of the past vibrant and alive during a time when the evidence
of the aging of our bodies was undeniable and death felt very close. They
reminded us of what once was, what had been, in our lives.

These images, individually and collectively, capture a sense of time
past and time passing: each individual photograph freezes a moment in
our lives. At the same time, as a collection, they give us a dizzying sense of
velocity, a sense of time passing rapidly, as if, as Billy Collins says in one
of our favorite poems, we have "speed lines trailing behind us as we rush
along the road of the world, as we rush down the long tunnel of time."

Initially, we did not plan to share these photographs with anyone beyond
our own family. Only after David's chemotherapy and radiation ended did
we consider a broader audience. The story of youth, aging, and change
over time is not ours alone. This is a story that we share with our entire
generation, and a story that can provide a window into the past for others
as well. It's a story about family photography over five decades, of a post-

war generation coming of age, and turning the camera upon itself.

Technically and stylistically, this book incorporates most of the forms of photography available over the last five decades, starting in a period when cameras and film were becoming more accessible and less expensive. Kodak Instamatic cameras were widespread at that time, although we never used one. Our earliest photos were taken with the 35mm single-lens reflex camera my father had given me. We also used Brownie Hawkeye, Polaroid, and single-use throw-away cameras. Later, David used more professional cameras like the Pentax 6x7, Sinar 4x5, Deardorff 8x10, and, eventually, full frame digital Canons. Currently, we, like the rest of the world, also use iPhones to make snapshots.

The threads that give coherence to this narrative are the story of our life together as we've aged and changed, and the story of how family photos have been made, stored, and viewed over the last 50 years.

We met 50 years ago, in the summer of 1970, when we were students at the University of California Santa Cruz. We were friends long before we became lovers. We took a few of the same classes – one on "The Origins of the Search for Meaning," and one on "Coptic Gnostic Literature" – both classic UCSC courses in their exploration of history, meaning, and the inner life.

We saw a few movies together – we both remember watching Truffaut's *400 Blows* in the college cafeteria and Bergman's *Persona* on a small TV with one of our classes. Our deeper relationship began in the summer of 1972, before our senior year, shortly after an actual movie date – a double bill with *Harold and Maude* and *Play it Again, Sam*.

After graduation in 1973, we spent a year in Switzerland, studying psychology at the C.G. Jung Institute. On school vacations we traveled. In September we went to the Greek island of Ios, and to Crete. We caught a ride to Munich in the fall. In December we went to Florence and Paris. In the spring we went to Oxford and spent a week in Baltimore, a small village on the southern tip of Ireland. In May we went to Geneva, Interlachen, and the Swiss Alps. We hitchhiked or took trains, taking photos wherever we went.

The following year we both enrolled in graduate programs at the University of Chicago. I finished a Ph.D. in Religion and Psychological Studies, and David completed a master's degree in the social sciences. In 1978 we moved back to California, to the area that was soon to become Silicon Valley, where we began our careers. David worked in his family's hardware business for a few years before turning to photography, while I pursued a career as professor, scholar, and university administrator. Our photographs from the early years do not document the rituals or ceremonies that are typically found in family photos – we graduated from college in 1973 but we have no graduation photos. We had several groups of good friends, but we never gathered them for group photos. We were married in 1976 but we have no significant wedding photographs. We didn't take a honeymoon, choosing instead to go camping with friends who had traveled 2,000 miles to join us for our informal backyard wedding. Our only "honeymoon" photos are from our camping trip to Fordyce Creek in the Sierras with friends. Our two daughters were born a few years later, but we have no formal baby pictures. The 1970s were a countercultural period, an era that was critical of formalities, pretentions, and traditional practices – including traditional photographic practices. The photographs in this book inevitably present a selective and incomplete view of our life together, but the absence of formal photographs of ceremonies and rituals reflects a reality: we avoided ceremony, and our rituals were informal and unlikely to be photographed.

Photography became a more significant pursuit for David in the late 1980s. He returned to graduate school at San Jose State University for a Master of Fine Arts degree and began a new career as artist and photography instructor in Bay Area colleges and universities in the early 90s. For over fifteen years we both taught at Santa Clara University. David's "serious" photographic work was more about culture than family – his MFA project, "Re:Collections," for example, documented collections of unusual objects – eggbeaters, tin cars, plumb bobs, robots, women's shoes, autographed paper napkins – gathered by individuals. His photos, mounted as large grids, created, in a sense, portraits of the collectors through the vivid portrayals of the objects they collected. He completed a series of short animated music videos focusing on the work of post-modern philosophers Nietzsche, Foucault, and Lacan. His later work included a ten-year project on a small village in West Africa, and a book on World War II wirephotos. He continued to document our family vacations and activities, and often cajoled our daughters into posing for him as he experimented with a new camera or a new film, but our family photos of this period were distinct from the culturally-focused fine art photography of his more serious work. Art photography and family photography fell into distinct categories at that time, merging only later into overlapping projects.

In our home, photos have been stored in two different places: the dark room and the closets. David's dark room is full of black and white negatives in archival sleeves and digital images stored on computer hard drives and backup systems. These are labeled and organized. The closets, on the other hand, at least until recently, were crowded with undated shoeboxes holding the unsorted, unlabeled prints and slide carousels that I began organizing during David's long illness.

In an earlier era, eighty or ninety years ago, photos would have been curated by family members and mounted in photo albums – we have albums of black and white images from the 1930s, '40s and '50s gathered by our parents and grandparents – small prints are corner-mounted on black paper, and hand-written text in lovely penmanship identifies people and places. Forty or fifty years ago, the photo album was replaced by the slide carousel: we often assembled a carousel of slides, projecting onto a screen or wall, and narrating our travels to friends and family. Twenty or thirty years ago we might have thumbed through holiday or vacation prints before storing them in shoeboxes in the closet. Today, Facebook and Instagram have replaced all three – the photo album, the carousel of slides, and the box of prints. Everyone has a cellphone, everyone is a photographer, all photographs are digital, and Facebook invites us to share images instantly and widely.

With cellphone cameras, images proliferate exponentially: it's easy to take lots of photos. We share them with a broad community: social media allows us to post images for wide viewing. The photos are intangible and ephemeral: we post, but we don't print. We worry that constant changes in software and media will make our digital images inaccessible: our old floppy disks are already illegible, CDs are challenging to view. How do these images on social media function today? How will they function in the future? Will any be printed? Will they be available in future years to our children, our grandchildren, or other viewers? Will photographs in the future still function for us as portals to the past as our memories fade?

Cancer Selfies

A day or so after David was released from the Intensive Care Unit to enter the cancer ward at Stanford Hospital in December 2016, he became conscious enough to ask what had happened. As soon as he understood the reality of his situation, he asked for his cellphone, requested assistance with a selfie, and posted it on Facebook with an optimistic note: *"In Stanford Hospital for lymphoma treatment. Long road ahead but prognosis is good. Great care by staff. Nice place to spend the holidays!"* The community response was powerful – friends and colleagues responded with love and encouragement from Burkina Faso, France, Italy, the

Netherlands, and throughout the U.S. The global response gave David a strong sense of support and encouraged a series of postings documenting the next months of his life: his gaunt face, the loss of his hair, the radiation mask, the PIC line, the intravenous tube, the inhalation technology, and the protective face mask required when his immune system was particularly vulnerable. Eventually, the series begin to show evidence of his healing – the first walk around the block without a walker, the first meal in a restaurant, the first visit to a museum, and the first trip with grandchildren. Some of these cancer selfies are included in this book. They highlight the way photographs are made, shared, and viewed today, illustrating the way that social media, in spite of its many flaws, can convey love, care, and community – and even contribute to the healing process. They document the illness that was the context for the re-discovery of the photographs in this book; they show, unmistakably, "where the time goes."

ISBN 978 90 5330 942 1

© 2020 David Pace & Diane Jonte – Pace
© 2020 Schilt Publishing & Gallery, Amsterdam
www.schiltpublishing.com

Edit
Victor Levie with David Pace & Diane Jonte – Pace

Design
Victor Levie, Amsterdam
www.levievandermeer.nl

Text correction
Kumar Jamdagni, Zwolle

Print & Logistics Management
Komeso GmbH, Stuttgart
www.komeso.com

Printing
Offizin Scheufele GmbH, Stuttgart
www.scheufele.de

Binding
Josef Spinner Grossbuchbinderei GmbH, Ottersweier
www.josef-spinner.de

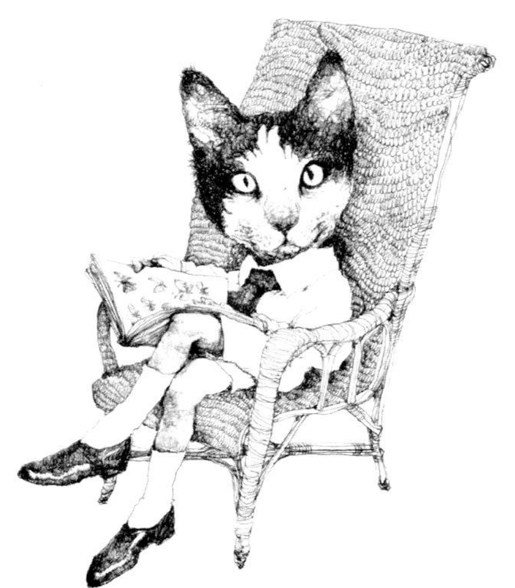

Distribution in North America
Ingram Publisher Services
One Ingram Blvd.
LaVergne, TN 37086
IPS: 866-765-0179
E-mail: customer.service@ingrampublisherservices.com

Distribution in the Netherlands and Flanders
Centraal Boekhuis, Culemborg

Distribution in all other countries
Thames & Hudson Ltd
181a High Holborn
London WC1V 7QX
Phone: +44 (0)20 7845 5000
Fax: +44 (0)20 7845 5055
E-mail: sales@thameshudson.co.uk

Schilt Publishing & Gallery books,
special editions, and prints
are available also online via
www.schiltpublishing.com

Inquiries via sales@schiltpublishing.com